BENCHMARK Series

MICROSOFT PowerPoint 2000

CORE CERTIFICATION

NITA RUTKOSKY

Pierce College at Puyallup
Puyallup, Washington

APPROVED COURSEWARE

Senior Editor	Sonja Brown
Developmental Editor	Mary Verrill
Cover Designer	Chris Vern Johnson
Art Director	Joan D'Onofrio
Text Designer	Jennifer Wreisner
Desktop Production Specialist	Leslie Anderson, Michelle Lewis, Jennifer Wreisner
Tester	Laura Bagley
Indexer	Nancy Fulton

Publishing Team—George Provol, Publisher; Janice Johnson, Director of Product Development; Lori Landwer, Marketing Manager; Shelley Clubb, Electronic Design and Production Manager.

Registered Trademarks—Microsoft, Windows, PowerPoint, Outlook, and the MOUS icon are registered trademarks of Microsoft Corporation in the United States and other countries. IBM is a registered trademark of IBM Corporation.

Acknowledgments—The author and publisher wish to thank these reviewers for technical assistance: Tony D. Gabriel, Computer Learning Center, Glendale, California; Denise Seguin, Instructor, Fanshawe College, London, Ontario; Janet Sheppard, Collin County Community College, Plano, Texas.

Library of Congress Cataloging-in-Publication Data
Rutkosky, Nita Hewitt.
    Microsoft PowerPoint 2000 : core certification / Nita Rutkosky.
        p.   cm. — (Benchmark series))
    ISBN 0-7638-0335-9 (text). — ISBN 0-7638-0336-7 (text & CD-ROM)
    1. Computer graphics. 2. Microsoft PowerPoint (Computer file)
3. Business presentations—Graphic methods—Computer programs.
4. Electronic data processing personnel—Certification. I. Title.
II. Series: Benchmark series (Saint Paul, Minn.).
T385.R88   1999
006.6'869—dc21   99-35151
                                                                                                                                                                         CIP

Text + CD: ISBN 0-7638-0336-7
Order Number 05358

© 2000 by Paradigm Publishing Inc.
        Published by **EMC**Paradigm
        875 Montreal Way
        St. Paul, MN 55102
        (800) 535-6865
        E-mail: **educate@emcp.com**
        Web Site: www.emcp.com

All rights reserved. No part of this book may be reproduced, stored in a retrieval system, or transmitted, in any form or by any means, electronic, mechanical, photocopying, recording, or otherwise, without prior written permission of Paradigm Publishing Inc.

Care has been taken to provide accurate and useful information about the Internet capabilities of Microsoft PowerPoint 2000. However, the authors, editor, and publisher cannot accept any responsibility for Web, e-mail, newsgroup, or chatroom subject matter nor content, nor for consequences from any application of the information in this book, and make no warranty, expressed or implied, with respect to the book's content.

Printed in the United States of America

10   9   8   7   6   5

Contents

Introduction	v

PowerPoint 2000 Core Level — Core P-1

Page numbers are indicated as "Core P" to denote Microsoft Office User Specialist (MOUS) PowerPoint 2000 Core Certification throughout this section.

Microsoft® PowerPoint 2000 Core Level MOUS Skills	2

Chapter 1

Preparing a PowerPoint Presentation — 3

Planning a Presentation	4
Creating a PowerPoint Presentation	4
Understanding the PowerPoint Window	5
Creating a Presentation Using a Template	7
Printing a Presentation	9
Printing a Presentation in Grayscale and Black and White	15
Expanding Drop-Down Menus	15
Saving a Presentation	15
Closing a Presentation	16
Completing Computer Exercises	16
Presentation Files	16
Creating a Folder	16
Planning a Presentation with the AutoContent Wizard	19
Opening a Presentation Document	20
Viewing a Presentation	20
Running a Slide Show	21
Starting the Slide Show on Any Slide	22
Using the Pen During a Presentation	22
Adding Transition and Sound Effects	25
Running a Slide Show Automatically	28
Setting and Rehearsing Timings for a Presentation	30
Preparing a Presentation in Outline View	31
Deleting a Presentation	36
Using Help	36
Getting Help from the Office Assistant	36
Using the Microsoft PowerPoint Help Dialog Box	37
Using Additional Help Features	40
Using ScreenTips	40
Chapter Summary	*41*
Commands Review	*42*
Thinking Offline	*43*
Working Hands-On	*45*

Chapter 2

Editing and Formatting a PowerPoint Presentation — 49

Editing Slides	49
Inserting and Deleting Text in Slides	50
Finding and Replacing Text in Slides	50
Inserting and Deleting Slides	51
Copying a Slide	52
Rearranging Text in Slides	54
Rearranging Object Boxes in a Slide	55
Rearranging Slides	55
Using Buttons on the Standard Toolbar	55
Completing a Spelling Check	57
Formatting a Presentation	60
Formatting Text in a Slide	60
Creating a New Line	62
Increasing/Decreasing Spacing Before/After Paragraphs	62
Formatting with a Master Slide	63
Formatting with Buttons on the Drawing Toolbar	66
Drawing an Object	68
Creating AutoShapes	68
Selecting an Object	68
Deleting an Object	69
Moving and Copying an Object	69
Sizing an Object	69
Formatting Objects	69
Creating a Text Box	72
Grouping and Ungrouping Objects	75
Flipping and Rotating an Object	75
Distributing and Aligning Objects	76
Formatting the Slide Color Scheme	78
Changing the Design Template	81
Creating a Blank Presentation and Applying a Design Template	83
Formatting with Format Painter	83
Promoting and Demoting Text in the Slide Pane	83
Formatting with Bullets and Numbers	86
Inserting Headers and Footers in a Presentation	89
Inserting a Header and/or Footer in Notes and Handouts	91
Adding Speaker Notes	91
Chapter Summary	*93*
Commands Review	*95*
Thinking Offline	*96*
Working Hands-On	*97*

Chapter 3

Adding Animation to Presentations — 103

Adding Animation Effects to a Presentation — 103
   Adding a Build to Slides — 106
Inserting Clip Art in a Presentation — 109
   Sizing and Scaling Images — 109
   Inserting Images from a Disk — 112
   Recoloring Clip Art Images in PowerPoint — 115
   Creating Watermarks — 116
Creating a Table in a Slide — 118
Creating Hyperlinks in a Presentation — 119
   Creating Hyperlinks from a Slide to the Web — 119
   Creating Hyperlinks from a Slide to a Word Document — 121
   Linking Slides within a Presentation with Action Buttons — 123
Importing Text from Word — 124
   Changing the Autolayout — 125
   Collecting and Pasting Multiple Items — 126
Publishing a Presentation to the Web — 127
   Previewing a Web Page — 128
Sending a Presentation via E-mail — 130
Chapter Summary — *132*
Commands Review — *133*
Thinking Offline — *133*
Working Hands-On — *135*

Chapter 4

Using WordArt and Creating Organizational Charts — 141

Using WordArt — 141
   Entering Text — 142
   Sizing and Moving WordArt — 143
   Changing the Font and Font Size — 144
   Customizing WordArt — 144
   Customizing WordArt with Buttons on the Drawing Toolbar — 148
Creating an Organizational Chart — 154
   Keying Information in an Organizational Chart — 155
   Sizing and Moving an Organizational Chart — 155
   Editing an Existing Organizational Chart — 157
   Adding Boxes to an Organizational Chart — 157
   Customizing an Organizational Chart — 159
   Changing the View in an Organizational Chart — 159
Chapter Summary — *161*
Commands Review — *162*
Thinking Offline — *163*
Working Hands-On — *164*

Chapter 5

Integrated Topic: Linking and Embedding Objects and Replacing Fonts — 169

Linking Objects — 170
Embedding Objects — 173
   Editing an Embedded Object — 174
Replace Fonts — 177
Create a New Presentation from Existing Slides — 178
Chapter Summary — *179*
Commands Review — *180*
Thinking Offline — *180*
Working Hands-On — *181*

PowerPoint 2000 Core Level Performance Assessments — 183

Assessing Core Proficiencies — 183
Writing Activities — 188
Internet Activity — 188

PowerPoint Core Level Index — 189

Introduction

Most new personal computers in the marketplace today are preloaded with the Microsoft® Windows® operating system or with Windows-based applications such as Microsoft PowerPoint® 2000. The PowerPoint 2000 software program is part of Microsoft Office 2000, one of the most popular Windows-based program suites, which includes Word, Excel, Access, PowerPoint, and additional applications in certain editions.

In this textbook, students gain a basic knowledge of PowerPoint 2000. They learn the beginning and intermediate features of PowerPoint, as well as ways in which this program interacts with Windows and the Internet.

Students do not need prior computer experience nor familiarity with using Windows in order to use this textbook. However, knowledge of basic high school freshman mathematics is required.

Approved Courseware for the Microsoft Office User Specialist (MOUS) Program

The logo on the cover of this text means that Microsoft has approved this text as courseware that teaches all of the skills that students need to master to pass the Microsoft Office User Specialist (MOUS) Core Certification exam in PowerPoint 2000. These skills and the corresponding page numbers of related instruction in the text are listed on the page that precedes chapter 1.

The MOUS program is used to test and validate a student's skills and thereby supply objective proof to an employer or prospective employer that the student knows how to use a program efficiently and productively. For more information on the MOUS program and where to take the certification exam, visit Microsoft's Web site at *www.microsoft.com* or the specific MOUS site at *www.mous.net*.

Focus on Certification

This text teaches the skills necessary for PowerPoint 2000 Core Level certification. Students learn to prepare a PowerPoint presentation and use various methods for editing and formatting a presentation. Students gain experience in adding animation, using WordArt, and creating organizational charts for use in presentations.

Chapter Structure

Each chapter contains the following sections:

- Performance Objectives that identify the specific learning goals of the chapter.
- Introductory material that provides an overview of new concepts and features.
- Step-by-step exercises at the computer, which allow students to practice using the features(s) presented in the chapter.
- Chapter Summary.
- Commands Review.
- Thinking Offline, a short-answer, knowledge self-check.
- Working Hands-On, skill assessments that require students to complete exercises without step-by-step instructions; this section includes an exercise that requires use of the Help feature as indicated by an icon.

Table of Contents

Additional simulation exercises called Performance Assessments at the end of each level require students to make decisions about document preparation and formatting. These applied exercises provide ample opportunity to practice new features as well as previously learned features. The Writing Activities offer students the opportunity to write and format business documents. In addition, there is an Internet Activity in which students explore the Internet and use PowerPoint or another Office application to report on the information that they discover. In this section, students demonstrate problem-solving, critical-thinking, and creative-thinking abilities as well as hands-on computer skills.

Completing Computer Exercises

Chapter 01C

Some computer exercises in the chapters require the student to access and use an existing file. Those student exercise files are saved on the CD-ROM that accompanies this textbook. The files for each chapter are saved in individual folders, as indicated by a CD icon and chapter folder name on the first page of each chapter. Note, however, that some chapters may have no data files to copy.

Before beginning a chapter, the student should copy the folder from the CD-ROM to a preformatted data disk. After completing the exercises in a chapter, the student should delete the chapter folder to ensure adequate storage space for the next chapter's files. Students should check with the instructor first, however. The inside back cover provides detailed instructions on how to use the CD-ROM and how to copy and delete folders.

Industry Standards from the SCANS Commission

This textbook covers the important goals of the Secretary's Commission on Achieving Necessary Skills (SCANS), a joint commission from the Department of Education and Labor. The overall goal of the commission was to establish interdisciplinary standards that should be required for all students. SCANS skill standards emphasize the integration of competencies from the areas of information gathering and research, technology, basic skills, and thinking skills.

In addition, all educators agree that curricula can be strengthened by classroom work that is authentic and relevant to learners, i.e., classroom work that connects context to content. Teaching in context helps students move away from a subject-specific orientation to an integrative learning that includes decision making, problem solving, and critical thinking. The concepts and applications material in each level of this book is designed to reflect an interdisciplinary emphasis, as well as implement the SCANS standards. SCANS places heavy emphasis on communication skills as well as on activity planning and follow-through, each of which is part of chapter and level exercises wherever appropriate.

Examples of context-relative and SCANS-related work are found in the chapter skill assessments called Working Hands-On, which reinforce acquired technical skills while providing practice in decision making and problem solving. Other examples, in the Performance Assessments sections, offer simulations that require students to demonstrate their understanding of the major skills and technical features within a framework of critical and creative thinking. The Writing Activities toward the end of each level make it clear that students are not just producers, but editors and writers as well.

Emphasis on Visual Learning

Microsoft Office programs such as PowerPoint operate within the Windows operating system, a graphical user interface (GUI) that provides a visually oriented environment by using icons to represent program features. This textbook also emphasizes a graphical environment with icons that represent specific learning components.

In keeping with Windows' graphical environment, figures that illustrate numerous steps done at the computer are labeled with "bubble" callouts corresponding to the steps. The student can easily follow the steps by seeing the exact spot on the computer screen where a certain action is required on their part.

Introduction

Icons offer additional visual learning cues. For example, a computer icon appears next to Performance Assessments. A hands-on-keyboard icon identifies the Writing Activities at the end of each level. A globe icon displays next to the Internet Activity at the end of each level.

Upon completion of the course, students will have mastered the basic-to-intermediate features and/or Core Level MOUS skills of PowerPoint 2000. They also will have practiced some basic skills in using Windows and acquired a solid foundation in the problem-solving and communication competencies so important in the contemporary workplace.

Learning Components that Accompany This Text

The following products for instructors and students correspond to this text and enhance its teaching possibilities. These products may be ordered by contacting an EMC/Paradigm Publishing Customer Care representative by phone at (800) 535-6865 or via E-mail at *educate@emcp.com* and supplying the order number as follows:

- **Textbook Web site at *www.emcp.com*.** Watch for updates, tips, and instructional activities for students and instructors at the Office 2000 Resource Center link.

- **Microsoft® PowerPoint 2000 Instructor's Guide with CD-ROM, Order number 41339.**
  The Instructor's Guide contains suggested course syllabi, grade sheets, and assignment sheets for Core and Expert Levels; comprehensive PowerPoint tests and answers to use as final exams; Supplemental Performance Assessments; and a list of PowerPoint slides available on the CD. For each chapter, the Instructor's Guide also provides a summary of chapter contents, Teaching Hints, Thinking Offline answers, and Working Hands-On model answers for all exercises and assessments in the text. The Instructor's CD-ROM contains everything found in the print Instructor's Guide plus model answer files for all exercises and PowerPoint slides for classroom use.

PowerPoint

CORE LEVEL

Preparing a PowerPoint Presentation

Editing and Formatting a PowerPoint Presentation

Adding Animation to Presentations

Using WordArt and Creating Organizational Charts

Integrated Topic: Linking and Embedding Objects and Replacing Fonts

Core Level Performance Assessments

MICROSOFT® POWERPOINT 2000

CORE LEVEL MOUS SKILLS

Coding No.	SKILL	Pages
PP2000.1	**Creating a presentation**	
PP2000.1.1	Delete slides	51-53
PP2000.1.2	Create a specified type of slide	7-10, 17-19
PP2000.1.3	Create a presentation from a template and/or a Wizard	7-9, 17-20
PP2000.1.4	Navigate among different views (slide, outline, sorter, tri-pane)	20-21
PP2000.1.5	Create a new presentation from existing slides	27
PP2000.1.6	Copy a slide from one presentation into another	52-54
PP2000.1.7	Insert headers and footers	89-93
PP2000.1.8	Create a Blank presentation	83-85
PP2000.1.9	Create a presentation using the AutoContent Wizard	19-20
PP2000.1.10	Send a presentation via e-mail	130-131
PP2000.2	**Modifying a presentation**	
PP2000.2.1	Change the order of slides using Slide Sorter view	55, 58
PP2000.2.2	Find and replace text	50-52
PP2000.2.3	Change the layout for one or more slides	125-127
PP2000.2.4	Change slide layout (modify the Slide Master)	63-66
PP2000.2.5	Modify slide sequence in the Outline pane	54, 58
PP2000.2.6	Apply a design template	81-82, 83-85
PP2000.3	**Working with text**	
PP2000.3.1	Check spelling	56, 57
PP2000.3.2	Change and replace text fonts (individual slide and entire presentation)	61, 63-65, 74, 76
PP2000.3.3	Enter text in tri-pane view	7, 52-54, 142
PP2000.3.4	Import Text from Word	124-126
PP2000.3.5	Change the text alignment	61, 64-65
PP2000.3.6	Create a text box for entering text	72-75
PP2000.3.7	Use the Wrap text in Text Box feature	72-75
PP2000.3.8	Use the Office Clipboard	126-127
PP2000.3.9	Use the Format Painter	83-84
PP2000.3.10	Promote and Demote text in Slide and Outline panes	32-35, 83-85
PP2000.4	**Working with visual elements**	
PP2000.4.1	Add a picture from the ClipArt Gallery	109-111
PP2000.4.2	Add and group shapes using WordArt or the Drawing Toolbar	75-77, 142-148
PP2000.4.3	Apply formatting	60-91, 115
PP2000.4.4	Place text inside a shape using a text box	72-75
PP2000.4.5	Scale and size an object including ClipArt	109-111
PP2000.4.6	Create tables within PowerPoint	118-119
PP2000.4.7	Rotate and fill an object	75-77
PP2000.5	**Customizing a presentation**	
PP2000.5.1	Add AutoNumber bullets	87-89
PP2000.5.2	Add speaker notes	91-93
PP2000.5.3	Add graphical bullets	86-89
PP2000.5.4	Add slide transitions	25-27
PP2000.5.5	Animate text and objects	103-109
PP2000.6	**Creating output**	
PP2000.6.1	Preview presentation in black and white	15, 18
PP2000.6.2	Print slides in a variety of formats	9-15, 18-19, 20, 23-24, 83-85, 127, 130
PP2000.6.3	Print audience handouts	18-19
PP2000.6.4	Print speaker notes in a specified format	92-93
PP2000.7	**Delivering a presentation**	
PP2000.7.1	Start a slide show on any slide	22-25
PP2000.7.2	Use on screen navigation tools	22-25
PP2000.7.3	Print a slide as an overhead transparency	84
PP2000.7.4	Use the pen during a presentation	22, 24-25
PP2000.8	**Managing files**	
PP2000.8.1	Save changes to a presentation	27, 30, 31
PP2000.8.2	Save as a new presentation	7, 15-16
PP2000.8.3	Publish a presentation to the Web	127-130
PP2000.8.4	Use Office Assistant	36-37
PP2000.8.5	Insert hyperlink	119-123

 Chapter 01C

Preparing a PowerPoint Presentation

PERFORMANCE OBJECTIVES

Upon successful completion of chapter 1, you will be able to:
- Plan a PowerPoint presentation.
- Create a PowerPoint presentation.
- Print a PowerPoint presentation.
- Save, open, and close presentations.
- View and preview a presentation.
- Run a presentation.
- Use the pen during a presentation.
- Add transitions and sound effects to a presentation.
- Run a slide show automatically.
- Set and rehearse timings for a presentation.
- Prepare a presentation in Outline view.
- Delete a presentation.
- Use the Office Assistant and Microsoft PowerPoint Help.

During a presentation, the person doing the presenting may use visual aids to strengthen the impact of the message as well as help organize the presentation. Visual aids may include transparencies, slides, photographs, or an on-screen presentation. With Microsoft's PowerPoint program, you can easily create visual aids for a presentation and then print copies of the aids as well as run the presentation. PowerPoint is a presentation graphics program that you can use to organize and present information.

PowerPoint provides a variety of output capabilities for presentations. A presentation prepared in PowerPoint can be run directly on the computer. In addition, black and white overheads can be created by printing slides on transparencies, or, color transparencies can be created if you have access to a color printer. Slides can be created in PowerPoint and then sent to a film processing company to be converted to 35mm slides. Also, printouts of slides can be made for use as speaker's notes, audience handouts, or outline pages.

Planning a Presentation

With PowerPoint, you can create slides for an on-screen presentation, or for an overhead or slide projector. You can also print handouts of the presentation, print an outline, or print the entire presentation. When planning a presentation, first define the purpose of the presentation. Is the intent to inform? educate? sell? motivate? and/or entertain? Additionally, consider the audience who will be listening to and watching the presentation. Determine the content of the presentation and also the medium that will be used to convey the message. Will a computer be used to display the slides of a presentation or will overhead transparencies be created from the slides? Basic guidelines to consider when preparing the content of the presentation include:

- **Determine the main purpose of the presentation.** Do not try to cover too many topics—this may strain the audience's attention or cause confusion. Identifying the main point of the presentation will help you stay focused and convey a clear message to the audience.
- **Determine the output:** Is the presentation going to be presented in PowerPoint? will slides be used? or will black and white or color transparencies be made for an overhead? To help decide the type of output needed, consider the availability of equipment, the size of the room where the presentation will be made, and the number of people who will be attending the presentation.
- **Show one idea per slide.** Each slide in a presentation should convey only one main idea. Too many thoughts or ideas on a slide may confuse the audience and cause you to stray from the purpose of the slide. Determine the specific message you want to convey to the audience then outline the message to organize ideas.
- **Maintain a consistent layout.** A consistent layout and color scheme for slides in a presentation will create continuity and cohesiveness. Do not get carried away by using too many colors and too many pictures or other graphic elements.
- **Keep slides easy to read and uncluttered.** Keep slides simple and easy for the audience to read. Keep words and other items such as bullets to a minimum. If the presentation is done with 35mm slides, consider using a dark background color for slides. Use a light background color when creating overhead transparencies.
- **Determine the output needed:** Will you be providing audience members with handouts? If so, will these handouts consist of a printing of each slide? an outline of the presentation? or a printing of each slide with space for taking notes?

Creating a PowerPoint Presentation

PowerPoint provides several methods for creating a presentation. You can use PowerPoint's AutoContent Wizard, which asks questions and then chooses a presentation layout based on your answers. You can also create a presentation using predesigned templates. PowerPoint's templates provide a variety of formatting options for slides. If you want to apply your own formatting to slides, you can choose a blank presentation. The steps you follow to create a presentation will vary depending on the method you choose. There are, however, basic steps you will complete. These steps are:

Chapter One

1. Open PowerPoint.
2. Choose a slide template (or choose a blank template if you want to apply your own formatting) or use PowerPoint's AutoContent Wizard.
3. Key the text for each slide, adding additional elements as needed such as graphic images.
4. Save the presentation.
5. Print the presentation as slides, handouts, notes pages, or an outline.
6. Run the presentation.
7. Close the presentation.
8. Exit PowerPoint.

Understanding the PowerPoint Window

When PowerPoint has been opened and you have chosen the specific type of presentation you want to create, you are presented with the PowerPoint window in the Normal view. What displays in the window will vary depending on what type of presentation you are creating. However, there are consistent elements of the PowerPoint window. Figure 1.1 contains callouts specifying the various elements of the PowerPoint window. These elements are described after the figure.

In figure 1.1, the Standard and Formatting toolbars are displayed as two separate toolbars. When you start PowerPoint, the Standard and Formatting toolbar may appear together in the same row. In this case, you will notice two buttons on the toolbar with a double right-pointing arrow and a down-pointing triangle displayed on them. These are the More Buttons buttons and are used to access the Standard and Formatting buttons that are not visible. There will be one More Button approximately halfway across the toolbar which will provide access to additional Standard toolbar buttons. The second More Buttons button at the right end of the toolbar will provide access to additional Formatting toolbar buttons.

More Buttons button

Click the down-pointing triangle on the More Buttons button to display a palette of additional buttons. Complete the following steps if you prefer to set up PowerPoint so that the Standard and Formatting toolbars are separate as shown in figure 1.1.

1. Click Tools, and then click Customize.
2. Click the Options tab in the Customize dialog box.
3. Click the Standard and Formatting toolbars share one row check box to deselect the option.
4. Click Close to close the Customize dialog box.

As an alternative to the steps listed above, you could position the pointer over the raised gray bar between the More Buttons button and the Font button until the pointer changes to a four-headed move icon, and then drag the Formatting toolbar down below the Standard toolbar.

figure 1.1 PowerPoint Window

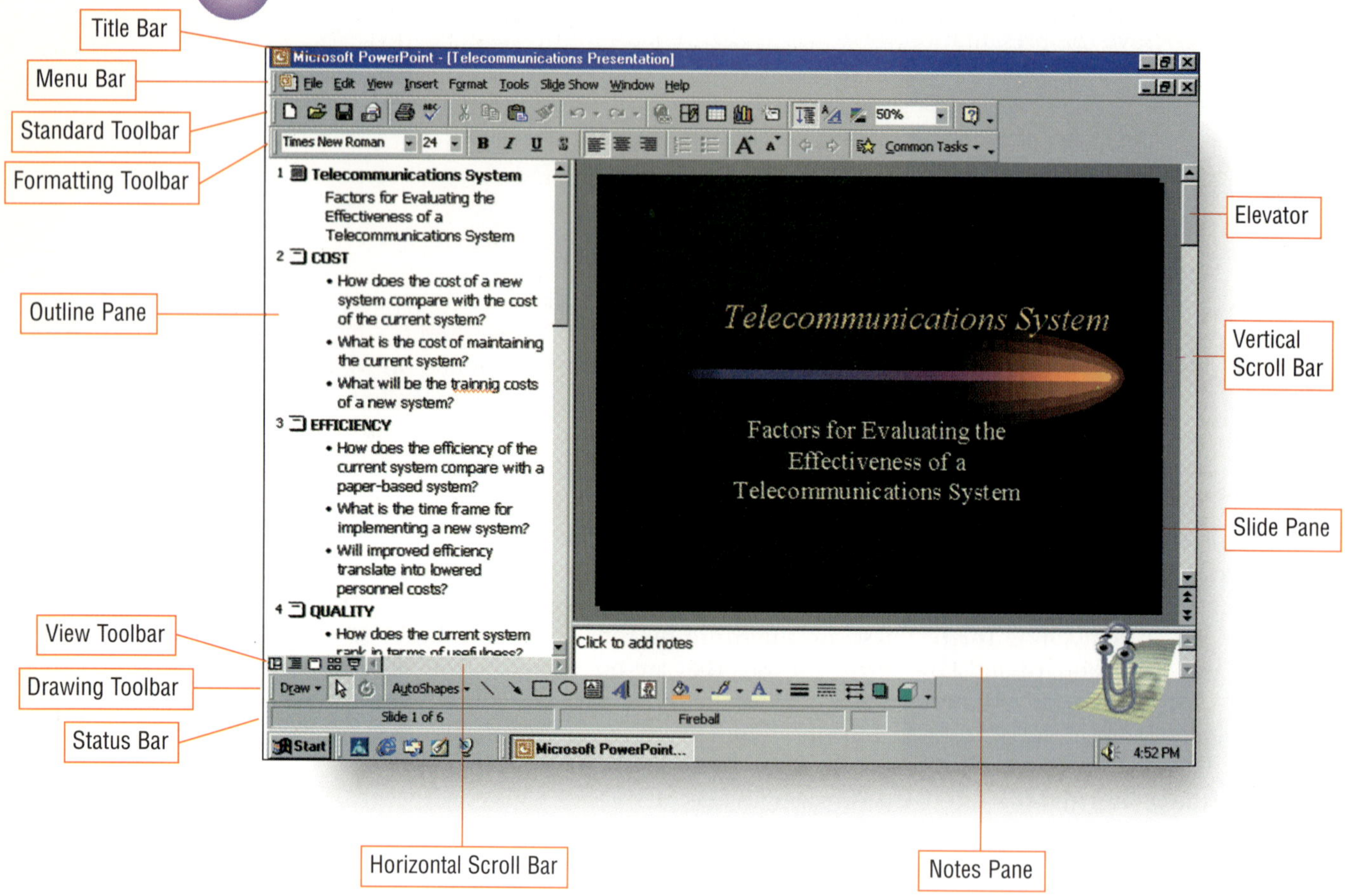

The PowerPoint window contains many elements that are similar to other Microsoft applications such as Word and Excel. For example, the PowerPoint window, like the Word window, contains a Title bar, Menu bar, Standard and Formatting toolbars, scroll bars, and a Status bar. The elements of the PowerPoint window include:

- **Title bar:** This bar displays the program name, a document title, a control menu, the Close button, and the Minimize and Restore buttons for resizing the window.
- **Menu bar:** PowerPoint commands are grouped into options that display on the Menu bar. For example, options for formatting slides can be found at the Format drop-down menu.
- **Standard toolbar:** This toolbar contains buttons for the most frequently used commands in PowerPoint such as cutting, copying, and pasting text; inserting hyperlinks, tables, and charts; and changing the zoom display.
- **Formatting toolbar:** Frequently used commands for formatting a PowerPoint presentation are grouped onto the Formatting toolbar. This toolbar contains options such as changing typeface and size, increasing and decreasing type size, adding type styles such as bold and italics, changing paragraph alignment, and adding animation effects.

- **Drawing toolbar:** With buttons on the Drawing toolbar, you can draw objects such as lines, arcs, and shapes. Buttons on this toolbar also contain options for adding attributes to objects, such as color, shading, and shadow.
- **Outline pane:** The contents of a presentation display in the Outline pane. At this pane, you can organize and develop the contents of the presentation. In a completed presentation, the Outline pane becomes the table of contents for the presentation.
- **Slide pane:** The slide pane is where slides are created and displayed. Here you can see how text looks on each slide and add elements such as clip art images, hyperlinks, and animation effects.
- **Notes pane:** Add notes to a presentation in the Notes pane.
- **Vertical scroll bar:** Use the vertical scroll bar to display specific slides in a presentation. The small box located on the vertical scroll bar is called the *elevator*. Drag the elevator on the vertical scroll bar and a yellow box displays specifying the slide number within the presentation. Use the elevator to move quickly to a specific slide.
- **Horizontal scroll bar:** The Outline pane contains a horizontal scroll bar you can use to shift text left or right in the Outline pane.
- **View toolbar:** The View toolbar, located at the left side of the horizontal scroll bar, contains buttons for changing the presentation view. For example, you can view individual slides, view several slides at once, view slide information as an outline, and also run the presentation.
- **Status bar:** Messages about PowerPoint features display in the Status bar, which is located toward the bottom of the PowerPoint window. The Status bar also displays information about the view.

PowerPoint, like other Microsoft applications, provides ScreenTips for buttons on toolbars. Position the arrow pointer on a button on any of the PowerPoint toolbars, and a ScreenTip displays (after one second) for the button.

Creating a Presentation Using a Template

To create a presentation using a PowerPoint template, you would complete the following steps:

1. Open PowerPoint by clicking the Start button on the Windows Taskbar, pointing to **P**rograms, and then clicking *Microsoft PowerPoint*.
2. At the PowerPoint dialog box shown in figure 1.2, select Design **T**emplate, and then click OK.
3. At the New Presentation dialog box shown in figure 1.3, make sure the Design Templates tab is selected. (If not, click the Design Templates tab.)
4. At the New Presentation dialog box with the Design Templates tab selected, click the desired template (the template displays in the Preview box at the right side of the dialog box), and then click OK. You can also double-click the desired template.
5. At the New Slide dialog box shown in figure 1.4, click the desired autolayout, and then click OK.
6. Key the desired text and/or insert the desired elements in the slide.
7. To create another slide, click the New Slide button on the PowerPoint Standard toolbar, and then double-click the desired autolayout.
8. When all slides have been completed, save the presentation by clicking the Save button on the Standard toolbar. At the Save As dialog box, key a name for the presentation, and then click **S**ave.

> Design templates provided by PowerPoint were designed by professional graphic artists who understand the use of color, space, and design.

> Use the Blank Presentation template if you want complete control over the presentation design.

New Slide

Save

Preparing a PowerPoint Presentation

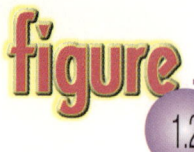

figure 1.2 PowerPoint Dialog Box

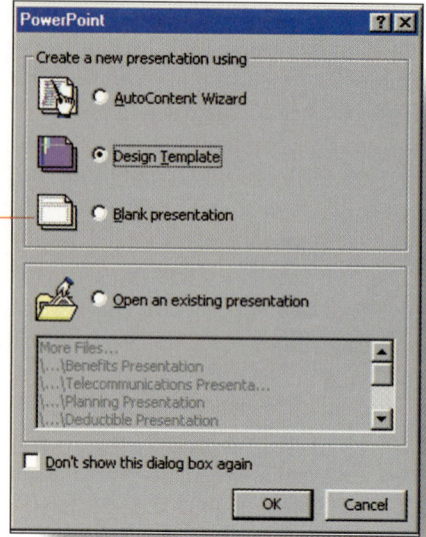

At this dialog box, choose the AutoContent Wizard, a design template, a blank presentation, or open an existing presentation.

figure 1.3 New Presentation Dialog Box

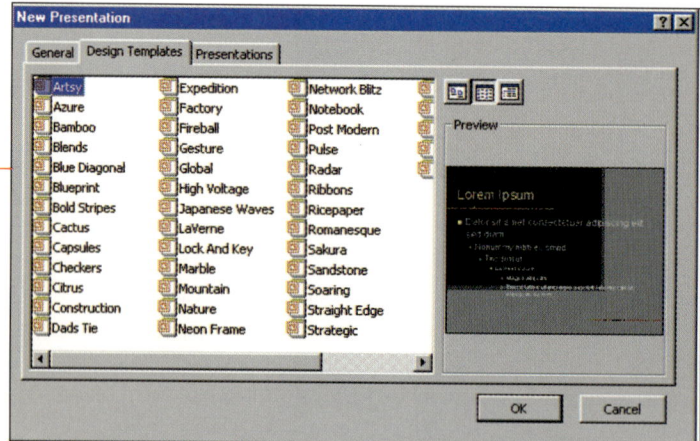

Choose a design template from this list and then preview it at the right.

New Slide Dialog Box

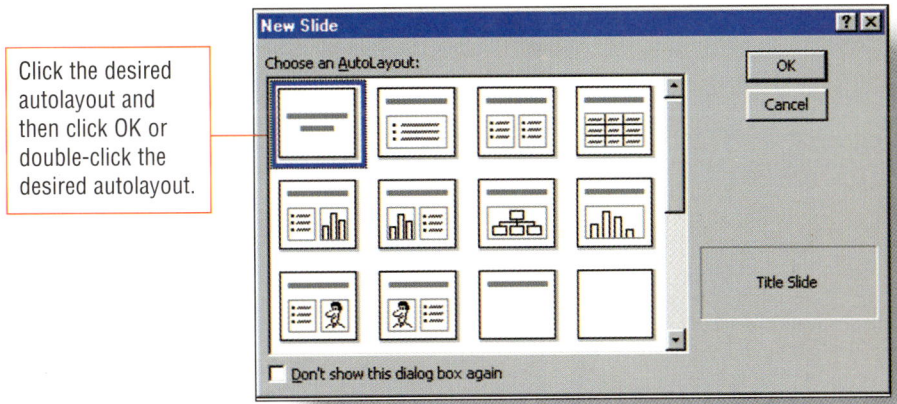

Click the desired autolayout and then click OK or double-click the desired autolayout.

When you choose an autolayout format at the New Slide dialog box, each slide will probably contain placeholders. A placeholder is a location on the slide where information is to be entered. For example, many slides contain a title placeholder. Click in this placeholder and then key the title of the slide. When text is entered into a placeholder, the placeholder turns into a text object. An autolayout format may include some or all of the following placeholders:

- **Title:** Used to hold the title of the slide.
- **Bulleted List:** Used for a bulleted list of related points or topics.
- **Clip Art:** Holds a picture, such as a clip art image, in a slide.
- **Chart:** Holds a chart, which is a visual representation of data.
- **Organization Chart:** Used to display an organizational chart in a slide.
- **Table:** Used for a table that is inserted from Microsoft Word.

Choose a template design at the New Presentation dialog box with the Design Templates tab selected as shown in figure 1.3. Display this dialog box when you first open PowerPoint by clicking Design Template at the PowerPoint dialog box. To display this dialog box if PowerPoint is already open, click File and then New. This displays the New Presentation dialog box where you can click the Design Templates tab.

Printing a Presentation

A presentation can be printed in a variety of formats. You can print each slide on a separate piece of paper; print each slide at the top of the page, leaving the bottom of the page for notes; print up to six slides or a specific number of slides on a single piece of paper; or print the slide titles and topics in outline form. Use the Print what option at the Print dialog box to specify what you want printed.

To display the Print dialog box, shown in figure 1.5, click File and then Print. At the Print dialog box, click the down-pointing triangle at the right side of the Print what text box, and then click the desired printing format.

Autolayouts make arranging elements in a slide easier.

Scroll down the Choose an AutoLayout list box to view additional autolayouts.

Printing a hard copy of your presentation helps reinforce your message.

Print Dialog Box

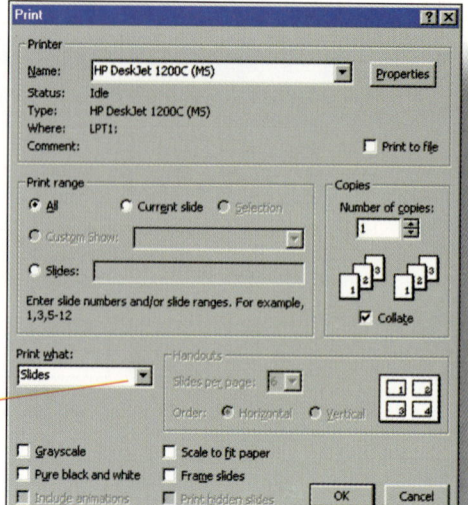

Click the down-pointing triangle to display a list of printing options.

As an example of what will print with the printing options, look at figures 1.6, 1.7, 1.8, and 1.9. Figure 1.6 shows the printing of the slides you will create in exercise 1 with the *Slides* option selected in the Print what text box at the Print dialog box. As you can see, each slide is printed on a separate piece of paper. Figure 1.7 shows the presentation as it will print when *Handouts* is selected and the Slides per page option in the Handouts is set at the default of *6*. The printing in figure 1.8 shows the slides printed in the *Notes Pages* format. At this printing, the slides are printed at the top of the page, leaving room at the bottom of the page for notes. The last printing figure, figure 1.9, shows the printing of the presentation in the *Outline View*.

Printing with Slides Selected at Print dialog box

Chapter One

Fig. 1.6 continued

Planning the Publication

STEP 2
Assess your target audience.

Planning the Publication

STEP 3
Determine the best format for your message based on your intended audience.

Planning the Publication

STEP 4
Decide what you want your readers to do after reading your message.

Planning the Publication

STEP 5
Collect examples of effective designs.

Printing with Handouts Selected at Print Dialog Box

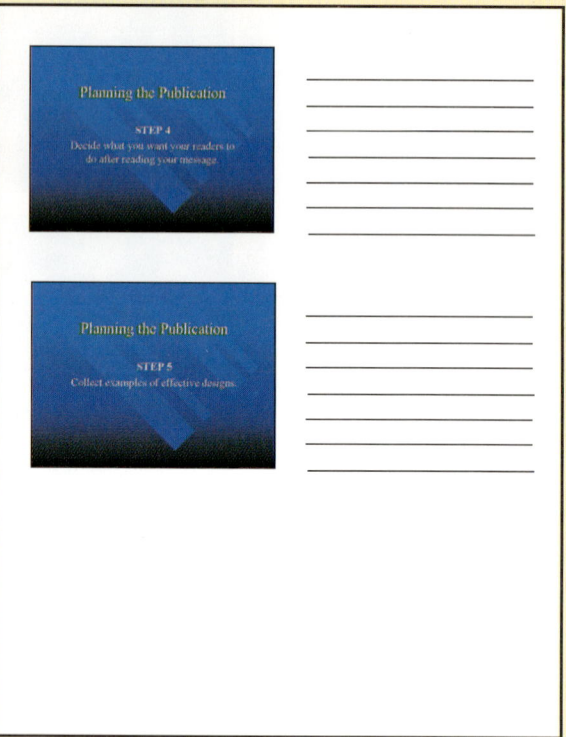

Printing with Notes Pages Selected at Print Dialog Box

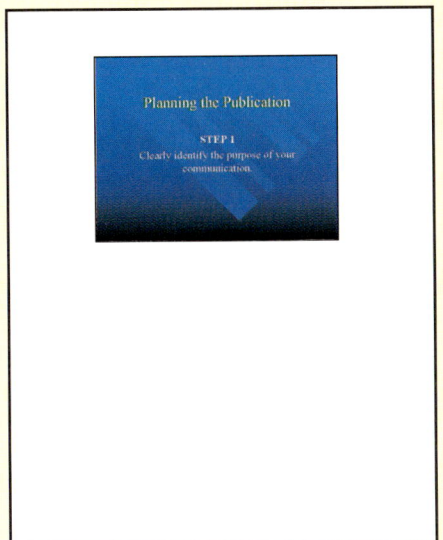
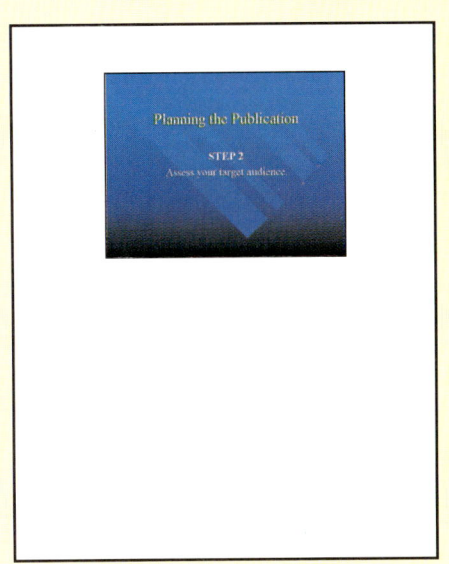

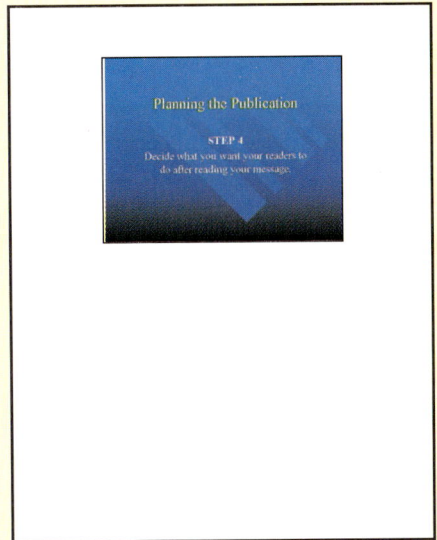

Preparing a PowerPoint Presentation

Fig 1.8 continued

figure 1.9

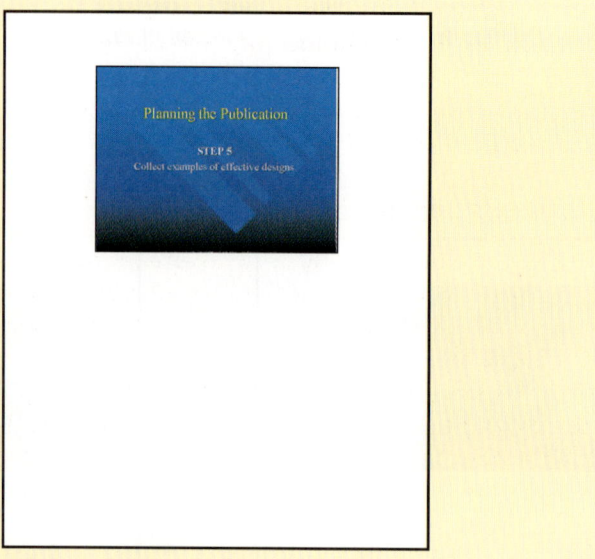

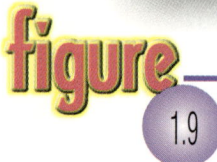

Printing with Outline View Selected at Print Dialog Box

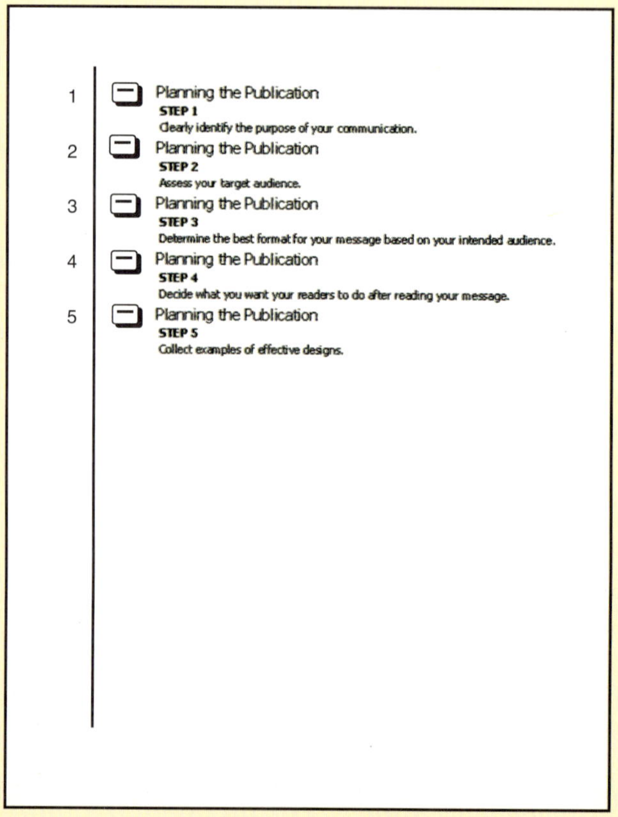

Printing a Presentation in Grayscale and Black and White

If you do not have access to a color printer or if you are going to photocopy slides and/or notes on a black and white photocopier, consider printing slides in grayscale or black and white. To do this, display the Print dialog box and then choose either Grayscale or Pure black and white. These options display in the lower left corner of the Print dialog box.

Previewing in Grayscale and Black and White

Before printing in grayscale or black and white, consider previewing the slides. Preview slides in grayscale by clicking the Grayscale Preview button on the Standard toolbar. If you are in Normal or Slide view, the slide displays in grayscale and a miniature slide displays showing the color formatting. Turn off Grayscale Preview by clicking the button again. If you want to preview slides in pure black and white (with no shades of gray), hold down the Shift key and then click the Grayscale Preview button.

Grayscale Preview

Expanding Drop-down Menus

When you open PowerPoint, the menus display a limited selection of basic commands called *first rank options*. At the bottom of each menu is a downward-pointing double arrow. To expand the drop-down menu and display additional options, known as *second rank options*, click the downward-pointing double arrow, double-click the menu option, or allow the pointer to rest on the menu option for approximately 5 seconds. The menu will expand and show all options. Second rank options are displayed with a lighter gray background.

As you create and edit presentations, the commands that you use most often are stored as personalized options and displayed on the drop-down menus when you select them. Expand the menu if an option that you require does not appear on the menu. Second-rank options become first-rank options after you have used them once.

To disable the personalized menu feature and always display all of the menu options, click Tools, click Customize, and then select the Options tab in the Customize dialog box. Click the Menus show recently used commands first check box to remove the check mark and click the Close button to close the Customize dialog box.

The instructions in this book assume that the personalized menu feature has been disabled. If the computer you are using has this feature enabled, you may need to expand the menus to find the options being discussed.

Saving a Presentation

After creating a presentation, save it by clicking File and then Save or by clicking the Save button on the Standard toolbar. This displays the Save As dialog box. By default, a PowerPoint presentation is saved to the *My Documents* folder. To save a presentation onto your data disk, you will need to change the active folder. To change to data disk that is located in drive A, click the down-pointing triangle to the right of the Save in text box, and then click *3½ Floppy (A:)*. After changing the default folder, key the presentation document name in the File name text box, and then click Save or press Enter.

Preparing a PowerPoint Presentation

P-15

Closing a Presentation

After creating, viewing, and/or printing a presentation, close the presentation. To do this click, the Close button at the right side of the Menu bar or click File and then Close. If any changes were made to the presentation that were not saved, you will be asked if you want to save the changes.

Completing Computer Exercises

At the end of sections within chapters and at the end of chapters, you will be completing hands-on exercises at the computer. These exercises will provide you with the opportunity to practice the presented functions and commands. The skill assessment exercises at the end of each chapter include general directions. If you do not remember how to perform a particular function, refer to the text within the chapter.

You will be instructed to save presentations in a folder for each chapter. Folders are used to organize files into logical units.

Presentation Files

In some exercises in this book you will be instructed to open a presentation from the Presentations folder on the CDROM that accompanies this textbook. Presentations, particularly presentations containing images, can be quite large in size and take up a considerable amount of space on your disk. For this reason, you will be instructed to open the presentation file from the Presentations folder on the CDROM instead of copying the file from the CDROM to your data disk.

Creating a Folder

At the beginning of each chapter and before completing any computer exercises, you will be instructed to either create a new folder on your disk to save the presentations in that you will be completing throughout the chapter, or to copy a folder from the CDROM that accompanies this textbook to your disk. Instructions for copying a folder are printed on the inside of the back cover of the textbook.

A new folder can be created at either the Open or Save As dialog boxes. Complete the following steps to create a new folder in PowerPoint on your data disk:

1. Click the Open button on the Standard toolbar to display the Open dialog box.
2. Insert your data disk in the floppy drive.
3. Click the down-pointing triangle at the right of the Look in text box, then click *3½ Floppy (A:)* from the drop-down list.
4. Click the Create New Folder button on the dialog box toolbar.
5. Key the folder name in the Name text box in the New Folder dialog box and then click OK or press Enter.
6. The new folder becomes the active folder.
7. Close the Open dialog box.

Chapter One

Creating and Printing a Presentation

1. Create a new folder on your disk named *Chapter 01C* by completing the following steps:
   a. Open PowerPoint by clicking the Start button, pointing to *Programs*, and then clicking *Microsoft PowerPoint*.
   b. Click OK at the PowerPoint dialog box..
   c. Click the down-pointing triangle to the right of the Look in text box, and click *3½ Floppy (A:)* from the drop-down list.
   d. Click the Create New Folder button on the dialog box toolbar.
   e. Key **Chapter 01C** in the Name text box, and then click OK or press Enter.
   f. Chapter 01C folder is now the active folder.
   g. Close the Open dialog box by clicking the close button at the right side of the dialog box title bar.

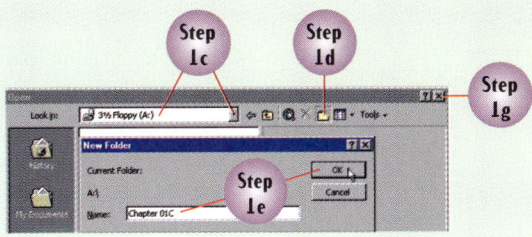

2. Prepare a presentation on the steps for planning a publication by completing the following steps:
   a. Click File and New.
   b. At the New Presentation dialog box, click the Design Templates tab.
   c. At the New Presentation dialog box with the Design Templates tab selected, double-click the *Blue Diagonal* template.
   d. At the New Slide dialog box, double-click the first autolayout in the list box. (The first autolayout is named Title Slide. The autolayout name displays in the lower right corner of the dialog box.)
   e. At the slide, click anywhere in the text *Click to add title*, and then key **Planning the Publication**.
   f. Click anywhere in the text *Click to add subtitle* and key the following:
      1) Turn on bold, key **STEP 1**, and then turn off bold.
      2) Press Enter and key **Clearly identify the purpose of your communication.**

   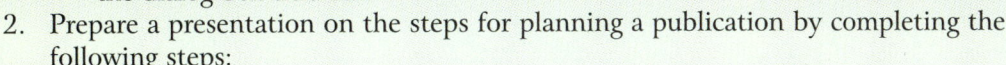

   g. Click the New Slide button located on the Standard toolbar.
   h. At the New Slide dialog box, double-click the first autolayout (Title Slide) in the list box. (This inserts another slide in the Presentation window.)
   i. Complete steps similar to those in 2e and 2f to create the following text. Do not key the text (*press Enter*); this is an instruction:
      Title   =   **Planning the Publication**
      Subtitle =   **STEP 2** (*press Enter*)
                    Assess your target audience.
   j. Click the New Slide button located on the Standard toolbar.
   k. At the New Slide dialog box, double-click the first autolayout (Title Slide) in the list box.

Preparing a PowerPoint Presentation

l. Complete steps similar to those in 2e and 2f to create the following text:
   Title   =   **Planning the Publication**
   Subtitle =   **STEP 3** *(press Enter)*
                Determine the best format for your message based on your intended audience.
m. Click the New Slide button located on the Standard toolbar.
n. At the New Slide dialog box, double-click the first autolayout (Title Slide) in the list box.
o. Complete steps similar to those in 2e and 2f to create the following text:
   Title   =   **Planning the Publication**
   Subtitle =   **STEP 4** *(press Enter)*
                Decide what you want your readers to do after reading your message.
p. Click the New Slide button located on the Standard toolbar.
q. At the New Slide dialog box, double-click the first autolayout (Title Slide) in the list box.
r. Complete steps similar to those in 2e and 2f to create the following text:
   Title   =   **Planning the Publication**
   Subtitle =   **STEP 5** *(press Enter)*
                Collect examples of effective designs.
s. Click in the slide outside the selected area. (This should deselect the box containing the subtitle.)

3. Save the presentation by completing the following steps:
   a. Click the Save button on the Standard toolbar.
   b. At the Save As dialog box, click the down-pointing triangle to the right of the Save in text box, and then click *3½ Floppy (A:)*.
   c. Double-click the Chapter 01C folder.
   d. Select the text in the File name textbox, key **Planning Presentation**, and then press Enter or click Save. Chapter 01C is now the default folder until you exit the PowerPoint.

4. Print all five slides on the same page by completing the following steps:
   a. Click File and Print.
   b. At the Print dialog box, click the down-pointing triangle to the right of the Print what option, and then click *Handouts* from the drop-down list.
   c. Make sure the number *6* displays in the Slides per page text box in the Handouts section of the dialog box.
   d. Click OK.

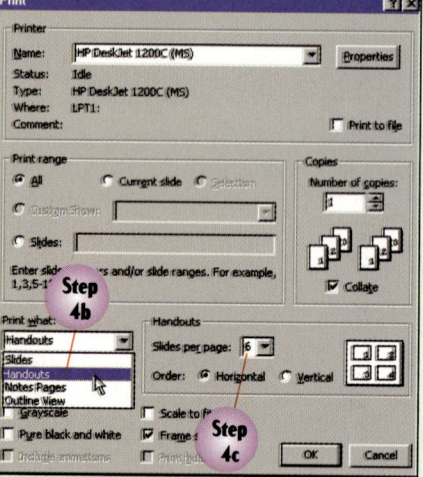

5. Preview and then print the slides in grayscale by completing the following steps:
   a. Click the Grayscale Preview button on the Standard toolbar.
   b. After viewing the presentation in grayscale, click the Grayscale Preview button to deactivate it.
   c. Preview the presentation in pure black and white by holding down the Shift key and then clicking the Grayscale Preview button on the Standard toolbar.
   d. Click the Grayscale Preview button again to deactivate it.
   e. Print the five slides on one page in grayscale by completing the following steps:

1) Click File and then Print.
   2) At the Print dialog box, click the Grayscale option (located in the lower left corner of the dialog box).
   3) Click the down-pointing triangle at the right of the Print what option and then click *Handouts* from the drop-down menu.
   4) Make sure the number *6* displays in the Slides per page text box in the Handouts section of the dialog box.
   5) Click OK.
6. Close Planning Presentation by clicking File and Close.
7. Exit PowerPoint by clicking File and then Exit.

Note: Do not delete Planning Presentation when you complete this chapter. You will need it in the next chapter.

Planning a Presentation with the AutoContent Wizard

PowerPoint contains an AutoContent Wizard that will help you in the planning and organizing of a presentation. You respond to certain questions from the Wizard and, based on your responses, the Wizard presents slides containing information on how to organize the presentation. For example, suppose you are an employee of an investment firm and have been asked to prepare a presentation on a variable annuity fund. You can use the AutoContent Wizard for help on how to organize this presentation. You will be doing this in exercise 2. The Wizard provides additional information on other types of presentations. Consider printing the information for these other presentations.

Getting Help from the AutoContent Wizard

1. Prepare slides for helping organize a presentation to market and sell a service by completing the following steps:
   a. Open PowerPoint by clicking the Start button on the Windows Taskbar, pointing to Programs, and then clicking *Microsoft PowerPoint*.
   b. At the PowerPoint dialog box, click AutoContent Wizard, and then click OK. (If PowerPoint is already open, click File and New. At the New Presentation dialog box with the General tab selected, double-click *AutoContent Wizard*.)
   c. At the AutoContent Wizard Start dialog box, click the Next> button that displays toward the bottom right side of the dialog box.
   d. At the AutoContent Wizard Presentation type dialog box, click the gray button containing Sales/Marketing, click *Product/Services Overview* in the list box, and then click the Next> button.

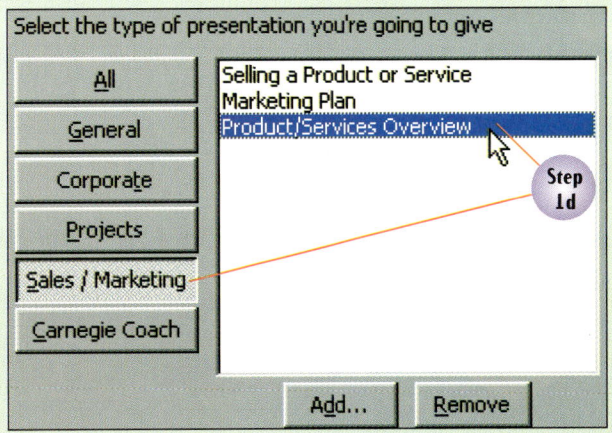

Preparing a PowerPoint Presentation P-19

e. At the AutoContent Wizard Presentation style dialog box, make sure the On-screen presentation option is selected, and then click the Next> button.
f. At the AutoContent Wizard Presentation options dialog box, make the following changes:
   1) Click inside the Presentation title text box and then key **McCormack Annuity Funds**.
   2) Press the Tab key. (This moves the insertion point to the Footer text box.)
   3) Key **Variable Annuity Fund**.
   4) Click the Next> button.

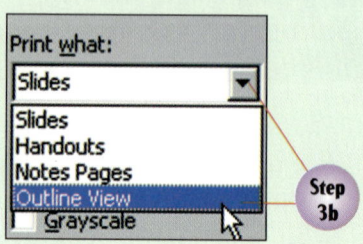

g. At the AutoContent Wizard Finish dialog box, click the Finish button.
h. The presentation created by the AutoContent Wizard displays in the Normal view. Scroll through the text in the Outline pane and read the information presented by the Wizard.

2. Save the presentation by completing the following steps:
   a. Click the Save button on the Standard toolbar.
   b. At the Save As dialog box, make sure Chapter 01C on your disk is the default folder, key **Selling Presentation** in the File name text box, and then press Enter or click Save.

3. Print the information on the slides provided by the Wizard in Outline View by completing the following steps:
   a. Choose File and Print.
   b. At the Print dialog box, click the down-pointing triangle to the right of the Print what option, and then click Outline View at the drop-down list.
   c. Click OK.

4. Close Selling Presentation. (If a dialog box displays asking if you want to save the changes, click Yes.)
5. Exit PowerPoint by clicking File and Exit.

Opening a Presentation Document

Open

A saved presentation document can be opened at the Open dialog box. To display this dialog box, click File and then Open or click the Open button on the Standard toolbar. At the Open dialog box, double-click the desired presentation document in the list box.

Viewing a Presentation

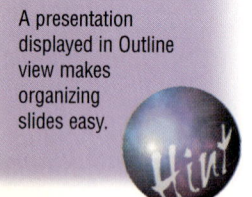
A presentation displayed in Outline view makes organizing slides easy.

PowerPoint provides a variety of viewing options for a presentation. The presentation view can be changed with options from the View drop-down menu or with viewing buttons that display on the View toolbar, shown in figure 1.10, located at the left side of the horizontal scroll bar. The viewing choices include:

- **Normal View:** This is the default view and displays three panes—outline, slide, and notes. With these three panes, you can work with all features in one place. This view is also referred to as tri-pane view.

Chapter One

- **Outline View:** The Outline view displays the organization of the presentation by headings and subheadings (see figure 1.9). Organize and develop the contents of the presentation in Outline view. Editing is probably easiest in this view since you simply click in the location you want to edit.
- **Slide View:** Use the Slide view to display individual slides. This view is useful for determining the effectiveness of elements that are positioned on the slide. Editing can also be performed in this view.
- **Slide Sorter View:** Choosing the Slide Sorter view displays all slides in the presentation in slide miniatures. In this view, you can easily add, move, rearrange, and delete slides.
- **Slide Show:** Use the Slide Show view to run a presentation. When you choose this view, the slide fills the entire screen.

Key and edit text in individual slides in Slide view.

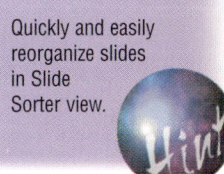

Quickly and easily reorganize slides in Slide Sorter view.

View Toolbar

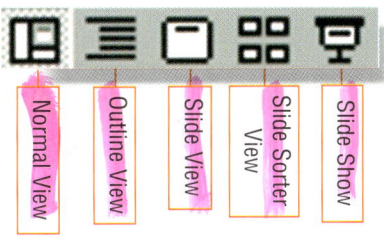

Change the view using either buttons on the View toolbar or options from the View drop-down menu. To use the View toolbar, click the desired button. To use the View option on the Menu bar, click View, and then click the desired view from the drop-down menu (except Outline view). The View drop-down menu contains the Notes Page option. Some presenters provide a hard copy of the information covered in the presentation. With PowerPoint, this can take the form of the slide printed at the top of the page with space available at the bottom of the page for the audience members to write notes. Choose the Notes Page view to see how the slide will display on the page along with the space for taking notes.

In the Slide view, change slides by clicking the Previous Slide or Next Slide buttons located at the bottom of the vertical scroll bar. You can also change to a different slide by using the mouse pointer on the scroll box (called the *elevator*) on the vertical scroll bar. To do this, position the mouse pointer on the elevator, hold down the left mouse button, drag up or down until a yellow box displays with the desired slide number, and then release the mouse button. The keyboard can also be used to change to a different slide. Press the Page Down key to display the next slide in the presentation or press the Page Up key to display the previous slide in the presentation.

Previous Slide

Next Slide

In addition to the Next Slide and Previous Slide buttons, you can use the Page Up and Page Down keys to move from one slide to another.

Running a Slide Show

Several methods can be used to run a slide show. Slides created in PowerPoint can be converted to 35mm slides or transparencies, or the computer screen can provide the output. An on-screen presentation saves the expense of producing slides, requires no projection equipment, and lets you use the computer's color capability.

If you are running a slide show in PowerPoint, there are several methods you can choose. You can run the slide show manually (you determine when to advance to the next slide), advance slides automatically, or set up a slide show to run continuously for demonstration purposes.

Slide Show

If you want to run a slide show manually, open the presentation, and then click the Slide Show button on the View toolbar or click <u>V</u>iew and then Slide Sho<u>w</u>. To control movement through slides in a slide show, refer to figure 1.11.

Commands for Controlling a Slide Show

To do this	Perform this action
Show next slide	Click left mouse button; or press one of the following keys: space bar, N, right arrow, down arrow, or Page Down
Show previous slide	Click right mouse button and click desired direction at the pop-up menu; or press one of the following keys: Backspace, P, left arrow, up arrow, or Page Up
Show specific slide	Key slide number and press Enter
Toggle mouse on or off	Key A or equal sign (=)
Switch between black screen and current slide	Key B or period (.)
Switch between white screen and current slide	Key W or comma (,)
End slide show and return to PowerPoint	Press one of the following keys: Esc, hyphen (-), or Ctrl + Break

Starting the Slide Show on Any Slide

Click the Slide Show button on the View toolbar and the presentation begins with the currently active slide. To begin a slide show on any slide, make the desired slide active and then click the Slide Show button. If you want to begin the presentation with the first slide, make sure it is the active slide before clicking the Slide Show button.

Using the Pen during a Presentation

If you move the mouse when running a presentation, the Slide Show menu icon displays in the lower left corner of the slide. Click this icon and a pop-up menu displays as shown in figure 1.12.

Chapter One

Slide Show Menu Icon Pop-up Menu

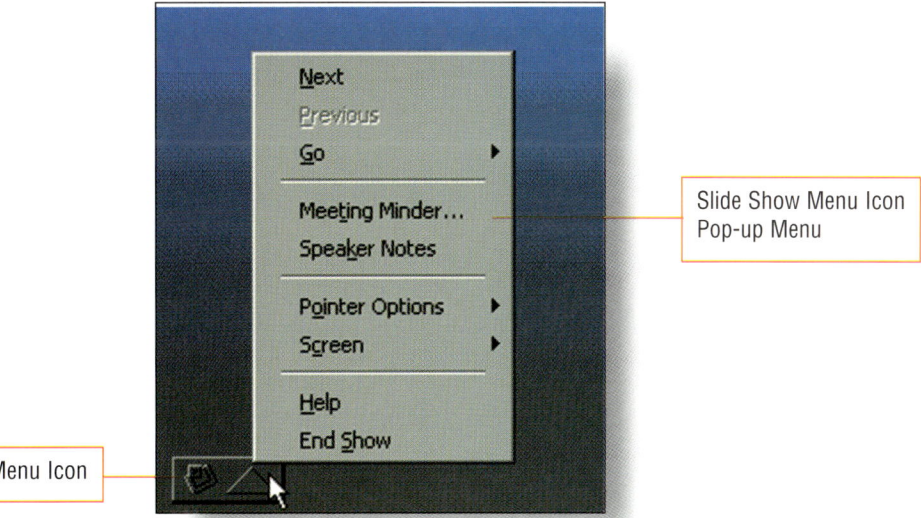

Slide Show Menu Icon Pop-up Menu

Slide Show Menu Icon

With options at this pop-up menu, you can perform such actions as navigating within the presentation, keying speaker notes, displaying a pen, changing the screen display, getting help, and ending the presentation.

Emphasize major points or draw the attention of the audience to specific items in a slide during a presentation using the pen. To use the pen on a slide, run the presentation, and when the desired slide displays, move the mouse to display the *Slide Show* menu icon and then click the icon. At the pop-up menu that displays, point to Pointer Options, and then click Pen. This removes the pop-up menu and displays the mouse pointer as a pen. Use the pen to draw attention to specific items in the slide. If you want to draw a straight horizontal or vertical line with the pen, hold down the Shift key while drawing. Change the color of the pen by clicking the Slide Show menu icon, pointing to Pointer Options, pointing to Pen Color, and then clicking the desired color at the side menu.

If you want to erase the marks you made with the pen, click the *Slide Show* menu icon, point to Screen, and then click Erase Pen. The Erase Pen option is only available when the pen is selected. When you are finished with the pen, click the *Slide Show* menu icon, point to Pointer Options, and then click Automatic.

Viewing, Printing, and Running a Presentation

1. Open Planning Presentation by completing the following steps:
   a. Open PowerPoint.
   b. At the PowerPoint dialog box, click Cancel.
   c. With a blank Presentation window displayed, click the Open button on the Standard toolbar.

d. At the Open dialog box, make sure Chapter 01C on your disk is the default folder, and then double-click *Planning Presentation* in the list box. 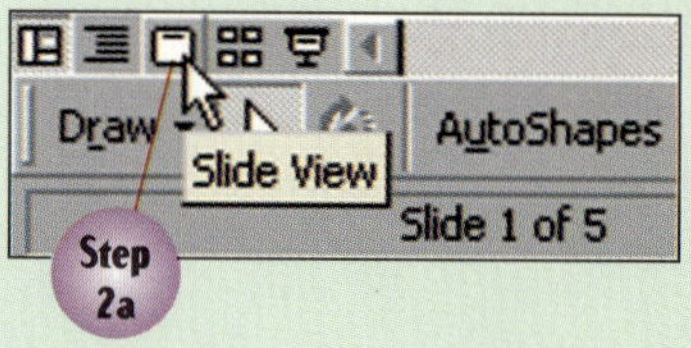
2. With Planning Presentation open, change the views by completing the following steps:
   a. Change to the Slide view by clicking the Slide View button on the View toolbar (located at the left side of the horizontal scroll bar).
   b. Click the Next Slide button located at the bottom of the vertical scroll bar until Slide 5 is visible.
   c. Position the mouse pointer on the elevator (the scroll box) on the vertical scroll bar, hold down the left mouse button, drag the elevator to the top of the vertical scroll bar until a yellow box displays with Slide 1 and the title of the slide, and then release the mouse button.
   d. Change to the Slide Sorter view by clicking the Slide Sorter View button on the View toolbar. 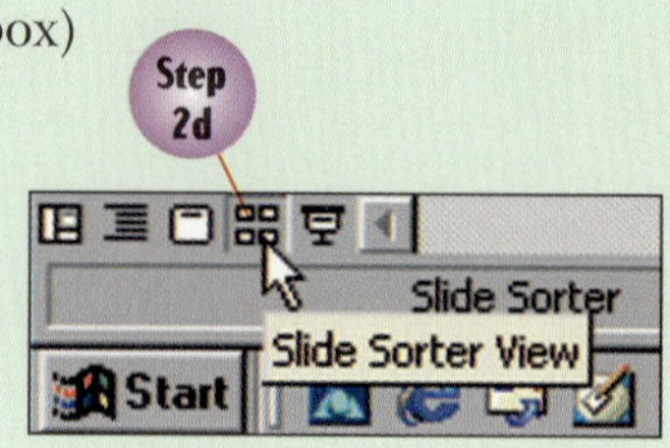
3. Print the presentation in outline view by completing the following steps:
   a. Choose File and Print.
   b. At the Print dialog box, change the Print what: option to *Outline View*.
   c. Click OK or press Enter.
4. Run the slide presentation on the screen by completing the following steps:
   a. In Slide Sorter view, click once on Slide 1. (This is to ensure that your slide show begins with the first slide.)
   b. Click the Slide Show button on the View toolbar. (This should cause Slide 1 to display and fill the entire screen.)
   c. After viewing Slide 1, click the left mouse button. (This causes Slide 2 to display.)
   d. Continue viewing and then clicking the left mouse button until all five slides have been viewed.
   e. At the black screen with the message *End of slide show, click to exit.*, click the left mouse button. This returns the presentation to the Slide Sorter view. 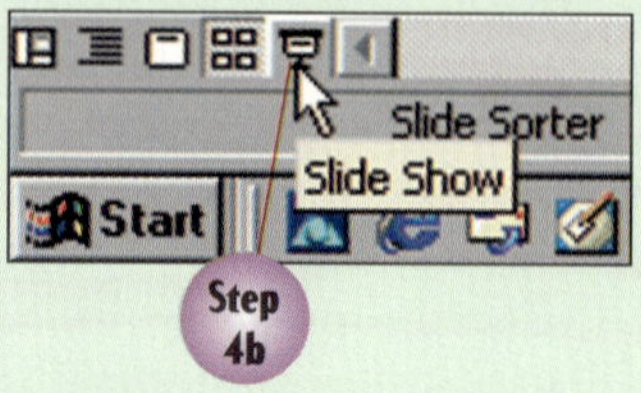
5. Run the presentation beginning with Slide 3 by completing the following steps:
   a. In Slide Sorter view, click Slide 3.
   b. Click the Slide Show button on the View toolbar.
   c. After viewing Slide 3, click the left mouse button.
   d. Continue viewing slides until the black screen displays. At this screen, click the left mouse button. (This returns the presentation to the Slide Sorter view.)
6. Run the presentation and use the pen to highlight specific words in the slides by completing the following steps:
   a. In Slide Sorter view, click Slide 1.
   b. Click the Slide Show button on the View toolbar.
   c. When Slide 1 displays, use the pen to underline a word by completing the following steps:
      1) Move the mouse to display the *Slide Show* menu icon.
      2) Click the *Slide Show* menu icon, point to Pointer Options, and then click Pen.
      3) Using the mouse, draw a circle around the text below *STEP 1*.

4) Hold down the Shift key and then use the mouse to draw a horizontal line below the word *identify*.
5) Erase the pen markings by clicking the *Slide Show* menu icon, pointing to S<u>c</u>reen, and then clicking <u>E</u>rase Pen.

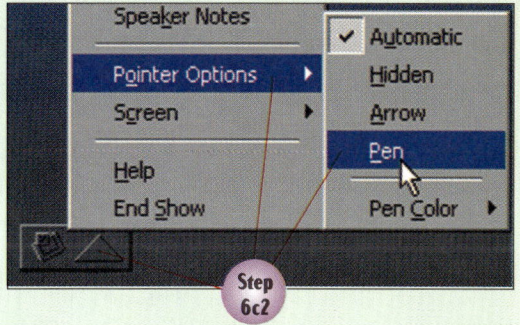

Step 6c2

6) Change the color of the pen by clicking the *Slide Show* menu icon, pointing to P<u>o</u>inter Options, pointing to Pen <u>C</u>olor, and then clicking Yellow.
7) Hold down the Shift key and use the mouse to draw a yellow line below the word *identify*.

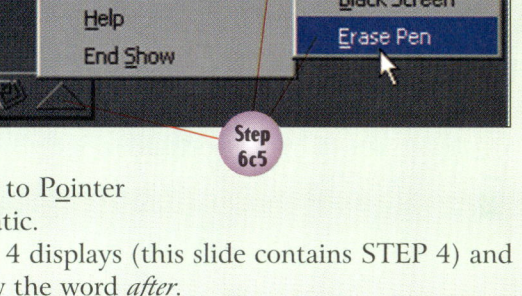

Step 6c5

8) Turn off the pen by clicking the *Slide Show* menu icon, pointing to P<u>o</u>inter Options, and then clicking A<u>u</u>tomatic.

d. Click the left mouse button until Slide 4 displays (this slide contains STEP 4) and then use the pen to underline in yellow the word *after*.
e. Turn off the display of the pen.
f. Click the left mouse to display Slide 5 and use the pen to underline in yellow the word *effective*.
g. Turn off the display of the pen.
h. Click the left mouse button and then, at the black screen, click the left mouse button again.

7. Close Planning Presentation and exit PowerPoint.

Adding Transition and Sound Effects

Interesting transitions and sounds can be applied to a presentation. A transition is how one slide is removed from the screen during a presentation and the next slide is displayed. Interesting transitions can be added such as blinds, boxes, checkerboards, covers, random bars, stripes, and wipes. To add transitions and sounds, open a presentation and then change to the Slide Sorter view. Select an individual slide or select all slides in the presentation, click Sli<u>d</u>e Show, and then click Slide <u>T</u>ransition. This displays the Slide Transition dialog box shown in figure 1.13.

Make a presentation more appealing by adding effects such as sound and transitions.

figure 1.13 Slide Transition Dialog Box

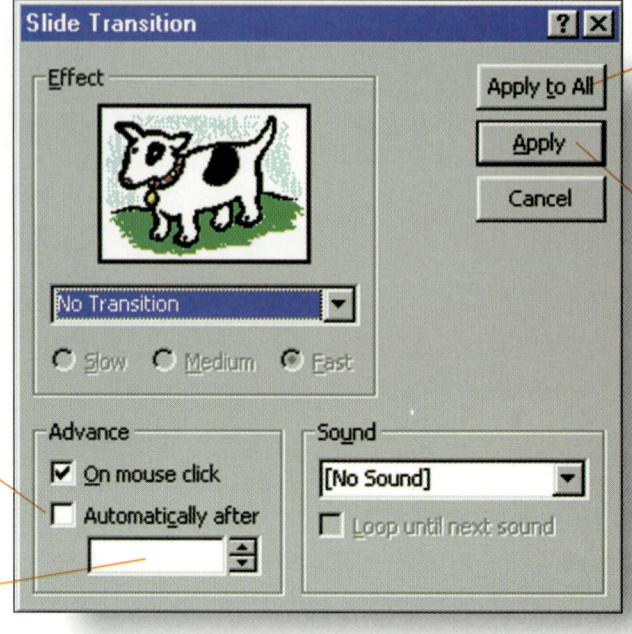

Click the Apply to All button to apply transition time to all slides.

Click the Apply button to apply transition time to selected slide only.

To advance slides automatically, insert a check mark in this check box.

Insert the desired number of seconds in this text box.

Slide Transition

Another method for displaying the Slide Transition dialog box shown in figure 1.13 is to click the Slide Transition button on the Slide Sorter toolbar. The Slide Sorter toolbar displays below the Standard toolbar in Slide Sorter view.

To add a transition effect, click the down-pointing triangle to the right of the Effect list box (located below the picture of the dog), and then click the desired transition at the drop-down menu. When you click the desired transition, the transition effect is displayed in the picture of the dog and the picture changes to a key.

As a slide is removed from the screen and another slide is displayed, a sound can be added. To add a sound, click the down-pointing triangle to the right of the Sound text box, and then click the desired sound. You can choose from a list of sounds such as applause, breaking glass, camera, laser, and much more. When a transition is added to a slide, a transition icon displays below the slide in Slide Sorter view.

Adding Transitions and Sounds to a Presentation

1. Open PowerPoint.
2. At the PowerPoint dialog box, click Open an existing presentation, and then click OK.
3. At the Open dialog box, make sure Chapter 01C on your disk is the active folder, and then double-click *Planning Presentation* in the list box.
4. Save the presentation with Save As and name it Planning Pres with Transitions by completing the following steps:
   a. Click File and then Save As.
   b. At the Save As dialog box, key **Planning Pres with Transitions** in the File name text box.
   c. Click Save or press Enter.
5. Add transition and sound effects by completing the following steps:
   a. Change to the Slide Sorter view.
   b. Click Slide Show on the Menu bar and then click Slide Transition.
   c. At the Slide Transition dialog box, add a transition effect by completing the following steps:
      1) Click the down-pointing triangle to the right of the Effect text box (containing the text *No Transition*).
      2) From the drop-down list that displays, click *Blinds Horizontal*.
   d. Add a sound effect by completing the following steps:
      1) Click the down-pointing triangle to the right of the Sound text box (containing the text *[No Sound]*).
      2) From the drop-down list that displays, click *Camera*.
   e. Click the Apply to All button. (This closes the Slide Transition dialog box and displays a transition icon below each slide.)

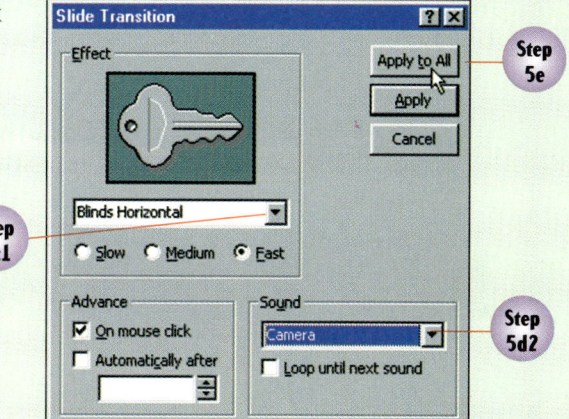

6. Run the presentation by clicking the Slide Show button on the View toolbar. (When the presentation is done, and the black screen displays with the message *End of slide show, click to exit.*, click the left mouse button or press the Esc key. This returns the presentation to the Slide Sorter view.)
7. Save the presentation again with the same name (Planning Pres with Transitions).
8. Close Planning Pres with Transitions.

Running a Slide Show Automatically

Set automatic times for slides in a presentation if you do not want to manually control slides during a presentation.

Slides in a slide show can be advanced automatically after a specific number of seconds with options at the Slide Transition dialog box. To automatically advance slides, click Automatically after (in the Advance section), and then key the number of seconds. If you want the transition time to affect all slides in the presentation, click the Apply to All button at the Slide Transition dialog box. If you want the transition time to affect only the selected slide, click the Apply button. The transition time is displayed below each affected slide in the presentation in Slide Sorter view.

To automatically run the presentation, make sure the first slide is selected, and then click the Slide Show button on the View toolbar. The first slide displays for the specified amount of time and then the next slide automatically displays.

In some situations, such as at a trade show or convention, you may want to prepare a self-running presentation. A self-running presentation is set up on a continuous loop and does not require someone to run the presentation. To design a self-running presentation, choose options at the Set Up Show dialog box shown in figure 1.14. To display this dialog box, open a presentation click Slide Show, and then Set Up Show.

figure 1.14

Set Up Show Dialog Box

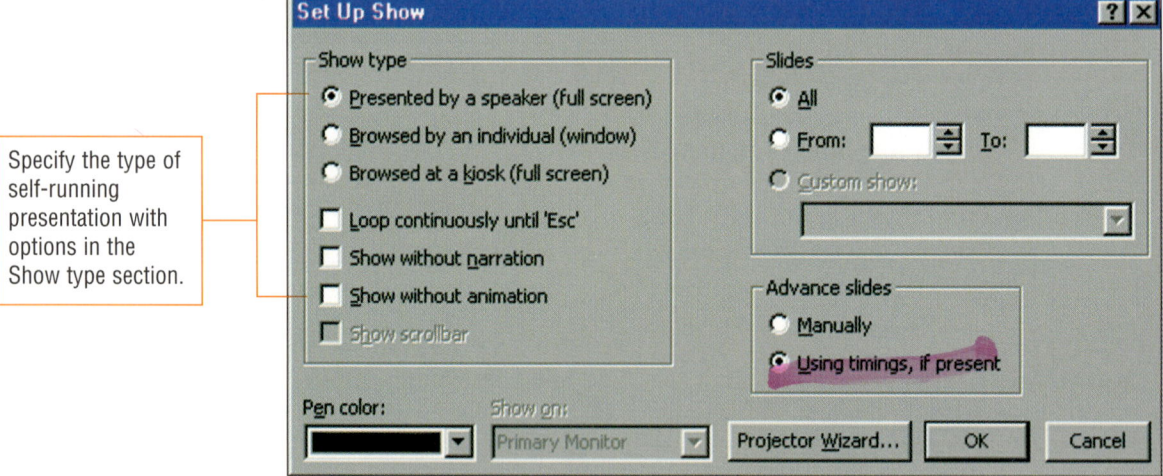

Specify the type of self-running presentation with options in the Show type section.

Click the Loop continuously until 'Esc' option and the presentation runs over and over again until the Esc key is pressed. With other options in the Show type section of the Set Up Show dialog, you can specify what a presentation shows when running. In the Advance slides section of the dialog box, specify whether the slides will be advanced manually or automatically. Use options in the Slides section to specify whether options are to be applied to all slides or specific slides within the presentation.

exercise 5

Preparing a Self-Running Presentation

1. Open History of Computers 1980s. (This presentation is located in the *Presentations* folder on the CD that accompanies this textbook.)
2. Save the presentation with Save As in the Chapter 01C folder on your disk and name it Self-Running History.
3. Add transition and sound effects and specify a time for automatically advancing slides by completing the following steps:
   a. Change to the Slide Sorter view.
   b. Click Slide Show and Slide Transition.
   c. At the Slide Transition dialog box, click Automatically after, and then key **5** in the seconds text box.
   d. Add a transition effect by completing the following steps:
      1) Click the down-pointing triangle to the right of the Effect text box (containing the text *No Transition*).
      2) From the drop-down list that displays, click *Box Out*.
   e. Add a sound effect by completing the following steps:
      1) Click the down-pointing triangle to the right of the Sound text box (containing the text *[No Sound]*).
      2) From the drop-down list that displays, click *Laser*.
   f. Click the Apply to All button. (This closes the Slide Transition dialog box and displays a transition icon below each slide as well as the transition time of 5 seconds.)
4. Set up the presentation to run continuously by completing the following steps:
   a. Click Slide Show and then Set Up Show.
   b. At the Set Up Show dialog box, click the Loop continuously until 'Esc' option. (Make sure All is selected in the Slides section and Using timings, if present is selected in the Advance slides section.)
   c. Click OK to close the dialog box.

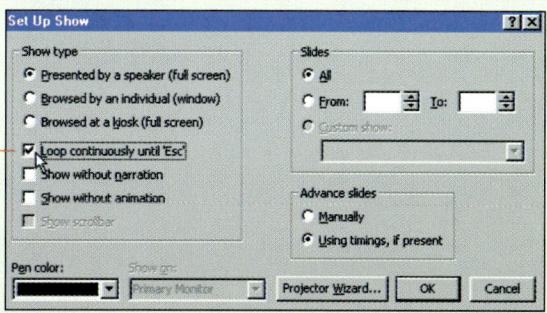

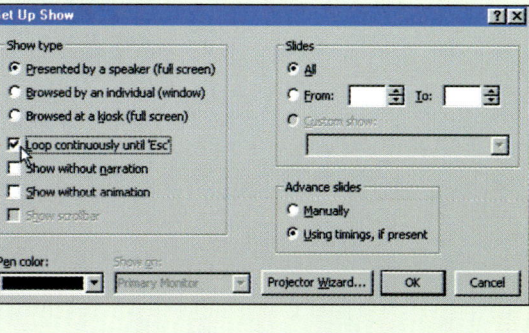

Preparing a PowerPoint Presentation

5. Make sure the first slide is selected and then run the presentation continuously by clicking the Slide Show button on the View toolbar.
6. After viewing the presentation at least twice, press the Esc key on the keyboard.
7. Save the presentation again with the same name (Self-Running History).
8. Close Self-Running History.

Setting and Rehearsing Timings for a Presentation

Setting a time at the Slide Transition dialog box sets the same time for each selected slide. In some presentations, you may want to specify a different amount of time for each slide and then rehearse the presentation to ensure that the time set is appropriate. To rehearse and set a time for each slide, you would complete these steps:

Rehearse Timings

1. Open the presentation.
2. Change to the Slide Sorter view.
3. Click the Rehearse Timings button on the Slide Sorter toolbar or click Sli<u>d</u>e Show and then <u>R</u>ehearse Timings.
4. The first slide in the presentation displays along with a Rehearsal dialog box shown in figure 1.15. The Rehearsal dialog box shows the time for the current slide and the total time for the presentation. The timer begins immediately. Click the Next button when the desired time displays; click the Pause button to stop the timer and leave the slide on the screen; or, click the Repeat button if you want the time for the current slide to start over.
5. When the desired time displays for the slide in the Rehearsal dialog box, click the Next button.
6. Continue in this manner until the time for all slides in the presentation has been specified.
7. After specifying the time for the last slide, a Microsoft PowerPoint dialog box displays with the total time of the presentation and asks if you want to record the new slide timings. At this dialog box, click <u>Y</u>es to save the new timings.

figure 1.15 *Rehearsal Dialog Box*

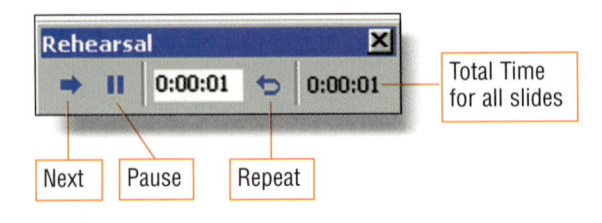

exercise 6

Rehearsing and Establishing Specific Times for Slides

1. Open Planning Presentation.
2. Save the presentation with Save As and name it Rehearsed Planning Pres.
3. Set specific times for each slide in the presentation by completing the following steps:
    a. Change to Slide Sorter view.
    b. Click the Rehearse Timings button on the Slide Sorter toolbar.
    c. With the first slide displayed, wait until the timer in the Rehearsal dialog box displays five seconds, and then click the Next button. (If you miss five seconds, click the Repeat button. This restarts the clock for the current slide.)
    d. With the second slide displayed, wait until the timer displays 5 seconds, and then click the Next button.
    e. Set 7 seconds for the third and fourth slides and 5 seconds for the fifth slide.
    f. After setting the time for the last slide, the Microsoft PowerPoint dialog box displays asking if you want to record the new timings. At this dialog box, click Yes.
4. Add a transition and sound effect to each slide by completing the following steps:
    a. Click the Slide Transition button located at the left side of the Slide Sorter toolbar.
    b. At the Slide Transition dialog box, click the down-pointing triangle at the right side of the Effect text box (containing the text *No Transition*), and then click *Dissolve* at the drop-down list. (You will need to scroll down the list to display *Dissolve*.)
    c. Click the down-pointing triangle at the right side of the Sound text box (containing the text *[No Sound]*) and then click *Camera* at the drop-down list.
    d. Click the Apply to All button.
5. Set up the presentation to run continuously by displaying the Set Up Show dialog box, clicking the Loop continuously until 'Esc' option, and then closing the dialog box.
6. Make sure Slide 1 is selected and then run the presentation by clicking the Slide Show button on the View toolbar. (The slide show will run automatically. The first and second slides will stay on the screen for five seconds, the third and fourth slides for seven seconds, and the fifth slide for five seconds.)
7. After viewing the entire presentation at least twice, press the Esc key on the keyboard.
8. Save the presentation again with the same name (Rehearsed Planning Pres).
9. Close Rehearsed Planning Pres.

Preparing a Presentation in Outline View

In exercise 1, you created a slide presentation using a PowerPoint template. With this method, a slide with formatting applied was presented in the Slide pane where you entered specific text. This was a short presentation of only five slides with a small amount of text on each slide. If you are creating a longer presentation with more slides and text, consider using the Outline view to help organize the topics for the slides. Figure 1.16 displays in Outline view the Networking Presentation you will be creating in exercise 7.

figure 1.16 Presentation in Outline View

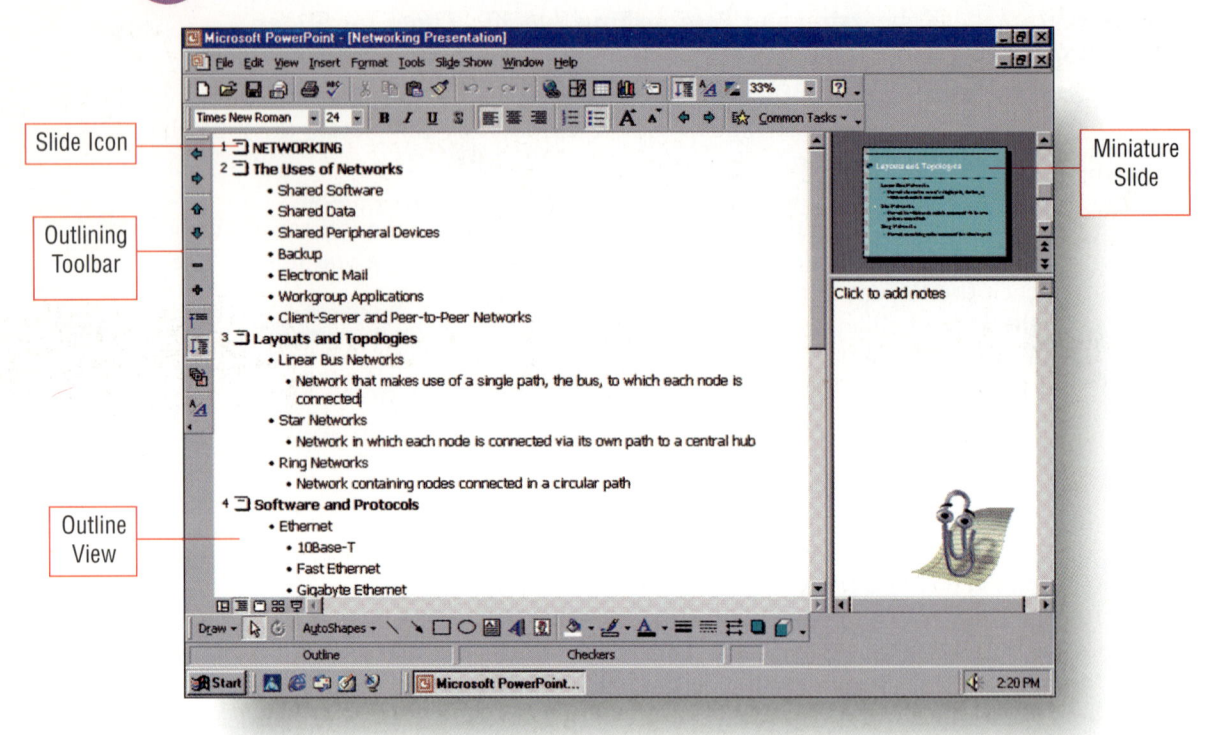

You can key text in the Outline pane in Normal view but consider changing to Outline view because this increases the size of the Outline pane allowing you to see more text. To prepare a presentation in the Outline view, you would complete the following steps:

1. At a blank PowerPoint screen, click File and New.
2. At the New Presentation dialog box, click the Design Templates tab.
3. At the New Presentation dialog box with the Design Templates tab selected, double-click the desired template.
4. At the New Slide dialog box, double-click the desired autolayout format.
5. With the blank slide displayed, click the Outline View button on the View toolbar.
6. Key the title of the first slide and then press Enter. (A miniature slide displays in the Slide pane so you can view the slide with the text you key.)
7. Click the Demote button on the Formatting toolbar or press the Tab key to move to the next tab stop and then key the first heading.

8. Continue keying the text for each slide in the presentation. Click the Demote button on the Formatting toolbar or press Tab to move the insertion point to the next tab stop (and automatically change the text formatting). Click the Promote button on the Formatting toolbar or press Shift + Tab to move the insertion point to the previous tab stop. Continue in this manner until all text is entered for the presentation.
9. When the presentation is completed, save it in the normal manner.

Promote

When keying text for a presentation in the Outline view, click the Demote button on the Formatting toolbar or press the Tab key to move the insertion point to the next tab stop. This moves the insertion point and also changes the formatting. The formatting will vary depending on the autolayout format you chose at the New Slide dialog box. For some autolayout formats, a slide title is set in a font such as 44-point Times New Roman bold. Text keyed at the first tab stop will be set in a smaller point size such as 32-point Times New Roman.

To move the insertion point to a previous tab stop, click the Promote button on the Formatting toolbar or press Shift + Tab. This moves the insertion point and also changes text formatting. Moving the insertion point back to the left margin will begin another slide. Slides are numbered at the left side of the screen and are followed by a slide icon as shown in figure 1.16.

PowerPoint contains an Outlining toolbar with buttons for editing in the Outline view (see figure 1.16). To display this toolbar, *right*-click any displayed toolbar, and then click *Outlining* at the drop-down list. You can also display the toolbar by clicking View, pointing to Toolbars, and then clicking *Outlining*. In the Outline view, the Outlining toolbar displays at the left side of the screen. This toolbar contains the same Promote and Demote buttons as the Formatting toolbar along with other buttons. Buttons on the Outlining toolbar are described in figure 1.17.

figure 1.17 — Outlining Toolbar Buttons

Click this button	Named	To do this
←	Promote	Move insertion point along with any text to the previous tab stop to the left
→	Demote	Move insertion point along with any text to the next tab stop to the right
↑	Move Up	Move insertion point along with any text up to the previous line

Preparing a PowerPoint Presentation

Icon	Name	Description
⬇	Move Down	Move insertion point along with any text down to the next line
−	Collapse	Display only the titles of the slides
+	Expand	Display all levels of the slides
⬆≡	Collapse All	Display only the titles of all of the slides
⬇≡	Expand All	Display titles and body text for all slides
	Summary Slide	Create a summary slide of presentation based on titles of slides you select
A/A	Show Formatting	Display all character formatting

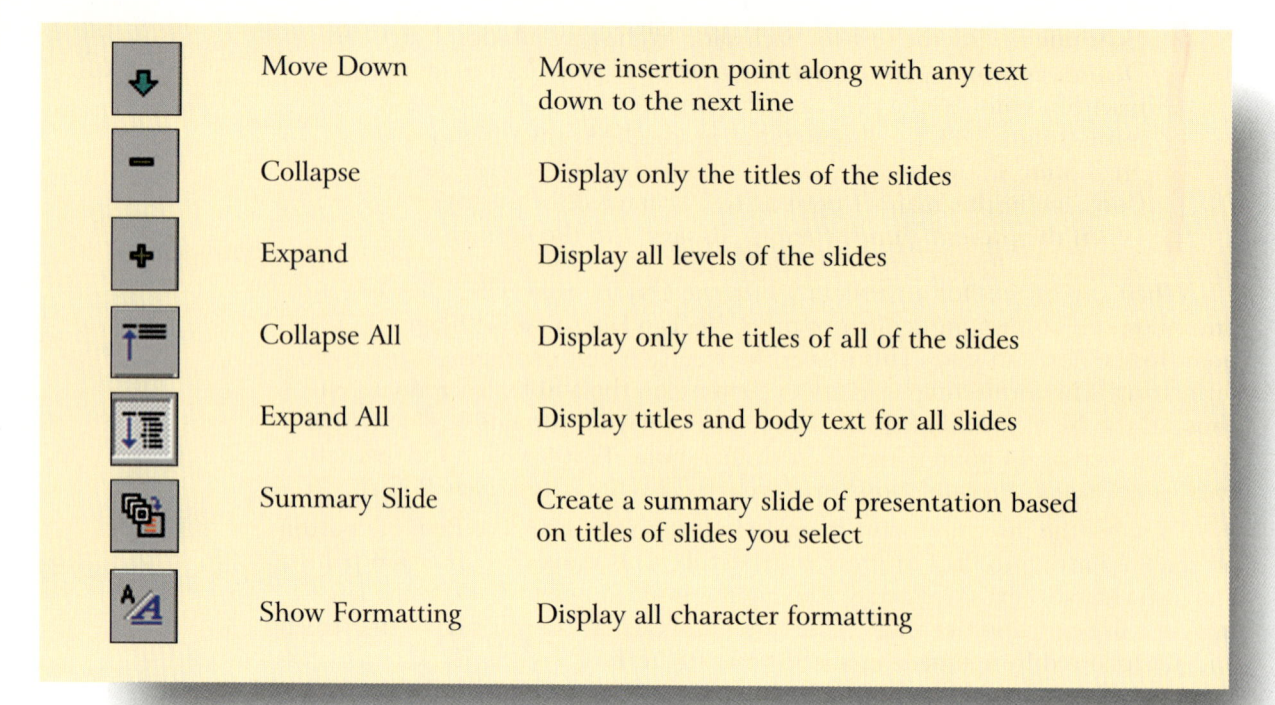

Expand All

Show Formatting

Two buttons available on the Outlining toolbar are also available on the Standard toolbar. These two buttons are Expand All and Show Formatting. Clicking either of these buttons on the Outlining toolbar or the Standard toolbar accomplishes the same thing.

exercise 7

Preparing a Presentation in Outline View

1. Create a presentation in Outline view by completing the following steps:
   a. With PowerPoint open and a blank screen displayed, click File and New.
   b. At the New Presentation dialog box, click the Design Templates tab.
   c. At the New Presentation dialog box with the Design Templates tab selected, double-click *Checkers*.
   d. At the New Slide dialog box, double-click the second autolayout in the list box (Bulleted List).
   e. With the empty slide displayed, click the Outline View button on the View toolbar. (Located at the left side of the horizontal scroll bar.)
   f. Turn on the display of the Outlining toolbar by clicking View, pointing to Toolbars, and then clicking Outlining.
   g. Create the outline shown in figure 1.18 by completing the following steps:
      1) Key the first slide title shown in figure 1.18 (NETWORKING) and press Enter.
      2) Key the second slide title shown in figure 1.18 (The Uses of Networks) and press Enter.

3) Click the Demote button on the Outlining toolbar or press Tab, key the text after the first bullet in figure 1.18 (Shared Software), and then press Enter.
4) Continue keying the text as it displays in figure 1.18. Click the Demote button or press Tab to move the insertion point to the next tab stop. Click the Promote button or press Shift + Tab to move the insertion back to a previous tab stop.

  h. Click the Collapse All button on the Outlining toolbar. (This displays only the title of each slide.)
  i. Click the Expand All button on the Outlining toolbar.
2. Save the presentation by completing the following steps:
  a. Click the Save button on the Standard toolbar.
  b. At the Save As dialog box, key **Networking Presentation** and press Enter or click Save.
3. View the slides by clicking the Slide Sorter View button on the View toolbar.
4. Print the four slides as notes pages by displaying the Print dialog box and changing the Print what option to *Notes Pages*.
5. Close Networking Presentation.

figure 1.18   Exercise 7

1 NETWORKING
2 The Uses of Networks
- Shared Software
- Shared Data
- Shared Peripheral Devices
- Backup
- Electronic Mail
- Workgroup Applications
- Client-Server and Peer-to-Peer Networks

3 Layouts and Topologies
- Linear Bus Networks
  - Network that makes use of a single path, the bus, to which each node is connected
- Star Networks
  - Network in which each node is connected via its own path to a central hub
- Ring Networks
  - Network containing nodes connected in a circular path

4 Software and Protocols
- Ethernet
- 10Base-T
- Fast Ethernet
- Gigabyte Ethernet
- Token Ring
- ARCNet
- AppleTalk

Deleting a Presentation

File management tasks in PowerPoint can be performed at the Open or Save As dialog box. To delete a PowerPoint presentation, display the Open dialog box, click the presentation you want deleted, and then click the Delete button on the dialog box toolbar. At the Confirm File Delete dialog box, asking if you are sure you want to delete the document, click Yes.

Delete

exercise 8

Deleting a PowerPoint Presentation

1. Delete three presentation documents by completing the following steps:
   a. With PowerPoint open, display the Open dialog box by clicking the Open button on the Standard toolbar.
   b. At the Open dialog box, click *Rehearsed Planning Pres* in the list box to select it.
   c. Click the Delete button on the dialog box toolbar.
   d. At the Confirm File Delete dialog box asking if you are sure you want to delete the presentation, click Yes.
   e. At the Open dialog box, delete Selling Presentation by completing steps similar to those in 1b through 1d.
   f. At the Open dialog box, delete Self-Running History by completing steps similar to those in 1b and 1d.
2. Close the Open dialog box.

Using Help

PowerPoint's Help feature is an on-screen reference manual containing information about all of PowerPoint's features and commands. PowerPoint's Help feature is similar to the Windows Help and the Help features in Word, Excel, and Access. Get help using the Office Assistant or turn off the Assistant and get help from the Microsoft PowerPoint Help dialog box.

Getting Help from the Office Assistant

The Office Assistant will provide information about specific topics. To get help using the Office Assistant, click the Office Assistant, or click Help and then Microsoft PowerPoint Help. This causes a box to display above the Office Assistant as shown in figure 1.19. If the Office Assistant is not visible, click the Microsoft PowerPoint Help button on the Standard toolbar.

figure 1.19 Office Assistant Help Box

When the Help box displays above the Office Assistant, the text *Type your question here, and then click Search* displays in the help box. This text is already selected, so all you need to do is key your question about the PowerPoint feature you need help on and then click the Search button, or click one of the categories listed above the text box preceded by the icon of a light bulb. The Office Assistant will display a list of related topics. At this list, click the desired topic and information will display in a Microsoft PowerPoint Help dialog box. After reading the information, click the Close button located in the upper right corner of the dialog box (contains an X).

The Microsoft PowerPoint Help dialog box contains a toolbar with buttons used to navigate through the Help screens. Use the Show button to expand the dialog box and display three tabs—Contents, Answer Wizard, Index. These tabs are discussed later in this section. If you move to various help items by clicking topics or hyperlinks, click the Back button to return to the previous window, or click the Forward button to move forward to a help item. Click the Print button to print a copy of the current topic on the printer. Use the Options button to display a drop-down menu with many of the same features as the toolbar buttons. Additional features on the Options drop-down menu include Home, Stop, Refresh, and Internet Options.

exercise 9

Using the Office Assistant to Learn How to Insert Symbols

1. Open Networking Presentation.
2. Use the Office Assistant to read information on inserting symbols in a slide by completing the following steps:
   a. Make sure the Office Assistant is visible. If it is not, click Help, and then click Show the Office Assistant.
   b. Click the Office Assistant.
   c. At the Help box that displays above the Office Assistant, key **How do I insert a symbol?**
   d. Click the Search button.
   e. At the list of topics that displays click *Insert a Symbol*. When you point at one of the topics, the pointer changes from a white arrow to a hand.
   f. In the Microsoft PowerPoint Help dialog box, read the information on inserting symbols and then print the help topic by clicking the Print button on the toolbar.
   g. Click the Close button located in the upper right corner of the dialog box (contains an X).
3. Close Networking Presentation.

Using the Microsoft PowerPoint Help Dialog Box

If the Office Assistant is turned off you can search for information on PowerPoint features using the Microsoft PowerPoint Help Dialog Box shown in figure 1.20. Three tabs display in the dialog box—Contents, Answer Wizard, and Index.

In the Contents tab a list of categories display preceded by an icon of a closed book. Most of these categories contain additional categories. To display the additional categories, double-click the category or click the small plus sign in the box displayed at the left of the category name. This causes the closed book icon to display as an open book icon. Double-click a topic below the category name to further expand the list or display the help topic associated for the item at the right side of the dialog box.

Click the Answer Wizard tab and a text box displays preceded by the question "What would you like to do?" Key your question in the text box and then click the Search button. This displays a list of categories in the Select topic to display list box. Click a topic in the list box and information about the topic displays at the right side of the dialog box.

With the Index tab selected, enter a keyword in the Type keywords list box, and then click the Search button. Topics related to the keyword display in the Choose a topic list box. Click a topic in this list box and information about the topic displays at the right side of the dialog box. You can also scroll through the alphabetical *Or choose k*eywords list box to display the desired topic.

While you are browsing through the Microsoft PowerPoint Help dialog box you will notice words or terms that are underlined and displayed in blue. These words or terms are hyperlinks. Click the blue underlined text to jump to the help text for the term. After reading the hyperlink help topic, return to the previous screen by clicking the Back button at the top of the dialog box. When you return to the previous help page, the hyperlink you just returned from will be displayed in a different color to indicate you have read the help associated with the item.

Click the Print button at the top of the Microsoft Excel Help dialog box to print the current help topic.

figure 1.20 **Microsoft PowerPoint Help Dialog Box with Contents Tab Selected**

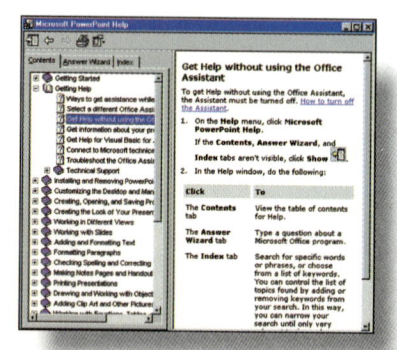

exercise 10

Turning Off the Office Assistant and Using the Help Dialog Box

1. Open Networking Presentation.
2. Turn off the Office Assistant by completing the following steps (if the Office Assistant is already turned off, skip this step):
   a. Click the Office Assistant.
   b. Click the Options button in the yellow box.

c. At the Office Assistant dialog box, click the Use the Office Assistant check box (this removes the check mark).
   d. Click OK to close the dialog box.
3. Use the Help feature with the Contents tab selected to find information on running and controlling a slide show by completing the following steps:
   a. Click Help on the Menu bar and click Microsoft PowerPoint Help.
   b. If necessary, click the Contents tab in the Microsoft PowerPoint Help dialog box.
   c. Double-click *Running and Controlling a Slide Show* in the Contents list box.
   d. Click the help topic *Start a slide show*.
   e. Read the list of topics displayed at the right side of the dialog box, then click one of the blue hyperlinked topics to jump to the help topic associated with the term.
   f. Return to the previous help page by clicking the Back button.
4. Use the Help feature with the Answer Wizard tab selected to find information on adding a sound effect by completing the following steps:
   a. Click the Answer Wizard tab.
   b. Key **How do I apply a sound effect to a slide?** in the What would you like to do? text box and then click the Search button.
   c. Read the information on inserting music or sound to a slide at the right side of the dialog box.
   d. Print the help topic.
5. Use the Help feature with the Index tab selected to find information on changing the layout of a slide by completing the following steps:
   a. Click the Index tab.
   b. Key **change** in the Type keywords text box and then click the Search button.
   c. Click the topic *Change the layout of a slide* that displays in the Choose a topic list box.
   d. Read the information on changing the layout of a slide that displays at the right side of the dialog box.
   e. Print the help topic.
6. Use the Contents tab, Answer Wizard tab, or the Index tab to find information on how to automatically correct text using AutoCorrect. Print the help topic you find associated with this item.
7. Close the Microsoft PowerPoint Help dialog box by clicking the close button at the upper right corner of the dialog box (contains an X).
8. Turn on the display of the Office Assistant by clicking Help and then Show the Office Assistant.
9. Click in the a blank area of the screen to remove the yellow box near the Office Assistant.
10. Close Networking Presentation.

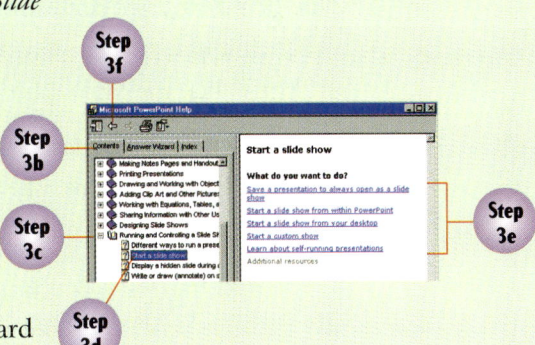

Using Additional Help Features

Click the <u>H</u>elp option on the Menu bar, and a variety of methods to obtain help are displayed. Choose the What's <u>T</u>his option to point to a specific item and display information about the item. For example, to display information about a button on a toolbar, click <u>H</u>elp, and then click What's <u>T</u>his. This causes the mouse pointer to display with a question mark attached to it. Click the button on the toolbar that you would like information on and a yellow box will display with some help text associated for the button.

Click Office on the <u>W</u>eb from the <u>H</u>elp drop-down menu and you are connected to the Microsoft Office Update Web site. From this site, you can get answers to most frequently asked questions about PowerPoint. You can also get up-to-date tips, templates, clip art, and Help files.

PowerPoint contains a self-repairing feature that will fix errors in PowerPoint. To run this feature, click <u>H</u>elp, and then click Detect and <u>R</u>epair. This displays the Detect and Repair dialog box with a message telling you that during the process you may be asked to provide the installation source and/or exit open applications. Click the <u>S</u>tart button to begin the detect and repair process.

The last option on the <u>H</u>elp drop-down menu, <u>A</u>bout Microsoft PowerPoint, displays information such as the release date, license number, and system information. You can also display information about Microsoft's technical support.

exercise 11

Using What's This

1. Open Networking Presentation.
2. Use the What's This feature by completing the following steps:
   a. Click <u>H</u>elp and then click What's <u>T</u>his. (This causes the mouse pointer to display with a question mark attached to it.)
   b. Click the E-mail button on the Standard toolbar (fourth button from the left).
   c. Read the information displayed in the yellow box and then click in the screen outside the yellow box to remove it.
   d. Click <u>H</u>elp and then click What's <u>T</u>his.
   e. Click the Animation Effects button on the Formatting toolbar.
   f. Read the information displayed in the yellow box and then click in the screen outside the yellow box to remove it.
   g. Click <u>H</u>elp and then click What's <u>T</u>his.
   h. Click a button on either the Standard or Formatting toolbar that you would like to know about.
   i. After reading the information displayed in the yellow box, click in the screen outside the yellow box to remove it.
3. Close Networking Presentation.

Using ScreenTips

PowerPoint includes a ScreenTips feature that is available in every dialog box and displays as a button containing a question mark. It is located just to the left of the close button in each dialog box. To use the ScreenTips feature, click the ScreenTips button, and then click an item in the dialog box. PowerPoint will display a brief explanation about the option.

exercise 12

Using ScreenTips

1. Open Networking Presentation.
2. Display information about items in the Print dialog box by completing the following steps:
   a. Display the Print dialog box.
   b. Click the ScreenTips button. (This button is located in the upper right corner of the dialog box just left of the close button and displays as a question mark.)
   c. Click the Collate option.
   d. Read the information on collating and then click in a blank area inside the dialog box to clear the yellow box.
   e. Click the ScreenTips button.
   f. Click the Properties button in the Printer section of the Print dialog box.
   g. Read the information on properties and then click in a blank area inside the dialog box to clear the yellow box.
3. Close the Print dialog box.
4. Close Networking Presentation.

chapter summary

➤ PowerPoint is a software program that lets you create slides for an on-screen presentation or for an overhead or slide projector. In PowerPoint, you can print handouts of the presentation, print an outline, or print the entire presentation.

➤ Before creating a presentation in PowerPoint, plan the presentation by defining the purpose and determining the content and medium.

➤ Follow these basic steps to create a PowerPoint presentation: 1) open PowerPoint; 2) choose a design template; 3) key the text for each slide; 4) save the presentation; 5) print the presentation as slides, an outline, or handouts; 6) run the presentation; and 7) close the presentation.

➤ The PowerPoint window contains the following elements: Title bar, Menu bar, Standard toolbar, Formatting toolbar, Drawing toolbar, Outline pane, Slide pane, Notes pane, Scroll bars, View toolbar, and Status bar.

➤ PowerPoint includes a variety of preformatted design templates you can use for creating a presentation.

➤ Many slides created with a PowerPoint template contain placeholders. A slide may contain all or some of the following placeholders: title, bulleted list, clip art, chart, organizational chart, and table.

- Presentations can be printed with each slide on a separate piece of paper; each slide at the top of the page, leaving room for notes; all or a specific number of slides on a single piece of paper; or slide titles and topics in outline form.
- Print a presentation in grayscale or black and white with options at the Print dialog box.
- Click the Grayscale Preview button on the Standard toolbar to preview the presentation in grayscale. Hold down the Shift key and then click the Grayscale Preview button to preview the presentation in black and white.
- Use PowerPoint's AutoContent Wizard to help in the planning and organizing of a presentation.
- Close a PowerPoint presentation document by clicking File and then Close. Open a presentation by clicking the Open button on the Standard toolbar and then double-clicking the desired presentation at the Open dialog box.
- View a presentation in one of the following five views: Normal view, which is the default and displays three panes—outline, slide, and notes; Outline view, which displays the presentation by headings and subheadings; Slide view, which displays individual slides in the presentation; Slide Sorter view which displays slides as minatures; and Slide Show view, which runs the presentation.
- A slide show can be run manually, where you determine when to advance to the next slide; automatically, where PowerPoint advances the slides; or continuously, for demonstration purposes.
- Use the pen during a presentation to emphasize major points or draw the attention of the audience to specific items in the slide. Display the pen by clicking the Slide Show menu icon, pointing to Pointer Options, and then clicking Pen. Draw a straight horizontal or vertical line by holding down the Shift key while drawing.
- Erase pen marks by clicking the Slide Show menu icon, pointing to Screen, and then clicking Erase Pen.
- A specific time can be set for how long each slide stays on the screen during a presentation.
- A presentation can be enhanced by adding transitions (how one slide is removed from the screen and replaced with the next slide) and sound.
- Consider preparing a presentation in Outline view to help organize the topics for the slides.
- File management tasks can be performed on PowerPoint presentations in the same manner as Word documents.
- PowerPoint includes an on-screen reference manual which you can use to find information on PowerPoint features and commands. The Help feature includes the Office Assistant, or you can search for a feature using Contents, the Answer Wizard, or an Index.

commands review

	Mouse
Open PowerPoint	Click Start button on Taskbar, point to *Programs*, and then click *Microsoft PowerPoint*
Display Print dialog box	Click File and Print
Preview presentation in grayscale	Click Grayscale Preview button on Standard toolbar
Preview presentation in black	Hold down Shift key and then click Grayscale and white button on Standard toolbar

Save presentation	Click Save button on Standard toolba, or click File and Save
Display Save As dialog box	Click File and Save As
Close a presentation	Click File and Close
Display Open dialog box	Click Open button on Standard toolbar. or click File and Open
Display Slide Transition dialog box	Click Slide Transition button on Slide Sorter toolbar, or click Slide Show and Slide Transition
Display Set Up Show dialog box	Click Slide Show and Set Up Show
Display Outlining toolbar	Click View, point to Toolbars, and then click *Outlining*; or right-click a toolbar and click *Outlining* at the drop-down list
Help	Click the Office Assistant, or click Help and Microsoft PowerPoint Help

thinking offline

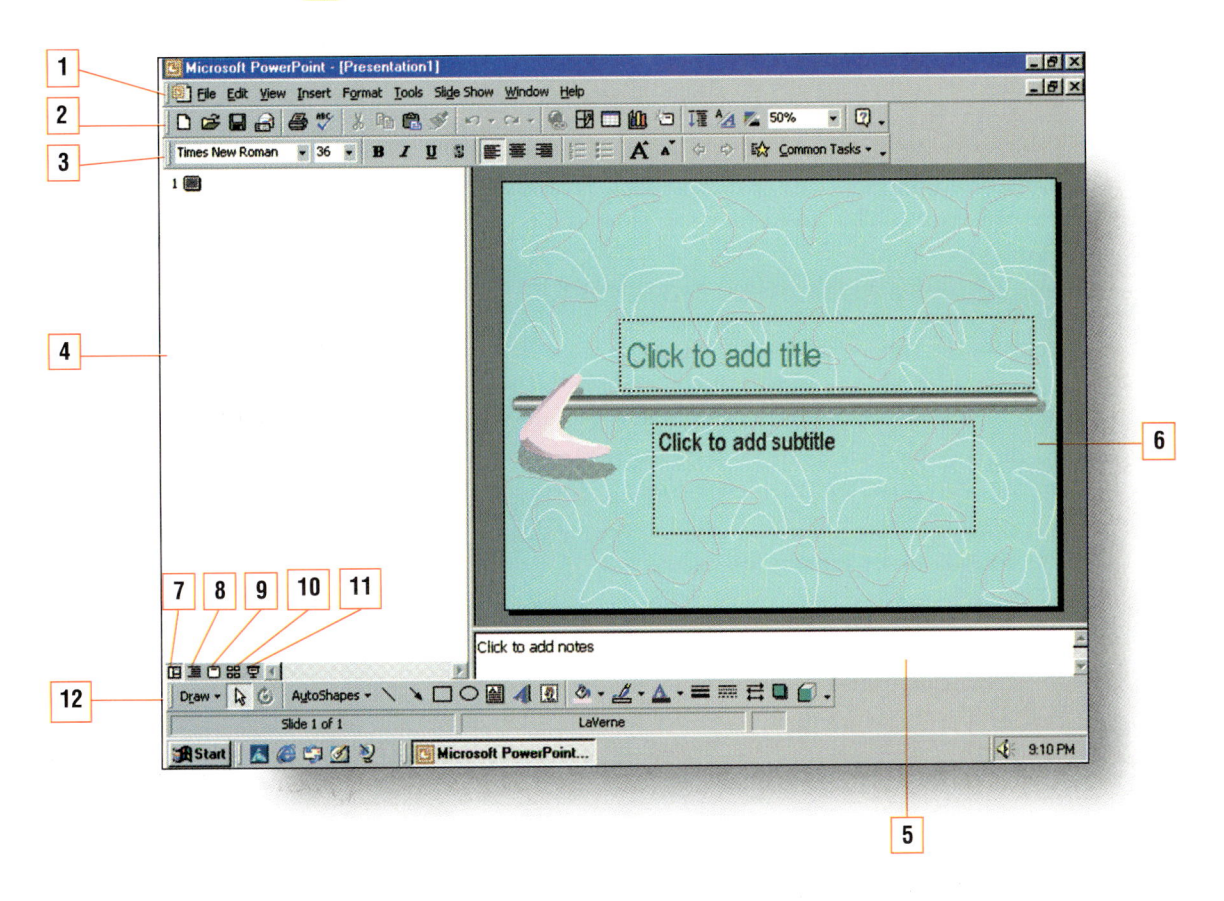

Preparing a PowerPoint Presentation

Identifying: Look at the PowerPoint screen shown above. This screen contains numbers with lines pointing to specific items. Write the name of the item after the number below that corresponds with the number in the PowerPoint screen.

1. menu bar
2. standard toolbar
3. formatting toolbar
4. outline page
5. notes page
6. slide show pane
7. normal view
8. outline view
9. slide view
10. slide sorter view
11. slide show
12. drawing toolbar

Completion: In the space provided at the right, indicate the correct term or command.

1. Click this button on the View toolbar to run a presentation. — slide show
2. Click this button on the View toolbar to display all slides in the presentation in slide miniatures. — slide sorter view
3. While running a presentation, click this button on the mouse to display the previous slide. — right
4. If a presentation contains six slides, click this option at the Print what drop-down menu at the Print dialog box to print all the slides on the same page. — handout
5. Hold down the Shift key and then click this button on the Standard toolbar to display the presentation in black and white. — grayscale
6. Use this during a presentation to emphasize major points or draw the attention of the audience to specific items in the slide. — pen
7. This term refers to how one slide is removed from the screen and replaced with the next slide. — transition
8. To display the Slide Transition dialog box, click this option on the Menu bar, and then click Slide Transition. — slide show
9. If a time has been added to a slide, the time displays at the bottom of the slide in this view. — slide sorter view
10. In Slide Sorter view, this toolbar displays below the Standard toolbar. — view slide sorter toolbar
11. Click the Loop continuously until 'Esc' option at this dialog box to specify that the presentation run continuously. — set up show
12. In the Outline view, click this button on the Outlining toolbar to move the insertion point to the next tab stop. — promote
13. In the Outline view, click this button on the Outlining toolbar to move the insertion point to the previous tab stop. — demote
14. This button displays in each dialog box and can be used to display a brief explanation of an option. — screen tip
15. Use this Help feature to display a yellow box with information about a button on the toolbar. — whats this

Chapter One

working hands-on

Assessment 1

1. Create a presentation with the text shown in figure 1.21 by completing the following steps:
    a. Open PowerPoint.
    b. At the PowerPoint dialog box, click Design Template, and then click OK.
    c. At the New Presentation dialog box, click the Design Templates tab (if necessary).
    d. At the New Presentation dialog box with the Design Templates tab selected, double-click the *Marble* template.
    e. At the New Slide dialog box, double-click the first autolayout in the list box (Title Slide).
    f. At the slide, click anywhere in the text *Click to add title* and key **DEDUCTIBLE INCOME**.
    g. Click anywhere in the text *Click to add subtitle* and key **Exceptions to Deductible Income**.
    h. Click the New Slide button located on the Standard toolbar and then create the second slide with the text shown in figure 1.21.
    i. Continue creating the remaining slides as shown in figure 1.21.
2. Save the presentation and name it Deductible Presentation.
3. Print all the slides on one page.
4. Close Deductible Presentation.

figure 1.21 Assessment 1

Slide 1	Title	=	DEDUCTIBLE INCOME
	Subtitle	=	Exceptions to Deductible Income
Slide 2	Title	=	EXCEPTION 1
	Subtitle	=	Any cost of living increase if increase becomes effective while disabled.
Slide 3	Title	=	EXCEPTION 2
	Subtitle	=	Reimbursement for hospital, medical, or surgical expense.
Slide 4	Title	=	EXCEPTION 3
	Subtitle	=	Reasonable attorney's fees incurred in connection with a claim for deductible income.
Slide 5	Title	=	EXCEPTION 4
	Subtitle	=	Benefits from any individual disability insurance policy.
Slide 6	Title	=	EXCEPTION 5
	Subtitle	=	Group credit or mortgage disability insurance benefits.

Assessment 2

1. Open Deductible Presentation.
2. Save the presentation with Save As and name it Enhanced Deductible Presentation.
3. Make the following changes to the presentation:
   a. Add the transition *Split Vertical Out* to all slides in the presentation.
   b. Add the cash register sound to all slides in the presentation.
4. Save the presentation again with the same name (Enhanced Deductible Presentation).
5. Run the presentation.
6. Close Enhanced Deductible Presentation.

Assessment 3

1. Create a presentation with the text shown in figure 1.22. You determine the template and the autolayout. (*Hint: Use the first autolayout for the first slide and the second autolayout for the remaining slides.*)
2. After creating the presentation, save it and name it Newsletter Presentation.
3. Print Newsletter Presentation as an outline.
4. Print Newsletter Presentation as individual slides.
5. Close Newsletter Presentation.

figure 1.22 Assessment 3

Slide 1	Title	=	PREPARING A COMPANY NEWSLETTER
	Subtitle	=	Planning and Designing the Layout
Slide 2	Title	=	Planning a Newsletter
	Bullets	=	• If a scanner is available, use pictures of different people from your organization in each issue. • Distribute contributor sheets soliciting information from employees. • Keep the focus of the newsletter on issues of interest to employees.
Slide 3	Title	=	Planning a Newsletter
	Bullets	=	• Make sure the focus is on various levels of employment; do not focus on top management only. • Conduct regular surveys to see if your newsletter provides a needed source of information.
Slide 4	Title	=	Designing a Newsletter

	Bullets	=	• Maintain consistent elements from issue to issue such as:
			   - Column layout
			   - Nameplate formatting and location
			   - Formatting of headlines
			   - Use of color

Slide 5   Title   =   Designing a Newsletter
           Bullets =   • Consider the following elements when designing a newsletter:
- Focus
- Balance
- White space
- Directional flow

Slide 6   Title   =   Creating a Newsletter Layout
           Bullets =   • Choose paper size
                           • Choose paper weight
                           • Determine margins
                           • Specify column layout

Assessment 4

1. Open Newsletter Presentation.
2. Save the presentation with Save As and name it Enhanced Newsletter Presentation.
3. Make the following changes to the presentation:
    a. Add a transition of your choosing to each slide.
    b. Add a sound of your choosing to each slide.
    c. Specify that all slides advance automatically after 5 seconds.
    d. Set up the presentation as continuous.
4. Save the presentation again with the same name (Enhanced Newsletter Presentation).
5. Run the presentation.
6. Close Enhanced Newsletter Presentation.

Assessment 5

1. Copy three presentations that you will use in the next chapter from the Chapter 01C folder to the root folder of your disk by completing the following steps:
    a. Display the Open dialog box with Chapter 01C on your disk as the active folder.
    b. Click the presentation named *Planning Presentation*.
    c. Hold down the Ctrl key and click *Newsletter Presentation*. This selects both Newsletter Presentation and Planning Presentation.
    d. Hold the Ctrl key and click *Networking Presentation*. This selects all three presentations.
    e. Point the tip of the mouse pointer over one of the selected presentations, right-click the mouse, and then select Copy from the shortcut menu.
    f. Click the Up One Level button on the dialog box toolbar to display the root (main) folder of the disk.
    g. Click in any white area inside the dialog box to make sure no folder names are selected, right-click the mouse, and then select Paste from the shortcut menu.
    h. Double-click the folder name Chapter 01C to make it the active folder.
2. Close the Open dialog box.

Assessment 6

1. A presentation created in PowerPoint can be sent to Word as an outline or as a handout. This might be helpful if you want to format or enhance the presentation using Word tools and features. Use PowerPoint's Help feature to learn about how to send slide images to Word. (*Hint: To get started, click the Office Assistant Title bar, key* **How do I send slide images to Word?** *and then click the Search button. At the list of choices that displays in the yellow box, click* Send notes, handouts, or an outline to Microsoft Word. *Continue using Help to determine the steps for sending a presentation to a Word document.*)
2. After reading the Help information, open Deductible Presentation and then send it to Word. (At the Write-Up dialog box, you choose the page layout.)
3. When the document displays in Word, print the document.
4. Close the Word document without saving it, exit Word, and then exit PowerPoint.

Chapter 02C

Editing and Formatting a PowerPoint Presentation

PERFORMANCE OBJECTIVES

Upon successful completion of chapter 2, you will be able to:
- Edit a PowerPoint presentation.
- Insert and delete slides in a presentation.
- Copy slides within and between presentations.
- Rearrange slides and rearrange objects within slides.
- Complete a spelling check.
- Format slides in a presentation.
- Format a master slide in a presentation.
- Draw objects and autoshapes with buttons on the Drawing toolbar.
- Select, move, copy, delete, and size objects.
- Draw text boxes and wrap text within an autoshape.
- Group, ungroup, flip, rotate, distribute, and align objects.
- Change slide color schemes, backgrounds, and design templates.
- Create a presentation with the Blank Presentation template.
- Format slides with Format Painter.
- Format slides with bullets and numbers.
- Insert the date and time, a header and footer, and page numbering in slides.
- Create, format, and print speaker notes.

In this chapter, you will learn to edit text and slides in a PowerPoint presentation, including inserting and deleting text and slides, rearranging slides, and formatting text and object boxes in slides. You will also learn how to change slide color schemes, apply different design templates, and insert elements in slides such as the date and time, a header and footer, and page numbering.

Editing Slides

Slides within a PowerPoint presentation can be edited. For example, text within individual slides can be inserted or deleted, slides can be deleted from the presentation, slides can be inserted into an existing presentation, and slides can be rearranged. Slides can be edited in several views—use the view that makes editing the easiest. For example, rearrange the order of slides in the Slide Sorter view; delete or insert text within slides in the Outline view or the Normal view.

Inserting and Deleting Text in Slides

To insert or delete text in an individual slide, open the presentation, change to the desired view, edit the text as needed, and then save the presentation again. If you want to delete more than an individual character, consider selecting the text first. Several methods can be used for selecting text as shown in Figure 2.1.

figure 2.1 Selecting Text

To do this	Perform this action
Select text mouse pointer passes through	Click and drag mouse
Select entire word	Double-click word
Select entire paragraph	Triple-click anywhere in paragraph
Select an entire sentence	Ctrl + click anywhere in sentence
Select all text in selected object box	Ctrl + A

Hint: Press Ctrl + F to display the Find dialog box.

Hint: Press Ctrl + H to display the Replace dialog box.

Finding and Replacing Text in Slides

Use the find and replace feature to look for specific text or formatting in slides in a presentation and replace with other text or formatting. Complete a find and replace in a PowerPoint presentation in the Normal view, Outline view, or the Slide view. Begin a find and replace by clicking Edit and then Replace. At the Replace dialog box shown in figure 2.2, key the text you want to find in the Find what text box, press the Tab key, and then key the replacement text in the Replace with text box. Click the Find Next button to find the next occurrence of the text or click the Replace All button to replace all occurrences in the presentation.

figure 2.2 Replace Dialog Box

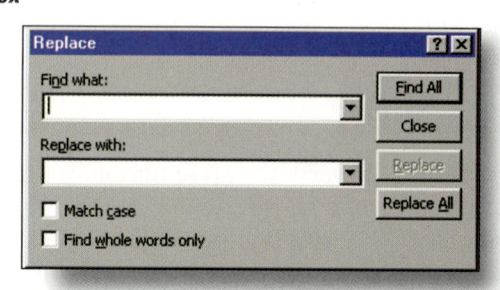

If you want to find specific text without replacing it with other text, click Edit and then Find. This displays the Find dialog box shown in figure 2.3. Key the text you want to find in the Find what text box and then click the Find Next button.

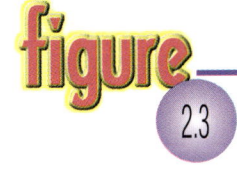

figure 2.3 *Find Dialog Box*

Inserting and Deleting Slides

An entire slide can be deleted from a presentation at the Slide Sorter, Outline view, or Outline pane. To delete a slide from a presentation, display the presentation in Slide Sorter view, click the slide you want to delete, and then press the Delete key. A slide can also be deleted in the Outline view or the Outline pane. To do this, change to the Normal view or Outline view, position the arrow pointer on the slide icon located next to the slide you want to delete until the arrow pointer turns into a four-headed arrow, and then click the left mouse button. (This selects all text for the slide.) With the text for the slide selected, press the Delete key.

Hint: Insert and/or delete slides in Slide Sorter view or in Outline view.

A new slide can be inserted into an existing presentation at the Slide Sorter view, Outline view, or Outline pane. To add a slide to a presentation in the Slide Sorter view, you would follow these basic steps:

1. Open the presentation to which you want the slide added.
2. Change to the Slide Sorter view.
3. Click the slide that will immediately precede the new slide. (For example, if the new slide should immediately follow Slide 3, click Slide 3.)
4. Click the New Slide button located on the Standard toolbar; click the Common Tasks button on the Formatting toolbar and click New Slide; or click Insert and New Slide.
5. At the New Slide dialog box, double-click the desired autolayout format.
6. At the Slide Sorter view, double-click the new blank slide. (This changes the presentation to the Normal view with the new slide displayed.)
7. Add the desired text to the new slide.
8. Save the presentation again.

(Before completing computer exercises, delete the Chapter 01C folder on your disk. Next, create the Chapter 02C folder. Instructions for deleting a folder are printed on the inside of the back cover of this textbook.)

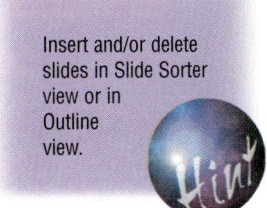

Editing and Formatting a PowerPoint Presentation

Copying a Slide

Slides in some presentations may contain similar text, objects, and formatting. Rather than creating a new slide, consider copying a slide. To do this, display the slides in Slide Sorter view and then select the slide you want to copy. Position the arrow pointer in the slide, hold down the Ctrl key and then the left mouse button. Drag to the location where you want the slide copied, release the mouse button, and then release the Ctrl key.

Copying a Slide Between Presentations

Slides can be copied within a presentation and also between presentations. To copy a slide between presentations, open the presentation containing the slide to be copied and change to the Slide Sorter view. Click the slide you want to copy and then click the Copy button on the Standard toolbar. Open the presentation into which the slide is to be copied and then display the slides in Slide Sorter view. Click in the location where you want the slide positioned and then click the Paste button. The copied slide will take on the template design of the presentation into which it is copied.

exercise 1

Finding and Replacing Text and Deleting, Inserting, and Copying Slides

1. Open PowerPoint and open Planning Presentation.
2. Save the presentation with Save As in the Chapter 02C folder on your disk and name it Edited Planning Presentation.
3. Find all occurrences of *Planning* in the presentation and replace with *Preparing* by completing the following steps:
   a. Click Edit and then Replace.
   b. At the Replace dialog box, key **Planning** in the Find what text box.
   c. Press the Tab key.
   d. Key **Preparing** in the Replace with text box.
   e. Click the Replace All button.
   f. At the Microsoft PowerPoint message telling you that 5 replacements were made, click OK.
   g. Click the Close button to close the Replace dialog box.
4. Find all occurrences of *Publication* and replace with *Newsletter* by completing steps similar to those in step 3.
5. Delete and insert slides in the Edited Planning Presentation by completing the following steps:
   a. At the Normal view, click the Next Slide button located at the bottom of the vertical scroll bar until Slide 4 displays.
   b. Edit Slide 4 by completing the following steps:

1) Position the I-beam pointer on the sentence below *Step 4* and then click the left mouse button. (This inserts a frame around the text.)
2) Edit the sentence so it reads *Decide what steps you want readers to take after reading the message.* (Use deleting and inserting commands to edit this sentence.)
   c. Click the Next Slide button to display Slide 5.
   d. Edit Slide 5 in the Outline pane so it reads *Collect and assess examples of effective designs.*
6. Add a new slide by completing the following steps:
   a. Click the Slide Sorter View button on the View toolbar.
   b. Click Slide 2 to select it.
   c. Click the New Slide button on the Standard toolbar.
   d. At the New Slide dialog box, double-click the first autolayout (Title Slide).
   e. At the Slide Sorter view, double-click the new slide (Slide 3). (This changes to the Normal view with Slide 3 displayed.)
   f. Click anywhere in the text *Click to add title* and key **Preparing the Newsletter**.
   g. Click anywhere in the text *Click to add subtitle* and key the following:
      1) Turn on bold, key **STEP 3**, and then turn off bold.
      2) Press Enter and key **Determine the available budget for the newsletter.**
7. Add another new slide by completing the following steps:
   a. Click the Slide Sorter View button on the View toolbar.
   b. Click Slide 4 to select it.
   c. Click the New Slide button on the Standard toolbar.
   d. At the New Slide dialog box, double-click the first autolayout (Title Slide).
   e. At the Slide Sorter view, double-click the new blank slide (Slide 5). (This changes to the Normal view with Slide 5 displayed.)
   f. Click anywhere in the text *Click to add title* and key **Preparing the Newsletter**.
   g. Click anywhere in the text *Click to add subtitle* and key the following:
      1) Turn on bold, key **STEP 5**, and then turn off bold.
      2) Press Enter and key **Specify the layout of elements to be included in the newsletter.**
8. Delete Slide 2 by completing the following steps:
   a. Click the Slide Sorter View button on the View toolbar.
   b. Click Slide 2 to select it.
   c. Press the Delete key.
9. Change to the Outline view and edit each slide so the step number matches the slide number.
10. Copy slides from a different presentation into the Edited Planning Presentation by completing the following steps:
    a. Change to the Slide Sorter view.
    b. Open the presentation named Company Newsletter located in the *Presentations* folder on the CD that accompanies this textbook.

    c. With the Company Newsletter presentation open, change to the Slide Sorter view.
    d. Click Slide 2, hold down the Shift key, and then click Slide 3. (This selects both slides.)
    e. Click the Copy button on the Standard toolbar.
    f. Click the button on the Taskbar representing Edited Planning Presentation.
    g. Click to the right of the last slide in the presentation and then click the Paste button on the Standard toolbar.
11. Save the presentation again with the same name (Edited Planning Presentation).
12. Print the presentation as six slides on one page. (Change the Print what option at the Print dialog box to Handouts.)
13. Close Edited Planning Presentation.
14. Close Company Newsletter.

Rearranging Text in Slides

Text in slides can be rearranged by deleting and inserting text. Text can also be rearranged in slides using Cut, Copy, and/or Paste options. For example, to move text in a slide, you would complete the following steps:

1. Click once in the object box containing the text to be moved.
2. Select the text to be moved.
3. Click the Cut button on the Standard toolbar.
4. Position the insertion point where you want the text inserted and then click the Paste button.

Text can also be moved from one slide to another by selecting the text, clicking the Cut button, displaying the slide where you want the text inserted, and then clicking the Paste button.

To copy text in or between slides, complete similar steps. Select the text to be copied, click the Copy button on the Standard toolbar, move the insertion point to the position where the text is to be copied, and then click the Paste button.

Rearranging Text in the Outline View or Outline Pane

Text in the Outline view or in the Outline pane can be moved using the mouse. To do this, position the mouse pointer on the slide icon or bullet at the left side of the text, until the arrow pointer turns into a four-headed arrow. Hold down the left mouse button, drag the arrow pointer (displays with a gray box attached) to the desired location, and then release the mouse button.

If you position the arrow pointer on the slide icon and then hold down the left mouse button, all the text in the slide is selected. If you position the arrow pointer on the bullet and then hold down the left mouse button, all text following that bullet is selected.

Dragging selected text with the mouse moves the selected text to a new location in the presentation. You can also copy selected text. To do this, click the slide icon or click the bullet to select the desired text. Position the arrow pointer in the selected text, hold down the Ctrl key, and then the left mouse button. Drag the arrow pointer (displays with a light gray box and a plus sign attached) to the desired location, release the mouse button, and then release the Ctrl key.

Rearranging Object Boxes in a Slide

An entire selected object box can be moved easily in a slide. To do this, click once in the object box (outside any text) to select it (white sizing handles should display around the box). If white sizing handles do not display around the box, position the arrow pointer on the border of the box (small gray lines), and then click the left mouse button. Position the arrow pointer on the border around the object box until the arrow pointer displays with a four-headed arrow attached. Hold down the left mouse button, drag the outline of the box to the desired position, and then release the mouse button.

Dragging a selected box with the mouse moves the box. You can also copy a selected box. To do this, hold down the Ctrl key while dragging the box with the mouse. When the outline of the box is in the desired position, release the mouse button, and then release the Ctrl key.

Sizing an Object Box

Click an object box in a slide and sizing handles display around the box. Use these sizing handles to increase or decrease the size of the box. To increase or decrease the size, position the arrow pointer on one of the white sizing handles until the arrow pointer turns into a double-headed arrow. Hold down the left mouse button, drag the outline of the box in to decrease the size or drag the outline out to increase the size, and then release the mouse button. You can increase or decrease the size of the box at the same time by using the sizing handles that display in each corner of the selected box.

Hint: The size of a selected object box can be changed by dragging a corner or side sizing handle.

Rearranging Slides

Slides can be rearranged easily in the Slide Sorter view. To do this, change to the Slide Sorter view, position the arrow pointer on the slide to be moved, hold down the left mouse button, drag the arrow pointer (with a square attached) to the desired position, and then release the mouse button.

Using Buttons on the Standard Toolbar

The Standard toolbar contains the Cut, Copy, and Paste buttons along with other buttons to quickly access commonly used features in PowerPoint. The buttons on the Standard toolbar are described in figure 2.4.

figure 2.4 — PowerPoint Standard Toolbar Buttons

Click this button	Named	To do this
	New	Display the New Presentation dialog box where a blank or preformatted template can be chosen to create a presentation
	Open	Display the Open dialog box to choose a previously saved presentation file
	Save	Save the current presentation with the same name; or, save a presentation at the Save As dialog box
	E-mail	Send a slide presentation as an e-mail attachment or use the current slide text as the e-mail message
	Print	Print the presentation currently open
	Spelling	Complete a spelling check on the text in the current presentation
	Cut	Remove selected text or object to the Windows Clipboard
	Copy	Insert a copy of selected text or object in the Windows Clipboard
	Paste	Insert the contents of the Clipboard into the current slide
	Format Painter	Copy formatting from selected text or object and apply it to another object
	Undo	Undo the most recent action
	Redo	Redo (or repeat) the most recent action
	Insert Hyperlink	Insert or edit the specified hyperlink
	Tables and Borders	Display the Tables and Borders dialog box containing buttons for drawing and customizing a table
	Insert Table	Insert a blank table with number of rows and columns you specify
	Insert Chart	Embed a graph in a slide using specified data

	New Slide	Display New Slide dialog box
	Expand All	Display all levels of the slides
	Show Formatting	Display all character formatting as it will appear on the slide
	Grayscale Preview	Display a presentation in black and white (rather than color)
53%	Zoom	Increase or decrease the display of a presentation
	Microsoft PowerPoint Help	Have Office Assistant provide help topics and tips to help accomplish tasks

Completing a Spelling Check

To perform a spelling check on a PowerPoint presentation, open a presentation and click the Spelling button on the Standard toolbar. Change or ignore selected text as required.

Spelling

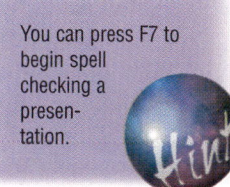

You can press F7 to begin spell checking a presentation.

exercise 2

Creating a Presentation and then Rearranging Slides

1. Create the slides for a presentation as shown in figure 2.5 by completing the following steps:
   a. At a blank PowerPoint screen, click File and New.
   b. At the New Presentation dialog box, click the Design Templates tab.
   c. At the New Presentation dialog box with the Design Templates tab selected, double-click the *Fireball* template.
   d. At the New Slide dialog box, double-click the first autolayout (Title Slide) in the list box.
   e. At the slide, key the text for the first slide shown in figure 2.5 by completing the following steps:
      1) Click anywhere in the text *Click to add title* and key **Telecommunications System**.
      2) Click anywhere in the text *Click to add subtitle* and key **Factors for Evaluating the Effectiveness of a Telecommunications System**.
   f. Click the New Slide button on the Standard toolbar.
   g. At the New Slide dialog box (with the second autolayout [Bulleted List] selected), click OK. (This inserts another slide in the Slide pane.)

Editing and Formatting a PowerPoint Presentation P-57

h. At the slide, key the text shown in the second slide in figure 2.5 by completing the following steps:
   1) Click anywhere in the text *Click to add title* and key **COST**.
   2) Click anywhere in the text *Click to add text* and key the text after the first bullet in the second slide in figure 2.5 (the text that begins *How does the cost of a new system compare...*).
   3) Key the text following the remaining bullets.
i. Click the New Slide button.
j. At the New Slide dialog box (with the second autolayout [Bulleted List] selected), click OK. (This inserts another slide in the Slide pane.) Key the text in the slide as shown for the third slide in figure 2.5.
k. Continue creating the remaining slides in figure 2.5 by completing steps similar to those in 1i and 1j.

2. When all six slides have been created, make Slide 1 the active slide, and then perform a spelling check by clicking the Spelling button. Change or ignore as required during the spelling check.
3. Save the presentation in the Chapter 02C folder on your disk and name it Telecommunications Presentation.
4. Print the six slides on one page.
5. Rearrange some of the slides in the presentation by completing the following steps:
   a. Change to the Slide Sorter view by clicking the Slide Sorter View button on the View toolbar.
   b. Move Slide 4 (QUALITY) before Slide 3 (EFFICIENCY). To do this, position the arrow pointer on Slide 4 (QUALITY), hold down the left mouse button, drag the arrow pointer (with a square attached) to the left of Slide 3, and then release the mouse button.
   c. Move Slide 2 (COST) after Slide 5 (TIME) by completing steps similar to those in 5b.
6. Print the six slides again on one page.
7. Move and copy text within and between slides in Outline view by completing the following steps:
   a. Click the Outline View button on the View toolbar.
   b. Move the first bulleted item in Slide 6 to the end of the list by completing the following steps:
      1) Scroll down and make sure all of the Slide 6 text displays.
      2) Position the mouse pointer on the first round bullet until it turns into a four-headed arrow.
      3) Hold down the left mouse button, drag the arrow pointer down until a thin horizontal line displays below the last bulleted item, and then release the mouse button. (Make sure that the thin black line displays before releasing the mouse button.)

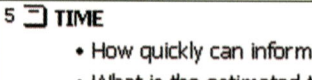

c. Copy a bulleted item from Slide 3 (EFFICIENCY) to Slide 4 (TIME) by completing the following steps:
   1) Position the mouse pointer on the last round bullet in Slide 3 until it turns into a four-headed arrow and then click the left mouse button. (This selects the text after the bullet.)
   2) With the text selected, click the Copy button on the Standard toolbar.
   3) Position the I-beam pointer immediately after the question mark in the second bulleted item in Slide 4 and then click the left mouse button.
   4) Press the Enter key. (This moves the insertion point down to the next line and inserts another bullet.)
   5) Click the Paste button on the Standard toolbar. (This pastes the item and also includes another bullet.)
   6) Press the Backspace key twice to remove the extra bullet.
8. Add a transition and sound of your choosing to all slides.
9. Save the presentation again with the same name (Telecommunications Presentation).
10. Run the presentation.
11. Print the presentation in Outline view.

figure 2.5 *Exercise 2*

12. Close Telecommunications Presentation.

| Slide 1 | Title | = | Telecommunications System |
| | Subtitle | = | Factors for Evaluating the Effectiveness of a Telecommunications System |

Slide 2	Title	=	COST
	Bullets	=	• How does the cost of a new system compare with the cost of the current system?
			• What is the cost of maintaining the current system?
			• What will be the training costs of a new system?

Slide 3	Title	=	EFFICIENCY
	Bullets	=	• How does the efficiency of the current system compare with a paper-based system?
			• What is the time frame for implementing a new system?
			• Will improved efficiency translate into lowered personnel costs?

Slide 4	Title	=	QUALITY
	Bullets	=	• How does the current system rank in terms of usefulness?
			• What is the current quality of transmission?
			• Is the current system effective in producing the required internal and external documents?

Slide 5　　Title　　　=　　TIME
　　　　　　Bullets　 =　　• How quickly can information be delivered?
　　　　　　　　　　　　　• What is the estimated training time for a new system?
　　　　　　　　　　　　　• What is the time frame for implementing a new system?

Slide 6　　Title　　　=　　EASE OF USE
　　　　　　Bullets　 =　　• Will there be a reduction in company efficiency during the transition?
　　　　　　　　　　　　　• Will the new system improve employee productivity?
　　　　　　　　　　　　　• How long before users feel comfortable with a new system?

Formatting a Presentation

PowerPoint provides a variety of design templates you can use to create a presentation. These templates contain formatting provided by the program. In some situations, the formatting provided by the template will be appropriate; in other situations you will want to change or enhance the formatting of a slide. Formatting can be applied to specific text in a slide or formatting can be applied to an object box.

Formatting Text in a Slide

Text formatting can include a variety of options such as changing fonts, changing font color, and changing paragraph alignment. The steps to change the formatting of a slide vary depending on the type of formatting desired. For example, to change the font of text in a slide, you would select the text first, and then change to the desired font. To change the alignment of a paragraph of text, you would position the insertion point on any character in the paragraph, and then choose the desired alignment.

The Formatting toolbar contains several buttons for applying formatting to text in a slide. The buttons, button names, and a description of what each button accomplishes are shown in figure 2.6.

figure 2.6 — PowerPoint Formatting Toolbar Buttons

Click this button	Named	To do this
Times New Roman	Font	Change selected text to a different font
28	Font Size	Change selected text to a different font size
B	Bold	Add or remove bolding to or from selected text
I	Italic	Add or remove italics to or from selected text
U	Underline	Add or remove underlining to or from selected text
S	Text Shadow	Add or remove a shadow to or from selected text
≡	Align Left	Left align text
≡	Center	Center align text
≡	Align Right	Right align text
≔	Numbering	Add or remove numbering to or from selected text
≔	Bullets	Add or remove bullets to or from selected text
A↑	Increase Font Size	Increase font size of selected text to the next available larger size
A↓	Decrease Font Size	Decrease font size of selected text to the next available smaller size
←	Promote	Move selected text to the previous level (left) in an outline
→	Demote	Move selected text to the next level (right) in an outline
⭐	Animation Effects	Turn on/off the display of the Animation Effects toolbar that contains buttons for adding motion and sound effects to objects in a slide
Common Tasks ▼	Common Tasks	Display a drop-down list with the options New Slide, Slide Layout, and Apply Design Template

Creating a New Line

Some of the slide autolayouts are designed to create bulleted text. You used one of these autolayouts when creating the Telecommunications Presentation. When creating bulleted text in a slide, pressing the Enter key causes the insertion point to move to the next line, inserting another bullet. There may be situations where you want to create a blank line between bulleted items to better separate them without creating another bullet. To do this, use the New Line command, Shift + Enter. When you insert a line with Shift + Enter, the new line is considered part of the previous paragraph. This lets you create a blank line without creating a bullet.

Increasing/Decreasing Spacing Before/After Paragraphs

With the New Line command you can insert a blank line without creating a bullet. If you want tighter control over the amount of spacing before or after paragraphs, use options from the Line Spacing dialog box shown in figure 2.7. Display this dialog box by clicking Format and then Line Spacing. Increase or decrease spacing before a paragraph by keying the desired line spacing measurement in the Before paragraph text box. Key a line spacing measurement in the After paragraph text box to control the amount of spacing after paragraphs. By default, the measurement used is Line spacing. This can be changed to *Points* by clicking the down-pointing triangle after the list box containing the word *Lines* and then clicking *Points* at the drop-down list.

figure 2.7 **Line Spacing Dialog Box**

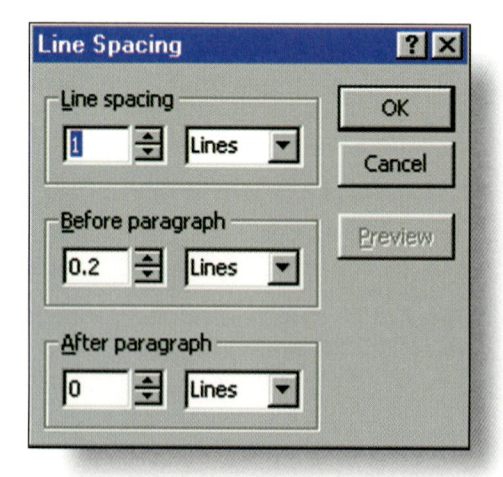

Formatting with a Master Slide

If you use a PowerPoint template, you may choose to use the formatting provided by the template, or you may want to customize the formatting. If you customize formatting in a presentation, PowerPoint's master slide can be very helpful in reducing the steps needed to format all slides in a presentation. If you know in advance that you want to change the formatting of slides, display the master slide, make the changes needed, and then create the presentation. If the presentation is already created, edit the presentation in a master slide. Any changes made to a master slide will affect all slides in the presentation.

To display the master slide, change to the Slide view, position the insertion point on the Slide View button on the View toolbar, hold down the Shift key (this causes the Slide View button to change to the Slide Master View or Title Master View button), and then click the left mouse button. You can also click View, point to Master, and then click Slide Master. This displays a master slide similar to the one shown in figure 2.8. At this slide, make any desired changes and then click the Slide View button (do not hold down the Shift key this time).

Hint: The Slide Master contains all the elements you want to display on a slide.

Hint: Control the formatting of all slides (except a title slide) at the Slide Master. Control the formatting of a title slide at the Title Master.

figure 2.8 *Master Slide*

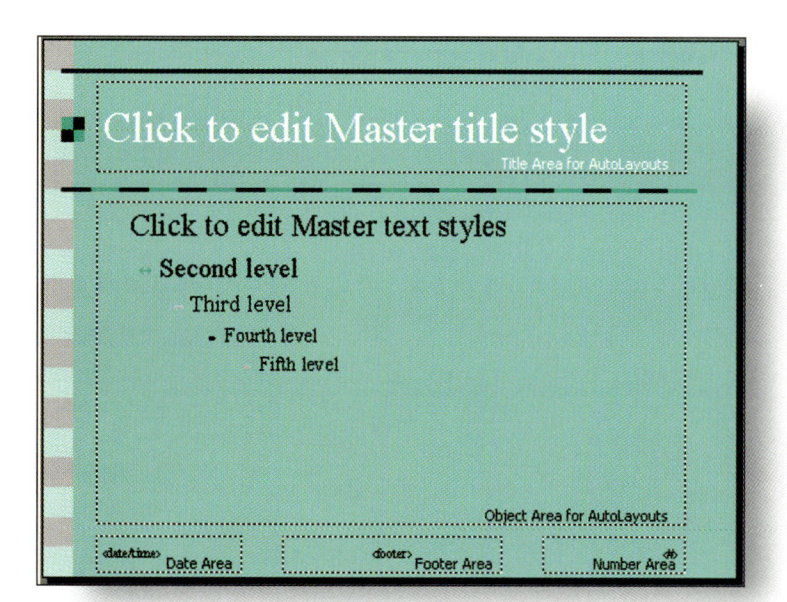

A Slide Master and/or a Title Master can be created in a presentation. If a slide was created using the first autolayout at the New Slide dialog box (Title Slide), holding down the Shift key and then clicking the Slide View button (or clicking View, pointing to Master, and then clicking Title Master) causes the Title Master slide to display. Any formatting changes made to this Title Master slide will affect only those slides in the presentation created with the Title Slide autolayout. If a slide was created using any other autolayout at the New Slide dialog box, holding down the Shift key and then clicking the Slide View button causes the Slide Master to display. Any formatting changes made to this Slide Master slide will affect all slides in the presentation that were created with any autolayout except the Title Slide autolayout.

In exercise 3, you will use a master slide to edit slides in an existing presentation. In exercise 4, you will edit a master slide and create slides for a presentation.

exercise 3

Formatting Text in a Presentation Using a Master Slide

1. Open Networking Presentation.
2. Save the presentation with Save As in the Chapter 02C folder on your disk and name it Formatted Network Pres.
3. Change the typeface and text color in slides using a master slide by completing the following steps:
   a. Change to the Slide Sorter view.
   b. Double-click Slide 1.
   c. With Slide 1 displayed in Slide view, position the arrow pointer on the Slide View button on the View toolbar, hold down the Shift key (the Slide View button turns into the Slide Master View button), and then click the left mouse button.
   d. With the master slide displayed, change the typeface and text color of the title by completing the following steps:
      1) Click in the object box containing the text **Click to edit Master title style**. (This selects the object box containing the text.)
      2) Click Format and Font.
      3) At the Font dialog box, click *Bookman Old Style* in the Font list box. (You will need to scroll up the list of typefaces to display Bookman Old Style. If this typeface is not available, choose a similar serif typeface.)
      4) Click the down-pointing triangle at the right of the Color text box.
      5) At the color pop-up menu, click the black color that displays in the Automatic section (the second color from the left).
      6) Click OK to close the dialog box.

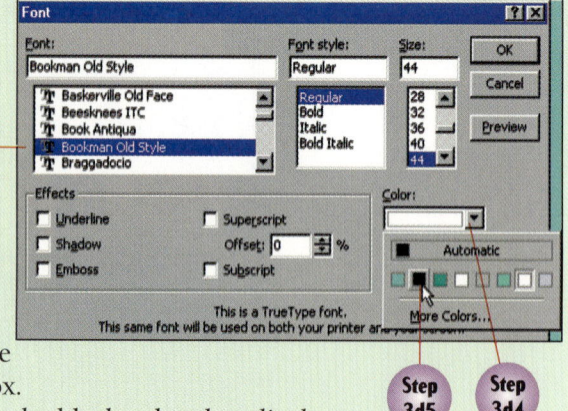

Chapter Two

e. Change the typeface and color of the text after bullets by completing the following steps:
   1) Click in the object box containing the bulleted text. (This selects the object box.)
   2) Position the arrow pointer on the first bullet until it displays as a four-headed arrow and then click the left mouse button. (This selects all text preceded by bullets.)
   3) With the text selected, click Format and Font.
   4) At the Font dialog box, click *Bookman Old Style* in the Font list box. (If this typeface is not available, choose a similar serif typeface.)
   5) Click the down-pointing triangle at the right of the Color text box.
   6) Click the More Colors option that displays at the bottom of the drop-down menu.
   7) At the Colors dialog box with the Standard tab selected, click the dark blue color that displays at the right side of the top row of colors.
   8) Click OK to close the Colors dialog box.
   9) Click OK to close the Font dialog box.
f. Click the Slide View button on the View toolbar. (This displays Slide 1 with the formatting applied.)
g. Click the Slide Sorter View button on the View toolbar to see how the slides display with the new formatting.

4. Center the text in the title object box and move the object box by completing the following steps:
   a. At the Slide Sorter view, double-click Slide 1.
   b. With Slide 1 displayed in Slide view, click in the object box containing the text *NETWORKING*. (This selects the object box.)
   c. Click the Center button on the Formatting toolbar. (This centers the text horizontally in the object box.)
   d. With the object box still selected, position the arrow pointer on the object box border until a four-headed arrow displays attached to the arrow pointer.
   e. Hold down the left mouse button, drag the outline of the object box until it is centered horizontally and vertically on the slide, and then release the mouse button.

5. Increase the line spacing after paragraphs for the text in Slide 2 by completing the following steps:
   a. Click the Next Slide button until Slide 2 displays.
   b. Click in the object box containing the bulleted text.
   c. Select the bulleted paragraphs of text.
   d. Click Format and Line Spacing.

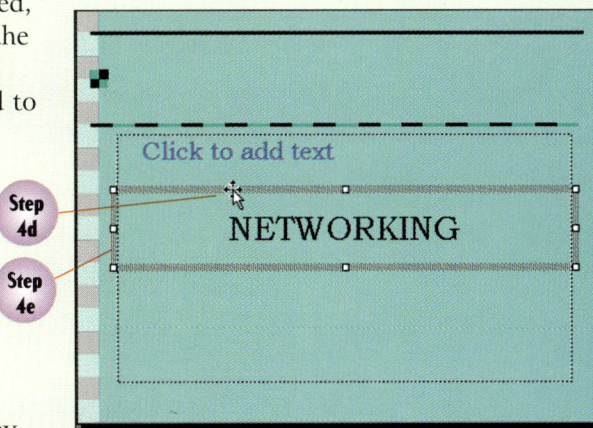

Editing and Formatting a PowerPoint Presentation

e. At the Line Spacing dialog box, make the following changes:
      1) Click the down-pointing triangle at the right of the text box containing the word *Lines* in the After paragraph section.
      2) At the drop-down list that displays, click *Points*.
      3) Select the *0* measurement in the After paragraph measurement box and key **6**.
      4) Click OK to close the Line Spacing dialog box.
   f. Deselect the text.
6. Add a transition and sound of your choosing to each slide.
7. Save the presentation again with the same name (Formatted Network Pres).
8. Run the presentation.
9. Print the presentation so all slides are printed on one page.
10. Close Formatted Network Pres.

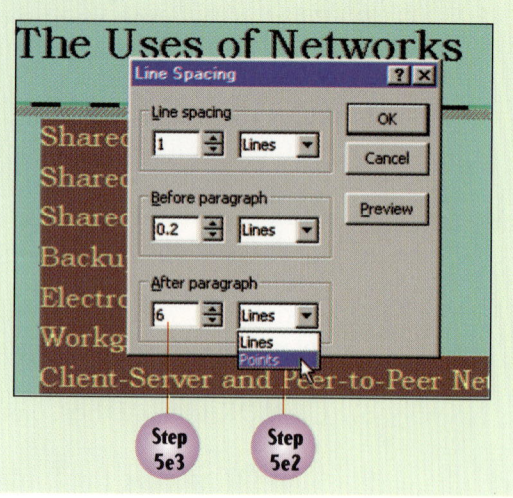

Formatting with Buttons on the Drawing Toolbar

Slides in a PowerPoint template contain placeholders where specific text or objects are inserted. Placeholders consist of an object box containing specific formatting. The formatting applied to placeholders in a template will vary depending on the template selected. These placeholders (object boxes) can be customized by changing such things as the background color or adding a border or shadow. These types of changes can be made with buttons on the Drawing toolbar. The Drawing toolbar displays toward the bottom of the screen in Normal view, Outline view, and Slide view. Figure 2.9 describes the buttons on the Drawing toolbar.

figure 2.9 PowerPoint Drawing Toolbar Buttons

Click this button	Named	To do this
Draw ▼	Draw	Group or ungroup drawn objects and customize and edit a drawn shape or autoshape
▧	Select Objects	Select text or objects
⟳	Free Rotate	Rotate selected object to any degree by dragging a corner of the object in the desired direction
AutoShapes ▼	AutoShapes	Display a palette of shapes that can be drawn in a slide (To draw a shape circumscribed within a perfect square, hold down the Shift key while drawing the shape.)

◣	Line	Draw a line in a slide
◥	Arrow	Insert a line with an arrowhead (To draw at 15-degree angles, hold down the Shift key.)
▢	Rectangle	Draw a rectangle in a slide (To draw a perfect square, hold down the Shift key while drawing the shape.)
○	Oval	Draw an oval in a slide (To draw a perfect circle, hold down the Shift key while drawing the shape.)
▤	Text Box	Add text outside a placeholder (To add text that does not wrap, click tool, click in slide, and then key text. To add text that does wrap, click tool, drag to create a box, and then key text.)
	Insert WordArt	Insert a Microsoft Office drawing object
	Insert Clip Art	Display Insert ClipArt dialog box containing clip art images that can be inserted in a slide
	Fill Color	Fill selected object with a color, pattern, texture, or shaded fill
	Line Color	Change color of selected line
A	Font Color	Format selected text with a color
≡	Line Style	Change thickness of selected line or change it to a compound line
	Dash Style	Change style of selected line, arc, or border to dashed
⇄	Arrow Style	Add arrowheads to a selected line, arc, or open freeform
	Shadow	Add or remove an object shadow
	3-D	Add or remove a 3-D effect

Editing and Formatting a PowerPoint Presentation

Drawing an Object

With buttons on the Drawing toolbar, you can draw a variety of shapes, such as circles, squares, rectangles, ovals. You can also draw straight lines, free form lines, and lines with arrowheads. If you drawn a shape with the Line button or the Arrow button, the shape you draw is considered a *line drawing*. If you draw a shape with the Rectangle or Oval button, the shape you draw is considered an *enclosed object*. If you want to draw the same shape more than once, double-click the shape button on the Drawing toolbar. After drawing the shapes, click the button again to deactivate it.

Use the Rectangle button on the Drawing toolbar to draw a square or rectangle in a slide. If you want to draw a square, hold down the Shift key while drawing the shape. The Shift key keeps all sides of the drawn object equal. Use the Oval button to draw a circle or an oval object. To draw a circle, hold down the Shift key while drawing the object.

Creating AutoShapes

With options from the AutoShapes button, you can choose from a variety of predesigned shapes. Click the AutoShapes button and a pop-up menu displays. Point to the desired menu option and a side menu displays. This side menu will offer autoshape choices for the selected option. For example, if you point to the Basic Shapes option, a number of shapes such as a circle, square, triangle, box, stop sign, and so on, display at the right side of the pop-up menu. Click the desired shape and the mouse pointer turns into cross hairs. Position the cross hairs in the slide, hold down the left mouse button, drag to create the shape, and then release the button.

Selecting an Object

After an object has been created in a slide, you may decide to make changes or delete the object. To do this, the object must be selected. To select an enclosed object, position the mouse pointer anywhere inside the object (the mouse pointer displays with a four-headed arrow attached) and then click the left mouse button. To select a line, position the mouse pointer on the line until the pointer turns into an arrow with a four-headed arrow attached, and then click the left mouse button. When an object is selected, it displays surrounded by white sizing handles. Once an object is selected, it can be edited (for example, by changing the fill and the line), it can be moved, or it can be deleted.

If a slide contains more than one object, you can select several objects at once using the Select Objects button on the Drawing toolbar. To do this, click the Select Objects button, position the cross hairs in the upper left corner of the area containing the objects, hold down the left mouse button, drag the outline to the lower right corner of the area containing the objects, and then release the mouse button. You can also select more than one object by holding down the Shift key as you click each object.

Each object in the selected area displays surrounded by white sizing handles. Objects in the selected area are connected. For example, if you move one of the objects in the selected area, the other objects move relatively.

Deleting an Object

An object you have drawn can be deleted from the slide. To do this, select the object, and then press the Delete key.

Moving and Copying an Object

Select an object and then move it by positioning the mouse pointer inside the object (mouse pointer displays with a four-headed arrow attached), holding down the left mouse button, and then dragging the outline of the object to the new location. If you select more than one object, moving one of the objects will move the other objects.

Moving an object removes the object from its original position and inserts it into a new location. If you want the object to stay in its original location and an exact copy to be inserted in a new location, use the Ctrl key while dragging the object.

Sizing an Object

With the sizing handles that appear around an object when it is selected, the size of the object can be changed. To change the size of the object, select it, and then position the mouse pointer on a sizing handle until it turns into a double-headed arrow. Hold down the left mouse button, drag the outline of the shape toward or away from the center of the object until it is the desired size, and then release the mouse button.

Formatting Objects

With buttons on the Drawing toolbar you can add fill color and/or shading to an object, change the line style, and change the line color. Click the down-pointing triangle at the right side of the Fill Color or Line Color button and a palette of color choices displays. Choose a color at this palette or click an option to display more fill or line colors and fill or line patterns.

exercise 4

Creating a Presentation and Formatting Objects Using a Master Slide

1. Prepare the presentation on enhanced services for McCormack Financial Services shown in figure 2.10 by completing the following steps:
   a. At a blank PowerPoint screen, click File and New.
   b. At the New Presentation dialog box, click the Design Templates tab.
   c. At the New Presentation dialog box with the Design Templates tab selected, double-click the *Neon Frame* template.
   d. At the New Slide dialog box, double-click the first autolayout (Title Slide).
   e. Create a Title Master slide for the presentation by completing the following steps:
      1) Position the arrow pointer on the Slide View button on the View toolbar, hold down the Shift key (this turns the button into Title Master View), and then click the left mouse button. (This displays a master slide.)
      2) With the master slide displayed, click anywhere in the text *Click to edit Master title style*.

3) Change the font to 44-point Arial bold italics.
4) With the text object box still selected (the box containing *Click to edit Master title slide*), add fill color by completing the following steps:
   a) Click the down-pointing triangle at the right side of the Fill Color button on the Drawing toolbar.
   b) At the pop-up menu that displays, click the second color from the right in the bottom row (a shade of green). 
5) Draw diamond shapes in the lower right corner of the slide by completing the following steps:
   a) Click the AutoShapes button on the Drawing toolbar.
   b) At the pop-up menu that displays, point to Basic Shapes (this causes a side menu to display).
   c) At the side menu, click the diamond shape (last shape in the top row).
   d) Hold down the Shift key (this draws the diamond circumscribed in a square) and then position the arrow pointer (displays as a crosshair) in the bottom right corner of the slide. (You will be drawing the diamond shape over text in the master slide. Do not worry about this—the text will not display in the regular slide.) 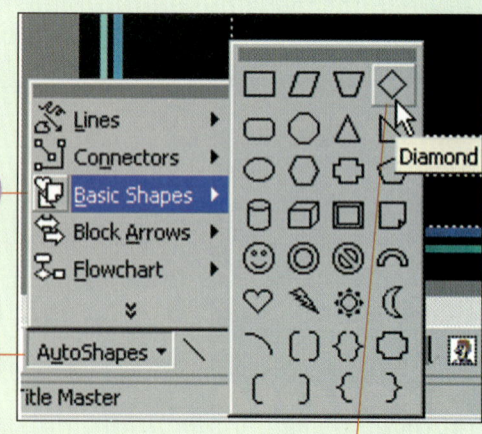
   e) With the Shift key still down, hold down the left mouse button, drag the mouse down and to the right until the diamond is about one-half of an inch tall, and then release the mouse button and then the Shift key. (If you do not like the size or position of the diamond, delete it. To do this, make sure the diamond is selected, and then press the Delete key.)
   f) If you need to move the diamond, make sure it is selected, position the arrow pointer inside the selected area, hold down the left mouse button, drag to the desired position, and then release the mouse button.
6) When the diamond is positioned in the desired location, copy it two times (you should end up with three diamond shapes in a row) by completing the following steps:
   a) With the diamond selected, position the arrow pointer inside the selected box.
   b) Hold down the Ctrl key and the left mouse button.

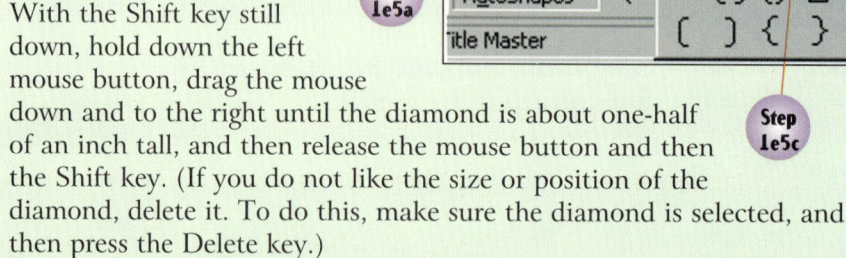

c) Drag the outline to the desired position, release the mouse button and then release the Ctrl key. Repeat these steps to create the third diamond shape.
7) Click anywhere in the text *Click to edit Master subtitle style*.
8) Change the font size to 40 points.
f. Click the Slide View button on the View toolbar. (This removes the master slide and displays a slide with the formatted elements.)
g. Key the text shown in figure 2.10 by completing the following steps:
1) Click anywhere in the text *Click to add title*.
2) Key **McCormack Annuity Funds**.
3) Click anywhere in the text *Click to add subtitle*.
4) Key **Enhanced Services**.

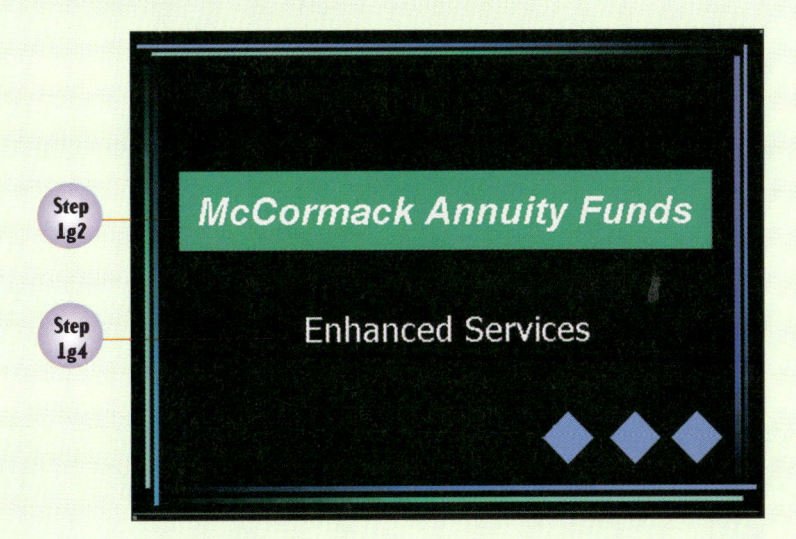

h. Click the New Slide button on the Standard toolbar.
i. At the New Slide dialog box, double-click the first autolayout (Title Slide).
j. At the next slide, key the text shown in the second slide in figure 2.10.
k. Continue creating the remaining four slides shown in figure 2.10 by completing steps similar to those in 1h through 1j.
2. View all slides in the presentation by clicking the Slide Sorter View button on the View toolbar. Make any necessary adjustments to the object boxes in the slides. For example, you may want to move some object boxes to better center the text on the slide.
3. Display Slide 1 in Slide view and increase the size of the subtitle Enhanced Services to 48 points.
4. Add a transition and sound of your choosing to all slides.
5. Save the presentation in the Chapter 02C folder on your disk and name it Enhanced Services Presentation.
6. Run the presentation.
7. Print all six slides on the same page.
8. Close Enhanced Services Presentation.

figure 2.10 Exercise 4

Slide 1	Title	=	McCormack Annuity Funds
	Subtitle	=	Enhanced Services
Slide 2	Title	=	Enhanced Services
	Subtitle	=	Set up future accumulations transfers
Slide 3	Title	=	Enhanced Services
	Subtitle	=	Receive automatic statement confirmation
Slide 4	Title	=	Enhanced Services
	Subtitle	=	Faster cash withdrawals
Slide 5	Title	=	Enhanced Services
	Subtitle	=	Personal service from 8 a.m. to 11 p.m. weekdays
Slide 6	Title	=	Enhanced Services
	Subtitle	=	Multiple transfers made with one telephone call

Creating a Text Box

With the Text Box button on the Drawing toolbar, you can create a box and then insert text inside the box. Text inside a box can be formatted in the normal manner. For example, you can change the font, alignment, or indent of the text.

Wrapping Text in an Autoshape

A text box can be drawn inside an autoshape. You can also click the Text Box button on the Drawing toolbar and then click in the autoshape. This positions the insertion point inside the shape where you can key text. If you want text to wrap within the autoshape, click Format and then AutoShape. At the Format AutoShape dialog box, click the Text Box tab. This displays the dialog box as shown in figure 2.11. At this dialog box, choose the Word wrap shape in AutoShape option. Choose the Resize AutoShape to fit text option if you want the size of the autoshape to conform to the text. Rotate text in a text box by choosing the Rotate text within AutoShape by 90° option.

figure 2.11

Format AutoShape Dialog Box with Text Box Tab Selected

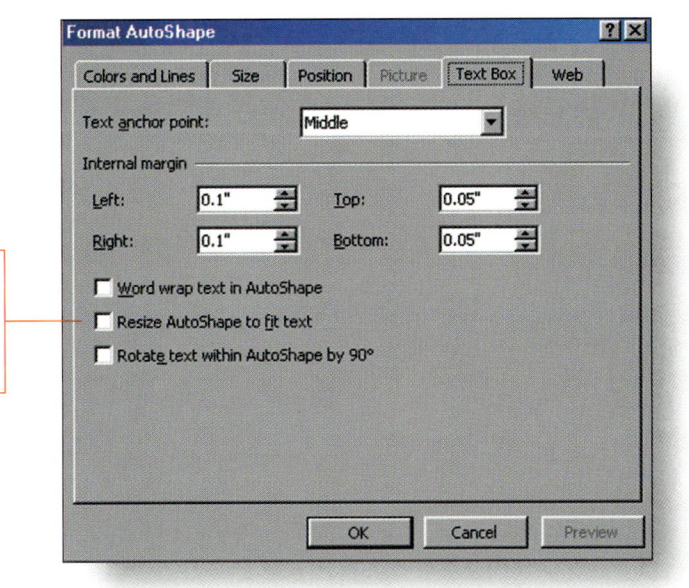

Specify how text is to wrap in the autoshape with these options.

exercise 5

Formatting at the Title Master Slide and Creating an AutoShape and Text Box

1. Open Enhanced Services Presentation.
2. Save the presentation with Save As in the Chapter 02C folder on your disk and name it Formatted Enhanced Presentation.
3. Format objects at the Title Master slide by completing the following steps:
   a. Display the presentation in Slide Sorter view.
   b. Double-click Slide 1.
   c. With Slide 1 displayed in Slide view, hold down the Shift key, and then click the Title Master View button on the View toolbar. (Remember that the Slide View button turns into the Title Master View button when the Shift key is held down.)
   d. Change the green fill color in the top box to a shade of blue and add a border to the object box by completing the following steps:
      1) Click anywhere in the text *Click to edit the Master title style*.
      2) Click the down-pointing triangle at the right side of the Fill Color button on the Drawing toolbar.
      3) At the pop-up menu that displays, click the last color at the right in the top row (matches the blue in the diamonds).

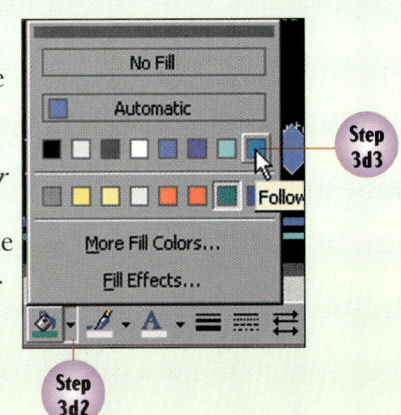

Step 3d3

Step 3d2

Editing and Formatting a PowerPoint Presentation

P-73

4) Click the Line Style button on the Drawing toolbar.
5) At the palette of line style choices that displays, click the first *4fi pt* single line choice from the top.
6) Click the down-pointing triangle at the right side of the Line Color button on the Drawing toolbar.
7) At the pop-up menu that displays, click the purple color (third color from the right in the top row).

e. Click the Slide View button on the View toolbar.

4. Create the slide shown in figure 2.12 by completing the following steps:
   a. Display Slide 6. (This is the last slide in the presentation.)
   b. Click the New Slide button on the Standard toolbar.
   c. At the New Slide dialog box, double-click the last autolayout in the third row (Blank).
   d. At Slide 7, insert the title shown in figure 2.12 by completing the following steps:
      1) Click the Text Box button on the Drawing toolbar.
      2) Position the cross hairs in the slide and then draw a text box in the slide that will hold the title *Enhanced Services Features*.
      3) After drawing the text box, change the font to 44-point Arial bold italic.
      4) Key the title **Enhanced Services Features**.
   e. Draw the diamond at the left by completing the following steps:
      1) Click the AutoShapes button on the Drawing toolbar, point to Basic Shapes, and then click Diamond.
      2) Hold down the Shift key and then draw the diamond the size and position shown in figure 2.12.
      3) Insert the text and wrap the text in the autoshape by completing the following steps:
         a) Click the Text Box button on the Drawing toolbar.
         b) Click inside the diamond shape.
         c) Click Format and then AutoShape.
         d) At the Format AutoShape dialog box, click the Text Box tab.
         e) At the Format AutoShape dialog box with the Text Box tab selected, click the Word wrap text in AutoShape option. (This inserts a check mark.)
         f) Click OK to close the dialog box.
         g) Change the font to 20-point Arial bold.

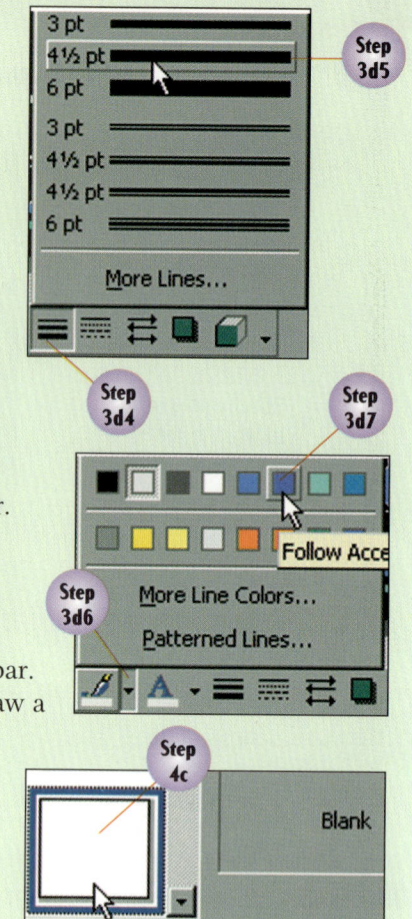

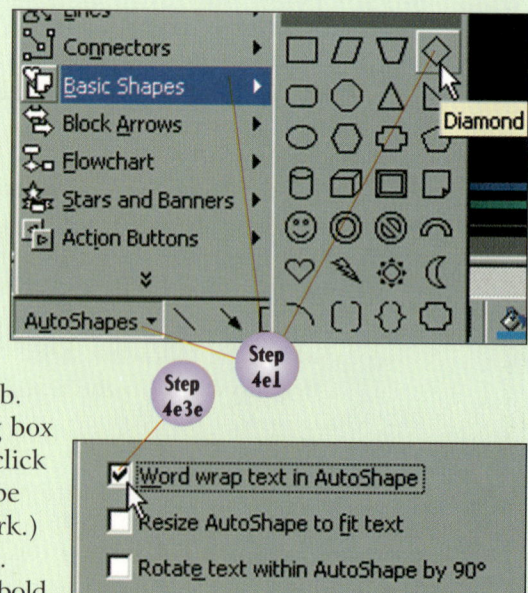

Chapter Two

h) Key the text **Personal Service**. (Make sure the word *Personal* is not split between two lines. If it is, increase the size of the diamond.)
  f. Copy the diamond to the right two times.
  g. Select the text in the middle diamond and then key **Easy to Use**.
  h. Select the text in the diamond at the right and then key **Fast and Accurate**.
5. Save the presentation again with the same name (Formatted Enhanced Presentation).
6. Print Slide 7 in grayscale.
7. Display Slide 1 and then run the presentation.
8. Close the presentation.

figure 2.12   **Exercise 5**

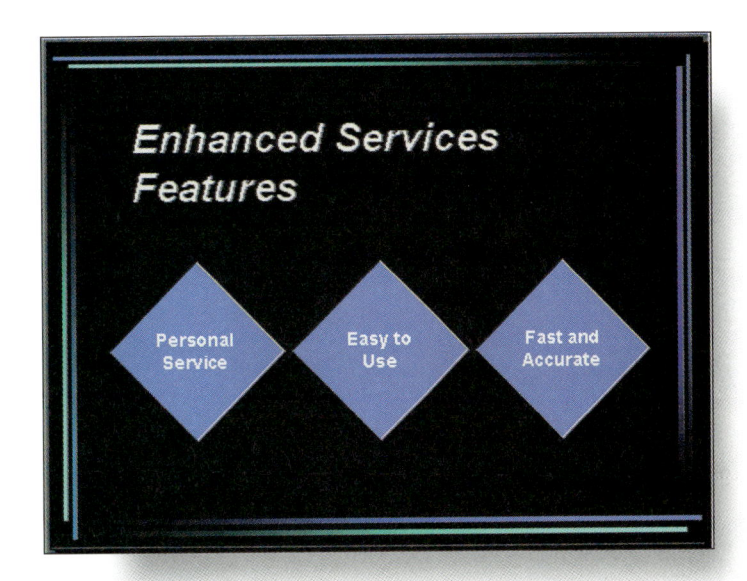

Grouping and Ungrouping Objects

You can group objects so you can work with them as if they were a single object. Grouped objects can be formatted, sized, moved, flipped, and/or rotated as a single unit. Group selected objects by clicking the Draw button on the Drawing toolbar and then clicking Group at the pop-up menu. Ungroup selected objects by clicking the Draw button and then clicking Ungroup.

Flipping and Rotating an Object

A selected object can be rotated and flipped horizontally or vertically. To rotate or flip an object, select the object, click the Draw button, point to Rotate or Flip, and then click the desired rotation or flip option at the side menu that displays. A drawn object can be rotated but a text box cannot.

Another method for rotating an object is to select the object and then click the Free Rotate button on the Drawing toolbar. This displays small green circles, called *rotation handles*, around the selected object. Use these rotation handles to rotate the object.

Distributing and Aligning Objects

Distribute and align selected objects with the D<u>r</u>aw button on the Drawing toolbar. To do this, select the objects, click the D<u>r</u>aw button on the Drawing toolbar, and then point to <u>A</u>lign or Distribute. This causes a side menu to display with options for aligning at the left, center, right, top, middle, or bottom and distributing horizontally and vertically. Depending on the objects selected, some of the options at the side menu may be inactive.

exercise 6

Creating, Grouping, Aligning, and Distributing AutoShapes

1. Open Formatted Enhanced Presentation.
2. Copy Slide 7 by completing the following steps:
   a. Display the slides in Slide Sorter view.
   b. Click Slide 7.
   c. Position the arrow pointer in Slide 7, hold down the Ctrl key and then the left mouse button. Drag to the right so the thin, vertical line displays at the right side of Slide 7, then release the mouse button and then the Ctrl key.
   d. Double-click the new Slide 8.
3. Create and format Slide 8 as shown in figure 2.13 by completing the following steps:
   a. Select *Features* in the title and then key **Launch Date**.
   b. Delete the diamonds by completing the following steps:
      1) Click the Select Objects button on the Drawing toolbar.
      2) Draw a border around the three diamonds.
      3) Press the Delete key.
   c. Click the Text Box button on the Drawing toolbar, draw a text box the size and location of the box containing *May 1, 2001*.
   d. With the insertion point inside the text box, change the font to 48-point Arial bold, click the Center button on the Formatting toolbar, and then key **May 1, 2001**.
   e. Draw the blue arrow that displays in the upper left side of the slide by completing the following steps:
      1) Click the A<u>u</u>toShapes button on the Drawing toolbar, point to Block A<u>r</u>rows, and then click the second arrow from the left in the third row from the bottom (Notched Right Arrow).
      2) Hold down the Shift key and then draw an arrow the approximate size and location of the arrow in the upper left side of the slide. (You will rotate this arrow later in the exercise.)

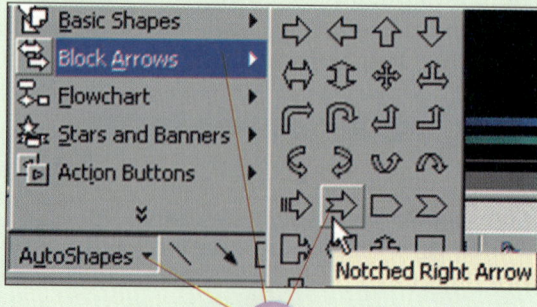

f. Copy the arrow three times to the approximate positions shown in figure 2.13. (You will rotate and flip the arrows later in the next steps.)
g. Group, flip, and then ungroup the arrows at the right by completing the following steps:
   1) Click the Select Objects button on the Drawing toolbar.
   2) Draw a border around the two arrows at the right side of the slide.
   3) Click the Draw button on the Drawing toolbar and then click Group at the pop-up menu.
   4) With the two arrows selected, click the Draw button, point to Rotate or Flip, and then click Flip Horizontal.
   5) Ungroup the arrows by clicking Draw and then clicking Ungroup at the pop-up list. 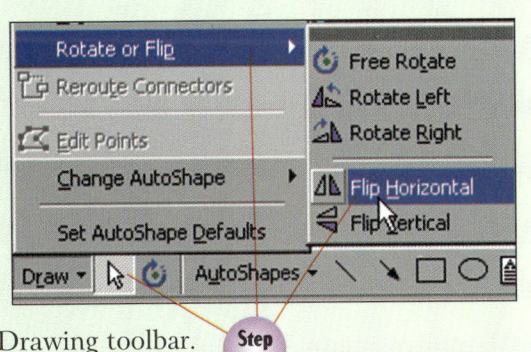
h. Rotate the arrow in the upper left side of the slide by completing the following steps:
   1) Click the upper left arrow.
   2) Click the Free Rotate button on the Drawing toolbar.
   3) Position the mouse pointer on one of the green rotation handles that displays around the arrow, hold down the left mouse button, drag to rotate the arrow (as shown in figure 2.13) and then release the mouse button.
   4) Click the Free Rotate button to deactivate it.
   5) Drag the arrow to the location shown in figure 2.13. 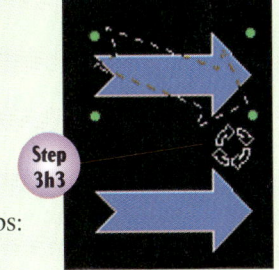
i. Complete steps similar to those in 3h to rotate the other three arrows so they display as shown in figure 2.13.
j. Align and distribute the arrows by completing the following steps:
   1) Click the Select Objects button on the Drawing toolbar.
   2) Draw a border around the top two arrows. (After the border is drawn, make sure both top arrows display surrounded by sizing handles.)
   3) Click the Draw button on the Drawing toolbar, point to Align or Distribute, and then click Align Top. 
   4) Draw a border around the bottom two arrows. (After the border is drawn, make sure both bottom arrows display surrounded by sizing handles.)
   5) Click the Draw button on the Drawing toolbar, point to Align or Distribute, and then click Align Bottom.
   6) Draw a border around the two arrows at the left side of the slide.
   7) Click the Draw button on the Drawing toolbar, point to Align or Distribute, and then click Align Left.
   8) Draw a border around the two arrows at the right side of the slide.
   9) Click the Draw button on the Drawing toolbar, point to Align or Distribute, and then click Align Right.
   10) Deselect the arrows.
4. Save the presentation again with the same name (Formatted Enhanced Presentation).
5. Display Slide 1 and then run the presentation.
6. Print only Slide 8 in grayscale.
7. Close Formatted Enhanced Presentation.

figure 2.13

Exercise 6

[Slide image: "Enhanced Services Launch Date — May 1, 2001"]

Formatting the Slide Color Scheme

PowerPoint design templates provide interesting and varied formatting effects and save time when preparing a presentation. Some of the formatting applied to slides by the design template can be formatted. For example, the color scheme and background of slides can be changed. To change the color scheme of a design template, open a presentation, click Format and then Slide Color Scheme. This displays the Color Scheme dialog box with the Standard tab selected as shown in figure 2.14.

figure 2.14

Color Scheme Dialog Box with Standard Tab Selected

Click the desired scheme in the Color schemes section and click the Apply button to apply the scheme to the active slide, or click the Apply to All button to apply the scheme to all slides in the presentation.

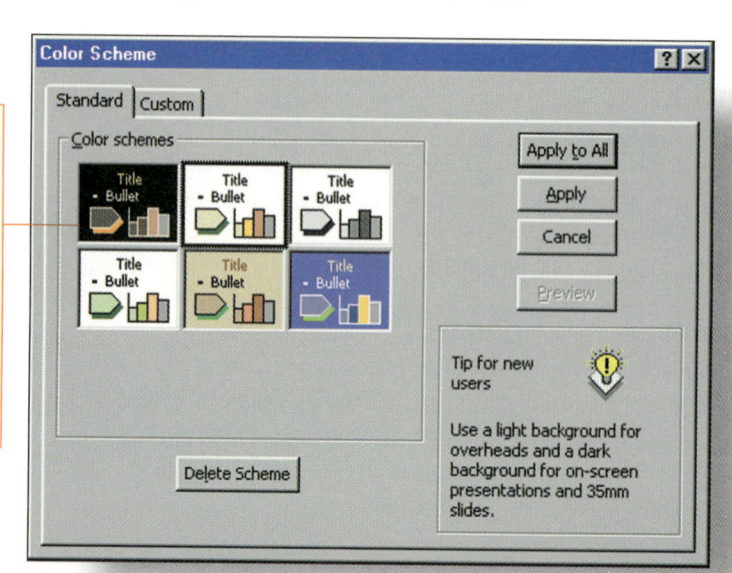

Chapter Two

Click a color scheme in the Color schemes section and click the Apply button to apply the color scheme to the selected slide. If you want the color scheme applied to all slides in the presentation, click the Apply to All button.

exercise 7

Formatting Slide Color Schemes

1. Open History of Computers 1980s. (This presentation is located in the *Presentations* folder on the Cd that accompanies this textbook.)
2. Save the presentation in the Chapter 02C folder on your disk with Save As and name it Formatted History Pres.
3. Change the color scheme by completing the following steps:
    a. Click Format and Slide Color Scheme.
    b. At the Color Scheme dialog box with the Standard tab selected, click the last color scheme in the bottom row.
    c. Click the Apply to All button.
4. Apply a transition of your choosing to each slide.
5. Save the presentation again with the same name (Formatted History Pres).
6. Run the presentation.
7. Print all six slides on one page.
8. Close Formatted History Pres.
9. Delete Formatted History Pres. (Check with your instructor before deleting this presentation.)

Customizing the Slide Color Scheme

Change the color for individual slide elements by clicking the Custom tab at the Color Scheme dialog box. This displays the dialog box as shown in figure 2.15. Click an item in the Scheme colors section and then click the Change Color button. At the Color dialog box for the selected element, click the desired color and then click OK.

Editing and Formatting a PowerPoint Presentation

figure 2.15 Color Scheme Dialog Box with Custom Tab Selected

Click the desired element scheme in the Scheme colors section and click the Change Color button.

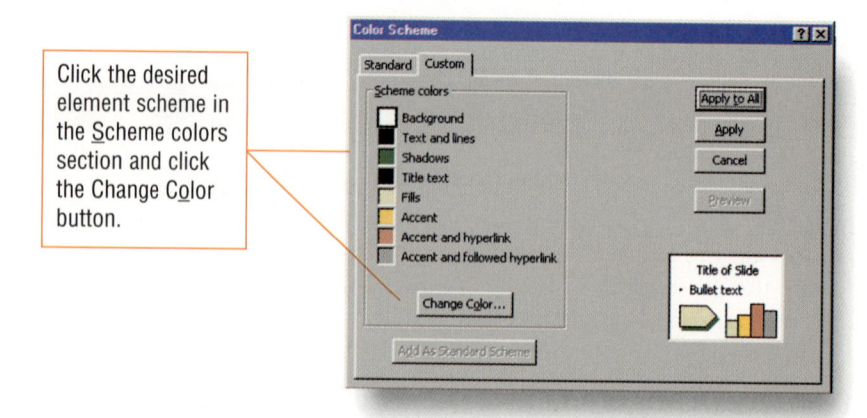

Background color can be changed with options at the Color Scheme dialog box with the Custom Tab selected or at the Background dialog box shown in figure 2.16. Display this dialog box by clicking Format and then Background. At the Background dialog box, click the down-pointing triangle at the right of the fill text box and then click the desired color at the drop-down list. Click the Apply button to apply the background color to the active slide, or click Apply to All to apply the background color to all slides.

figure 2.16 Background Dialog Box

Click this down-pointing triangle to display a palette of color choices.

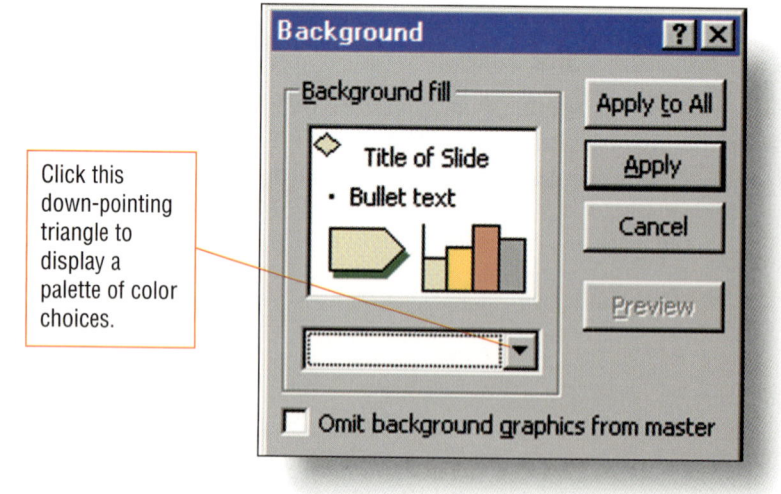

exercise 8

Customizing the Slide Color Scheme

1. Open History of Computers 1980s. (This presentation is located in the *Presentations* folder on the CD that accompanies this textbook.)
2. Save the presentation in the Chapter 02C folder on your disk with Save As and name it Customized History Pres.
3. Customize the slide color scheme by completing the following steps:
   a. Click Format and Slide Color Scheme.
   b. At the Color Scheme dialog box, click the Custom tab.
   c. At the Color Scheme dialog box with the Custom tab selected, change the background color by completing the following steps:
      1) Click the color box preceding Background in the Scheme colors section of the dialog box.
      2) Click the Change Color button.
      3) At the Background Color dialog box, click a light blue color of your choosing.
      4) Click OK to close the Background Color dialog box.
   d. At the Color Scheme dialog box, make the following changes:
      1) Change the Shadows color to dark blue by completing steps similar to those in 3c.
      2) Change the Accent color to light green by completing steps similar to those in 3c.
   e. Click the Apply to All button.
4. Save the presentation again with the same name (Customized History Pres).
5. Run the presentation.
6. Print all six slides on one page.
7. Close Customized History Pres.
8. Delete Customized History Pres. (Check with your instructor before deleting this presentation.)

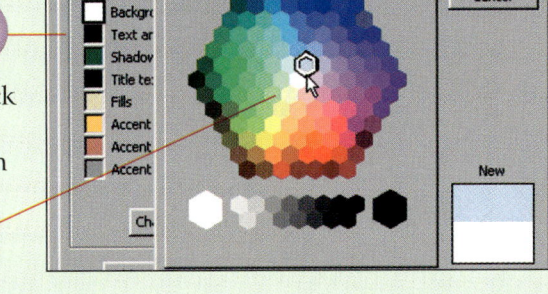

Changing the Design Template

When preparing presentations for this chapter and the previous chapter, you chose the design template first and then created each slide. A different design template can be applied to an existing presentation. To do this, click Format and then Apply Design Template; or, click the Common Tasks button on the Formatting toolbar and then click Apply Design Template at the drop-down menu. This displays the Apply Design Template dialog box shown in figure 2.17. This dialog box contains the same design templates that are available at the New Presentation dialog box with the Design Templates tab selected. Click a design template in the list box and then click the Apply button.

Hint: If you change the design template for an existing presentation, check to see how the new design formatting affects text and objects in slides. You may need to make some adjustments.

figure 2.17 Apply Design Template Dialog Box

exercise 9

Changing the Design Template

1. Open History of Computers 1980s. (This presentation is located in the *Presentations* folder on the CD that accompanies this textbook.)
2. Save the presentation in the Chapter 02C folder on your disk with Save As and name it New Design History Pres.
3. Choose a different design template by completing the following steps:
   a. Click the Common Tasks button on the Formatting toolbar and then click Apply Design Template at the drop-down menu.
   b. At the Apply Design Template dialog box, click *LaVerne* in the list box. (You will need to scroll down the list to display *LaVerne*.)
   c. Click the Apply button.
4. Run the presentation to see how it appears with the new design template applied.
5. Print all six slides on one page.
6. Save and close New Design History Pres.
7. Open Telecommunications Presentation.
8. Apply a different design template of your choosing to this presentation.
9. Run the presentation to see how it appears with the new design template applied.
10. Print all six slides on one page.
11. Close Telecommunications Presentation without saving the changes.
12. Delete New Design History Pres. (Check with your instructor before deleting this presentation.)

Creating a Blank Presentation and Applying a Design Template

Many of the presentations you have created in this and the previous chapter have been based on a design template. You can also create a blank presentation and then apply your own formatting or apply a design template. To create a blank presentation click File and then New. At the New Presentation dialog box with the General tab selected, double-click *Blank Presentation*. Create the presentation using the view you prefer and then apply formatting or apply a design template.

Preparing a Transparency

When preparing a presentation, consider using a design template with a darker background for a presentation that will be run with PowerPoint or that will be made into 35mm slides. If you are going to print slides as transparencies, consider using a lighter background. Choosing an appropriate color for a presentation or transparency is as easy as changing the design template. In exercise 10, you will apply a design template with a light background and then print one of the slides as a transparency. (Before completing this exercise, check with your instructor to see if you should print on an actual transparency or on normal paper.)

Formatting with Format Painter

If you create a blank presentation and decide to apply your own formatting, consider using the Format Painter. Use Format Painter to apply the same formatting in more than one location in a slide or slides. To use the Format Painter, apply the desired formatting to text, position the insertion point anywhere in the formatted text, and then double-click the Format Painter button on the Standard toolbar. Using the mouse, select the additional text to which you want the formatting applied. After applying the formatting in the desired locations, click the Format Painter button to deactivate it.

If you need to apply formatting in only one other location, click the Format Painter button once. The first time you select text, the formatting is applied and the Format Painter is deactivated.

Promoting and Demoting Text in the Slide Pane

In chapter 1, you created a presentation in the Outline view and used buttons on the Outlining toolbar to promote and demote bulleted text. You can also demote and promote bulleted text in the Slide pane. Press the Tab key to demote text in a slide or press Shift + Tab to promote text. If the Outlining toolbar is on, you can also promote and demote bulleted text with the Promote and Demote buttons.

exercise 10

Creating and Formatting a Blank Presentation

1. Create a blank presentation with the information shown in figure 2.18 by completing the following steps:
    a. Click File and then New.
    b. At the New Presentation dialog box, click the General tab.

    c. At the New Presentation dialog box with the General tab selected, double-click *Blank Presentation* in the list box.
    d. At the New Slide dialog box, double-click the first autolayout (Title Slide).
    e. Using the view you prefer, key the title and subtitle for Slide 1 as shown in figure 2.18.
    f. Create the remaining slides shown in figure 2.18. (Use the Bulleted List autolayout for Slides 2 through 5.)
2. Suppose you are going to print transparencies for the slides in this presentation. To do this, apply a design template with a light background by completing the following steps:
    a. Change to the Slide Sorter view.
    b. Click F*o*rmat and then App*l*y Design Template.
    c. At the Apply Design Template dialog box, double-click *Citrus* in the list box.
3. Change the font style and color of the terms using Format Painter by completing the following steps:
    a. Double-click Slide 4.
    b. Select the term *Balance:* (be sure to select the colon).
    c. Display the Font dialog box, change the Font style to *Bold Italic*, change the color to the green that follows the color scheme, and then close the dialog box.
    d. Deselect *Balance:* and then click anywhere in *Balance:*.
    e. Double-click the Format Painter button on the Standard toolbar.
    f. Using the mouse, select *Color Wheel:*.
    g. Using the mouse, select each of the other terms in Slide 4 *(Contrast:, Gradient:, Hue:)*.
    h. Display Slide 5 and then use the mouse to select each of the terms (including the colon) in the slide.
    i. Click the Format Painter button to deactivate it.
    j. Deselect the text.
4. Print only Slide 2 as a transparency by completing the following steps: *(Note: Check with your instructor to determine if you should print on an actual transparency or if you should print on paper.)*
    a. In Slide Sorter view, click Slide 2.
    b. Insert the transparency in your printer. (This step is optional.)
    c. Click F*i*le and then *P*rint.
    d. At the Print dialog box, click the Curr*e*nt slide option in the Print range section.
    e. Click OK.
5. Save the presentation in the Chapter 02C folder on your disk and name it Color Presentation.
6. Print all five slides on one page.
7. Close Color Presentation.

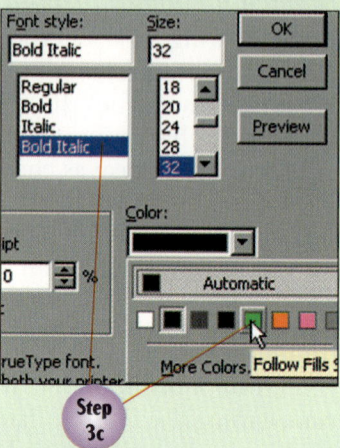

figure 2.18 *Exercise 10*

Slide 1	Title	=	COMPANY PUBLICATIONS
	Subtitle	=	Using Color in Publications
Slide 2	Title	=	Communicating with Color
	Bullets	=	• Color in a publication can:
			- Elicit feelings
			- Emphasize important text
			- Attract attention
			• Choose one or two colors
			• Use "spot color" by using color only in specific areas
Slide 3	Title	=	Printing the Publication
	Bullets	=	• Print all copies on a color printer
			• Print on a color printer and duplicate with a color photocopier
			• Print on color paper
			• Print on specialty paper
Slide 4	Title	=	Color Terminology
	Bullets	=	• Balance: Amount of light and dark in a picture
			• Color Wheel: Device used to illustrate color relationships
			• Contrast: Amount of gray in a color
			• Gradient: Gradual varying of color
			• Hue: Variation of a color such as green-blue
Slide 5	Title	=	Color Terminology
	Bullets	=	• Pixel: Each dot in a picture or graphic
			• Resolution: The number of dots that make up an image on a screen or printer
			• Reverse: Black background on white foreground or white type against a colored background
			• Saturation: Purity of a color

Formatting with Bullets and Numbers

Each design template contains a Bulleted List autolayout. The appearance and formatting of the bullets in this autolayout varies with each template. You can choose to use the bullet provided by the design template or you can insert different bullets and also can change to numbering.

Changing Bullets

Customize bullets with options at the Bullets and Numbering dialog box with the Bulleted tab selected as shown in figure 2.19. Display this dialog box by clicking in a bulleted list placeholder, and then clicking Format and Bullets and Numbering. At the dialog box, choose one of the predesigned bullets from the list box, change the size of the bullets by percentage in relation to the text size, change the bullet color, and display bullet pictures and characters.

figure 2.19　Bullets and Numbering Dialog Box with Bulleted Tab Selected

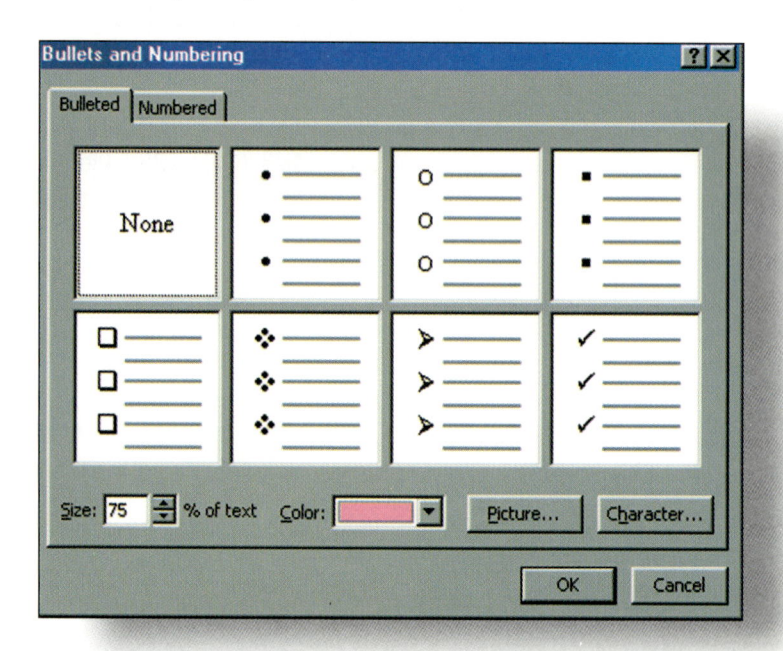

Click the Picture button located towards the bottom of the dialog box and the Picture Bullet dialog box with the Pictures tab selected displays as shown in figure 2.20. Click the desired bullet in the list box and then click the Insert clip button.

Chapter Two

figure 2.20
Picture Bullet Dialog Box with Pictures Tab Selected

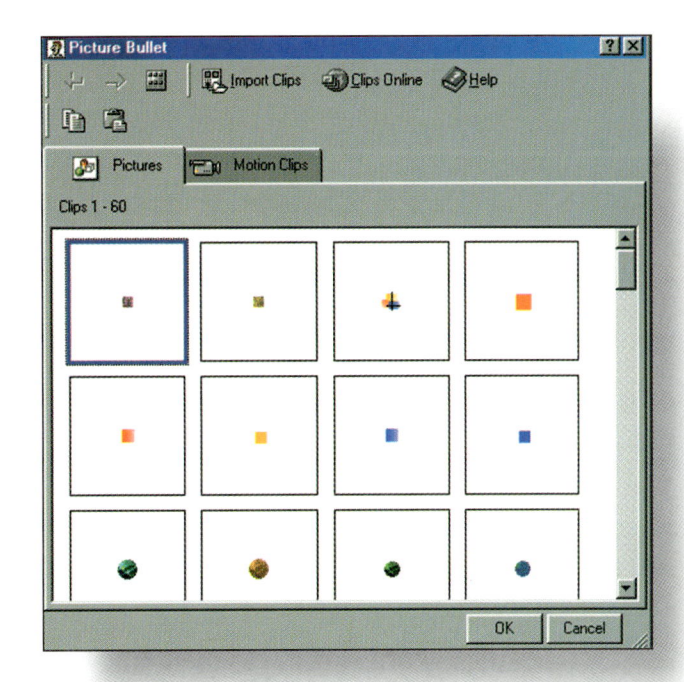

Click the Character button located towards the bottom right corner of the Bullets and Numbering dialog box and the Bullet dialog box displays. This dialog box contains the same character and symbols choices as the Insert Symbol dialog box.

Inserting Numbering

A bulleted list can be easily changed to numbers. To do this, select the bulleted list and then click the Numbering button on the Formatting toolbar. You can also change to numbering by selecting the list and then displaying the Bullets and Numbering dialog box with the Numbers tab selected. Display this dialog box by clicking Format and the Bullets and Numbering. At the Bullets and Numbering dialog box, click the Numbered tab. This dialog box contains many of the same options as the Bullets and Numbering dialog box with the Bulleted tab selected.

exercise 11

Changing Bullets and Applying Numbering

1. Open Color Presentation.
2. Change the first-level bullets in slides 2 through 5 by completing the following steps:
   a. Display Slide 2 in Slide view.
   b. Hold down the Shift key and then click the Slide View Master button on the View toolbar.
   c. Click in the text *Click to edit Master text styles*.
   d. Click Format and then Bullets and Numbering.
   e. At the Bullets and Numbering dialog box with the Bulleted tab selected, click the up-pointing triangle at the right side of the Size option until *85* displays in the text box.
   f. Click the Picture button that displays towards the bottom of the dialog box.
   g. At the Picture Bullets dialog box with the Pictures tab selected, click the second bullet from the left in the second row (this is a gold, square bullet).
   h. Click the Insert clip button.
   i. Click the Slide View button. (This removes the master slide.) 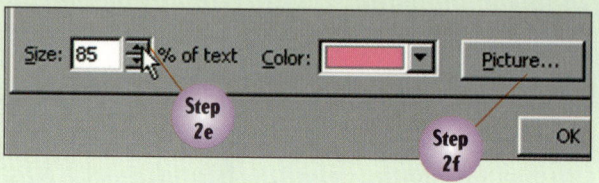 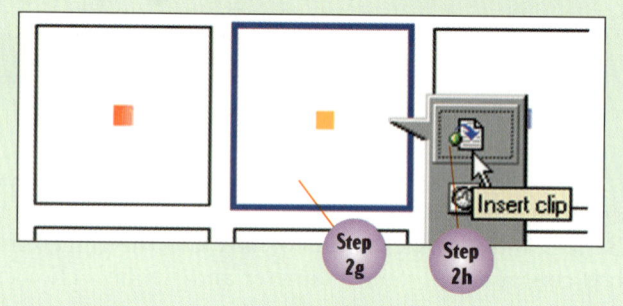
3. Print only Slide 2.
4. Change the second-level bullets in Slide 2 by completing the following steps:
   a. Make sure Slide 2 is displayed in Slide view.
   b. Hold down the Shift key and then click the Slide Master View button on the View toolbar.
   c. Click in the text *Second level*.
   d. Click Format and then Bullets and Numbering.
   e. At the Bullets and Numbering dialog box with the Bulleted tab selected, click the Character button that displays in the bottom right corner of the dialog box.
   f. At the Bullet dialog box, click the down-pointing triangle at the right side of the Color option, and then click the green color that follows the color scheme.
   g. Click the up-pointing triangle at the right side of the Size text box until *75* displays in the box.
   h. Click the pen image (first image [in the second square] from the left in the top row).
   i. Click OK to close the dialog box.
   j. Click the Slide View button. (This removes the master slide.)

Chapter Two

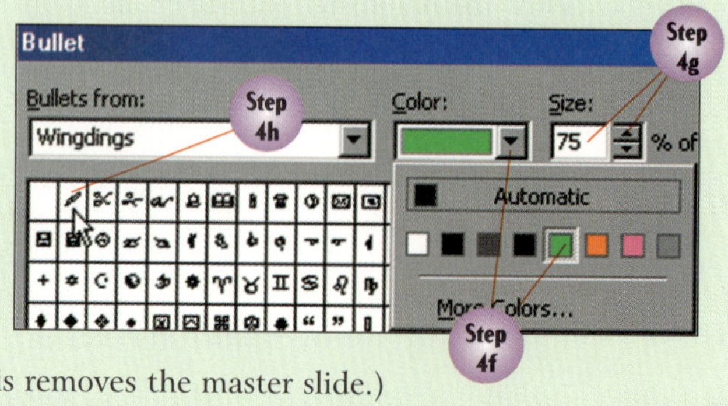

5. Print only Slide 2.
6. Save the presentation with the same name (Color Presentation).
7. Change the first-level bullets to numbers in Slides 2 through 5 by completing the following steps:
   a. Make sure Slide 2 is displayed in Slide view.
   b. Hold down the Shift key and then click the Slide Master View button on the View toolbar.
   c. Click in the text *Click to edit Master text styles*.
   d. Click the Numbering button on the Formatting toolbar.
   e. Change the color of the numbers by completing the following steps:
      1) Click Format and then Bullets and Numbering.
      2) At the Bullets and Numbering dialog box, make sure the Numbered tab is selected.
      3) Click the down-pointing triangle at the right side of the Color option and then click the orange color that follows the color scheme.
      4) Click OK to close the dialog box.
   f. Click the Slide View button. (This removes the master slide.)
8. Save the presentation again with the same name (Color Presentation).
9. Display Slide 1 and then run the presentation.
10. Print all five slides on one page.
11. Close the presentation.

Inserting Headers and Footers in a Presentation

Insert information that you want to appear at the top or bottom of each slide or on note and handout pages with options at the Header and Footer dialog box. If you want the information to appear on all slides, click View and then Header and Footer. This displays the Header and Footer dialog box with the Slide tab selected as shown in figure 2.21.

figure 2.21 **Header and Footer Dialog Box with Slide Tab Selected**

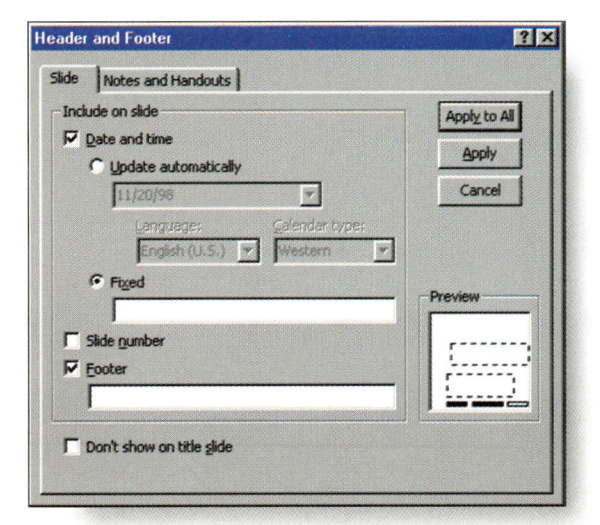

Include the date and time as fixed or automatic. To include a fixed date and time, click in the Fixed text box and then key the desired text. If you want the date and/or time inserted and then automatically updated when the presentation is opened, click the Update automatically option. Specify the format for the date and/or time by clicking the down-pointing triangle at the right side of the Update automatically text box and then click the desired format at the drop-down list. If you want the slide number inserted in a presentation, click the Slide number check box. Key any footer text desired in the Footer text box. Click the Apply button to apply the element(s) to the current slide. If you want the element(s) inserted in all slides, click the Apply to All button. Elements added to a slide or slides are previewed in the Preview section of the dialog box.

exercise 12

Inserting the Date, Time, Slide Number, and a Footer in a Presentation

1. Open Telecommunications Presentation.
2. Insert the date, time, slide number, and a footer into the presentation by completing the following steps:
   a. Click View and then Header and Footer.
   b. At the Header and Footer dialog box with the Slide tab selected, if necessary, click Date and time to insert a check mark in the check box.
   c. Click the Update automatically option.
   d. Click the down-pointing triangle at the right side of the Update automatically text box and click the option that displays the date in numbers followed by the time (i.e., 12/01/99 12:35 PM).
   e. Click the Slide number option to insert a check mark in the check box.
   f. Click in the Footer check box and key **Telecommunications** in the Footer text box.
   g. Click the *Don't show on title slide* option to insert a check mark in the check box.
   h. Click the Apply to All button.
3. Save the presentation again with the same name (Telecommunications Presentation).
4. Run the presentation to see how the inserted text displays in the slides (the date, time, page number, and footer will not display on the first slide.)
5. Print all six slides on one page.
6. Close Telecommunications Presentation.

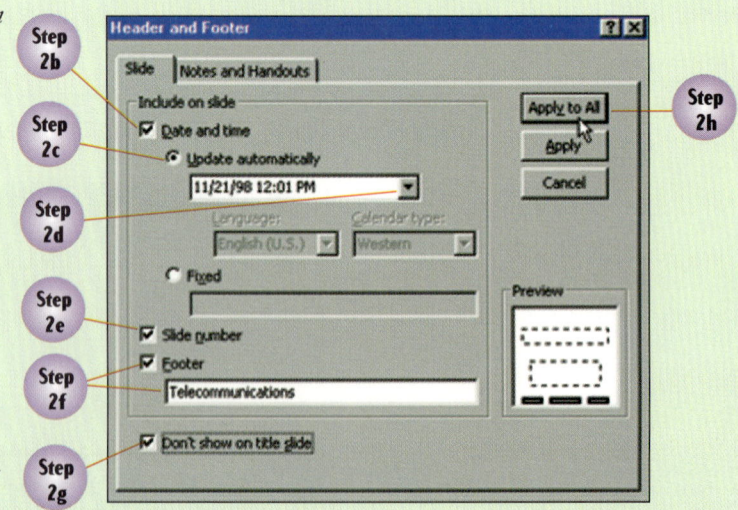

Inserting a Header and/or Footer in Notes and Handouts

Elements selected at the Header and Footer dialog box with the Slide tab selected are inserted in slides in a presentation. If you want elements inserted in notes or handouts, choose options at the Header and Footer dialog box with the Notes and Handouts tab selected as shown in figure 2.22.

figure 2.22 *Header and Footer Dialog Box with Notes and Handouts Tab Selected*

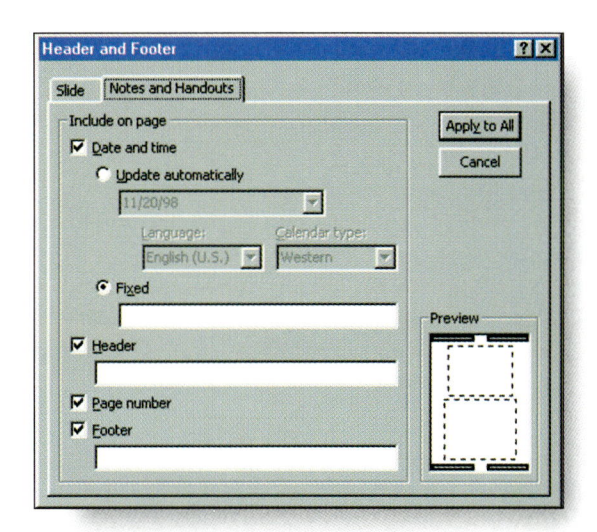

At the Header and Footer dialog box with the Notes and Handouts tab selected, choose to insert the date and/or time fixed or automatically, include a header and/or footer, and include page numbering. Choices made at this dialog box print when the presentation is printed as notes pages, handouts, or an outline.

Adding Speaker Notes

If you are going to give your presentation in front of an audience, consider creating speaker notes for some or all of the slides. Create speaker notes containing additional information about the slide that will help you during the presentation. Speaker notes do not display on a slide when the presentation is running. Speaker notes print when *Notes Pages* is selected in the Print what option of the Print dialog box.

To insert speaker notes, display slides in the Normal view, click in the Notes pane, and then key the information. Another method for inserting speaker notes is to display the presentation in Notes Page view. To do this, click View and then Notes Page. This displays the active slide with a text box below. Click inside the text box and then key the speaker note information. Format speaker notes in the normal manner. For example, you can change the font, change the text alignment, and insert bullets or numbering.

Editing and Formatting a PowerPoint Presentation

You can create and/or display speaker notes while a presentation is running. To do this, run the presentation, and then display the desired slide. Move the mouse to display the *Slide Show* menu icon. Click the *Slide Show* menu icon and then click Speaker Notes at the pop-up menu. This displays the Speaker Notes dialog box. View, key, or edit text at this dialog box and then click the Close button.

exercise 13

Inserting a Header, Footer, and the Date in Notes and Handouts

1. Open Telecommunications Presentation.
2. Insert a header and footer, the date, and page numbering in notes and handouts by completing the following steps:
   a. Click View and then Header and Footer.
   b. At the Header and Footer dialog box, click the Notes and Handouts tab.
   c. At the Header and Footer dialog box with the Notes and Handouts tab selected, click the Update automatically option. (Check to make sure the current date displays in the Update automatically text box. If not, click the down-pointing triangle at the right side of the text box, and then click the desired date style at the drop-down list.)
   d. Click in the Header text box and key **Technology Evaluation**.
   e. Click in the Footer text box and key **Telecommunications System**.
   f. Make sure there is a check mark in the Page number check box.
   g. Click the Apply to All button.
3. Add and format speaker notes by completing the following steps:
   a. Display Slide 2 in Normal view.
   b. Click in the Notes pane. (This pane displays below the slide and contains the text *Click to add notes*.)
   c. Click the Bold button on the Formatting toolbar and then click the Center button.
   d. Key **Distribute Case Study handout.**, press Enter, and then key **Discuss Case Study 1 and Case Study 4**.
   e. Display Slide 4 in Normal view.
   f. Click in the Notes pane.
   g. Click the Bold button on the Formatting toolbar and then click the Center button.
   h. Key **Elicit comments from participants regarding the current system.**, press Enter, and then key **Ask what changes individuals would like to make**.

4. Print slides 2 and 4 as notes pages by completing the following steps:
   a. Display the Print dialog box.
   b. Click the down-pointing triangle to the right of the Print what option and then click *Notes Pages* at the drop-down list.
   c. Click in the Slides text box and then key **2,4**.
   d. Click OK. (This prints each slide [slides 2 and 4] towards the top of the page on a separate piece of paper with the header, footer, date, page number, and speaker notes included.)
5. Save the presentation with the same name (Telecommunications Presentation).
6. Close Telecommunications Presentation.

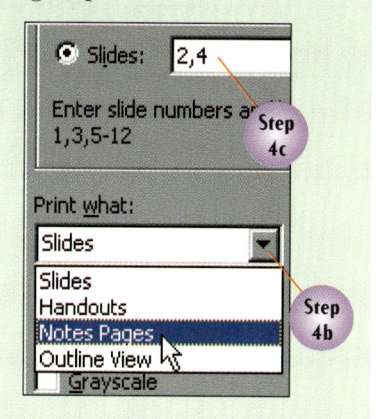

chapter summary

- Text in individual slides can be inserted or deleted, slides can be deleted from a presentation, slides can be inserted into an existing presentation, and slides can be rearranged.
- When editing a slide or text within a slide, use the view that makes editing the easiest. For example, rearrange the order of slides in the Slide Sorter view, delete or insert text within slides in the Normal view, Outline view, or Slide view.
- Use the find and replace feature to search for specific text or formatting in slides and replace with other text or formatting.
- To delete a slide from a presentation, display the presentation in Slide Sorter view, click the slide to be deleted, and then press the Delete key.
- To delete a slide in Outline view or in the Outline pane, position the arrow pointer on the slide icon located next to the slide to be deleted until the arrow pointer turns into a four-headed arrow, click the left mouse button, and then press Delete.
- Add a new slide to a presentation in the Slide Sorter view. A new slide will be inserted immediately following the selected slide.
- Copy a slide in a presentation at the Slide Sorter view by clicking the slide, holding down the Ctrl key, dragging to the location where you want the slide copied, releasing the left mouse button, and then the Ctrl key.
- Slides can be copied between presentations using the Copy and Paste buttons on the Standard toolbar.
- Move text within and between slides with the Cut and Paste buttons on the Standard toolbar. Copy text within and between slides with the Copy and Paste buttons.
- Click the Spelling button on the Standard toolbar to perform a spelling check on slides in a presentation.
- A selected object box can be moved in a slide by dragging it with the mouse.
- A selected object box can be copied in a slide by dragging it with the mouse while holding down the Ctrl key.

- Rearrange slides in Slide Sorter view by dragging the selected slide with the mouse.
- Formatting such as changing fonts, changing font color, and changing paragraph alignment can be applied to text in slides.
- To create a blank line between bulleted paragraphs without inserting a bullet, use the New Line command, Shift + Enter.
- Increase or decrease spacing before or after paragraphs with options at the Line Spacing dialog box.
- Formatting applied to a master slide will affect all slides in a presentation. Formatting can be applied to a master slide as the presentation is being created, or formatting can be applied to a master slide in an existing presentation.
- To display a master slide, change to the Slide view, hold down the Shift key, and then click the Slide View button (which changes to the Slide Master or Title Master View button).
- Use buttons on the Drawing toolbar to draw a variety of shapes and lines
- A shape drawn with the Line or Arrow buttons is considered a line drawing. A shape drawn with the Rectangle or Oval buttons is considered an enclosed object.
- A variety of predesigned shapes is available from the AutoShapes button on the Drawing toolbar.
- To select an enclosed object, position the mouse pointer anywhere inside the object and then click the left mouse button. To select a line, position the mouse pointer on the line until the pointer turns into an arrow with a four-headed arrow attached, and then click the left mouse button.
- To select several objects at once, click the Select Objects buttons, and then draw a border around the objects. You can also select more than one object by holding down the Shift key and then clicking each object.
- To delete an object, select it, and then press the Delete key.
- To move an object, select it, and then drag it to the desired location.
- To copy an object, select it, and then hold down the Ctrl key while dragging the object.
- Use the sizing handles that display around a selected object to increase or decrease the size of the object.
- Apply formatting to an object such as fill color, shading, line color, and shadows with buttons on the Drawing toolbar.
- Create a text box by clicking the Text Box button on the Drawing toolbar and then drawing the box in the document screen.
- A text box can be drawn inside an autoshape.
- Choose a text wrapping style for text inside of an autoshape with options at the Format AutoShape dialog box with the Text Box tab selected.
- Group objects you want to work with as a single unit. Grouped objects can be formatted, sized, flipped, and/or rotated as a unit. Grouped objects can be ungrouped.
- Flip or rotate a selected object by clicking the Draw button on the Drawing toolbar, pointing to Rotate or Flip, and then clicking the desired rotation or flip option.
- Distribute and align selected objects with the Draw button on the Drawing toolbar.
- Change formatting to placeholders (object boxes) such as changing background color or adding a border or shadow with buttons on the Drawing toolbar located toward the bottom of the PowerPoint window. If changes are to affect all slides in a document, make changes at the master slide.
- Choose a different slide color scheme at the Color Scheme dialog box.
- Customize individual elements of a slide with options at the Color Scheme dialog box with the Custom tab selected.

- Apply a different design template to a presentation with options at the Apply Design Template dialog box.
- Create a presentation with little formatting using the Blank Presentation template. This template is available at the New Presentation dialog box with the General tab selected.
- Use a design template with a darker background for a presentation that will run in PowerPoint or that will be made into 35mm slides. Use a template with a lighter background if the slides will be printed as transparencies.
- Use Format Painter to apply the same formatting to more than one location in a slide or slides.
- Change bullets with options at the Bullets and Numbering dialog box with the Bulleted tab selected. Click the Picture button at this dialog box to display the Picture Bullet dialog box containing bullet pictures or click the Character button to display the Bullet dialog box containing bullet symbols.
- Click the Numbering button on the Formatting toolbar to apply numbers to selected paragraphs of text, or display the Bullets and Numbering dialog box with the Numbered tab selected.
- Insert elements in a slide or slides such as the date and time, slide number, and a footer with options at the Header and Footer dialog box with the Slide tab selected.
- Insert elements in notes and handouts such as the date and time, page number, and a header and footer with options from the Header and Footer dialog box with the Notes and Handouts tab selected.
- Add speaker notes in Normal View by clicking in the Notes pane and then keying the information, or by displaying the presentation in Notes Page view.

commands review

	Mouse/Keyboard
Display Replace dialog box	Click Edit and then click Replace
Display the Find dialog box	Click Edit and Find
Start a spelling check	Click the Spelling button on the Standard toolbar
Insert a New Line command	Press Shift + Enter
Display the Line Spacing dialog box	Select object box, click Format and Line Spacing
Display master slide	Position arrow pointer on Slide View button, hold down Shift key, click left mouse button
Display Format AutoShape dialog box	With autoshape selected, click Format and AutoShape
Display the Color Scheme dialog box	Click Format and Slide Color Scheme
Display the Background dialog box	Click Format and Background
Display the Apply Design Template dialog box	Click Format and Apply Design Template; or click the Common Tasks button on the Formatting toolbar and click Apply Design Template
Display New Presentation dialog box	Click File and New
Display Bullets and Numbering dialog box	Click Format and then Bullets and Numbering
Display the Header and Footer dialog box	Click View and then Header and Footer
Notes Page View	Click View Notes Page

Editing and Formatting a PowerPoint Presentation

thinking offline

Completion: In the space provided at the right, indicate the correct term, command, or number.

1. Rearrange slides in a presentation in this view. — *Outline* ~~slide sorter~~ slide view
2. Delete or insert text within slides in the Normal view, Outline view, or this view. — ~~slide sorter~~ slide view
3. If Slide 2 is selected in a presentation in Slide Sorter view, and the New Slide button is clicked, this is the number of the new slide. — 3
4. To copy a selected object, hold down this key while dragging the object. — Ctrl
5. Press these keys to access the New Line command. — Shift + enter
6. Increase spacing before and after paragraphs with options at this dialog box. — line spacing
7. A variety of predesigned shapes is available from this button on the Drawing toolbar. — Autoshapes
8. Click this button on the Drawing toolbar to display rotation handles around the selected object. — free rotate
9. Choose a text wrapping style for text inside an autoshape with options at the Format AutoShape dialog box with this tab selected. — text box
10. Change the color for individual elements in a slide with options at the Color Scheme dialog box with this tab selected. — Standard custom
11. The Blank Presentation template is available at the New Presentation dialog box with this tab selected. — general
12. Use this feature to apply the same formatting in more than one location in a slide or slides. — format painter
13. Click this button at the Bullets and Numbering dialog box to display the Bullet dialog box. — Character bullet tab
14. One method for displaying the Apply Design Template dialog box is to click this button on the Formatting toolbar and then click Apply Design Template at the drop-down menu. — format common tasks
15. If you want page numbering to print in an outline, click the Page number option at the Header and Footer dialog box with this tab selected. — notes + handouts

working hands-on

(Note: If you are using a disk for saving presentations, consider deleting the following presentations before completing assessment 1: Color Presentation, Edited Planning Presentation, Formatted Enhanced Presentation, Formatted Network Pres, Planning Presentation, and Telecommunications Presentation.)

Assessment 1

1. Create a presentation with the text shown in figure 2.23 by completing the following steps:
    a. At a blank PowerPoint screen, click File and New.
    b. At the New Presentation dialog box, click the Design Templates tab.
    c. At the New Presentation dialog box with the Design Templates tab selected, double-click the *Marble* template.
    d. At the New Slide dialog box, double-click the first autolayout in the list box (Title Slide).
    e. At the slide, click anywhere in the text *Click to add title* and key **BENEFITS PROGRAM**.
    f. Click anywhere in the text *Click to add subtitle* and key **Changes to Plans**.
    g. Click the New Slide button located on the Standard toolbar.
    h. At the New Slide dialog box, double-click the second autolayout.
    i. Create the second slide with the text shown in figure 2.23. (Use the New Line command, Shift + Enter, and press Enter as indicated in italics.)
    j. Continue creating the remaining slides as shown in figure 2.23.
2. When all the slides are created, increase the line spacing after the bulleted paragraphs in Slide 5 to 12 points. (Be sure to change to *Points* before you change the measurement.)
3. Complete a spelling check on the presentation.
4. Make the following changes to the slides:
    a. Display Slide 2 in Slide view and make the following changes:
        1) Change to the Slide Master view.
        2) Click anywhere in the text *Click to edit Master title style*, change the font to 48-point Bookman Old Style, and change the color to white.
        3) Click anywhere in the text *Click to edit Master text styles*, change the font to 30-point Bookman Old Style, and change the color to yellow. (You will need to click the More Colors option to display the Colors dialog. At this dialog box, choose a yellow color.)
        4) Click the Slide View button to remove the Master slide.
    b. Display Slide 1 in Slide view and make the following changes:
        1) Select the title *BENEFITS PROGRAM*, change the font to 50-point Bookman Old Style, and then change the color to yellow. (Use the same yellow color you selected in step 4a3.)
        2) Select the subtitle *Changes to Plans*, change the font to 48-point Bookman Old Style, and then change the color to white.
5. Add a transition and sound of your choosing to each slide.
6. Save the presentation in the Chapter 02C folder on your disk and name it Benefits Presentation.
7. Run the presentation.
8. After running the presentation, print all the slides on one page.
9. Close Benefits Presentation.

figure 2.23 **Assessment 1**

Slide 2	Title	=	INTRODUCTION
	Bullets	=	• Changes made for 2000 *(Press Shift + Enter and then Enter.)*
			• Description of eligibility *(Press Shift + Enter and then Enter.)*
			• Instructions for enrolling new members *(Press Shift + Enter and then Enter.)*
			• Overview of medical and dental coverage
Slide 3	Title	=	INTRODUCTION
	Bullets	=	• Expanded enrollment forms *(Press Shift + Enter and then Enter.)*
			• Glossary defining terms *(Press Shift + Enter and then Enter.)*
			• Telephone directory *(Press Shift + Enter and then Enter.)*
			• Pamphlet with commonly asked questions
Slide 4	Title	=	WHAT'S NEW
	Bullets	=	• New medical plan, Plan 2002 *(Press Shift + Enter and then Enter.)*
			• Changes in monthly contributions *(Press Shift + Enter and then Enter.)*
			• Paying with pretax dollars *(Press Shift + Enter and then Enter.)*
			• Contributions toward spouse's coverage
Slide 5	Title	=	COST SHARING
	Bullets	=	• Increased deductible
			• New coinsurance amount
			• Higher coinsurance amount for retail prescription drugs
			• Co-payment for mail order drugs
			• New stop loss limit

Assessment 2

1. Create a presentation with the text shown in figure 2.24. You determine the template and the autolayout. Add a transition and sound of your choosing to each slide in the presentation.
2. After creating the presentation, complete a spelling check.
3. Save the presentation in the Chapter 02C folder on your disk and name it Trends Presentation.
4. Run the presentation.
5. Print the slides as handouts with six slides per page.
6. Close Trends Presentation.

figure 2.24 Assessment 2

Slide 1	Title	=	TRENDS IN TELECOMMUNICATIONS
	Subtitle	=	Current and Future Trends
Slide 2	Title	=	Trend 1
	Subtitle	=	Continued movement toward the deregulation of telecommunications services
Slide 3	Title	=	Trend 2
	Subtitle	=	Continued expansion and enhancement of local and wide area networks
Slide 4	Title	=	Trend 3
	Subtitle	=	Movement toward integrated services digital networks
Slide 5	Title	=	Trend 4
	Subtitle	=	Movement toward standardization of data communication protocols
Slide 6	Title	=	Trend 5
	Subtitle	=	Increased use of wireless radio-based technology
Slide 7	Title	=	Trend 6
	Subtitle	=	Continued growth of photonics (fiber optics)
Slide 8	Title	=	Trend 7
	Subtitle	=	Expansion of video teleconferencing

Slide 9	Title	=	Trend 8
	Subtitle	=	Increased power in electronic workstations
Slide 10	Title	=	Trend 9
	Subtitle	=	More sophisticated software
Slide 11	Title	=	Trend 10
	Subtitle	=	Continued growth of voice processing
Slide 12	Title	=	Trend 11
	Subtitle	=	Greater use of optical storage technologies

Assessment 3

1. Open Trends Presentation.
2. Save the presentation with Save As and name it Edited Trends Presentation.
3. Make the following edits to the presentation:
   a. Display the presentation in Slide Sorter view.
   b. Move Slide 2 between Slide 5 and Slide 6.
   c. Move Slide 10 between Slide 7 and Slide 8.
   d. Renumber the trends numbers in the titles to reflect the correct order.
   e. Display Slide 4 in Slide view, delete the subtitle text, and then key **Multimedia in integrated systems**.
   f. Display Slide 8 in Slide view, delete the subtitle text, and then key **Information as a strategic resource**.
4. Apply a different design template of your choosing.
5. Insert the current date and slide number on all slides in the presentation. (Make sure there is no check mark in the Don't show on title slide option at the Header and Footer dialog box.)
6. Save the presentation again with the same name (Edited Trends Presentation).
7. Run the presentation.
8. Print the presentation as handouts with six slides per page.
9. Close Edited Trends Presentation.

Assessment 4

1. Open Enhanced Services Presentation.
2. Save the presentation with Save As and name it Revised Enhanced Services Pres.
3. Make the following change to the presentation:
   a. Find all occurrences of *Enhanced* and replace with *Premium*.
   b. Create the header *McCormack Annuity Funds*, the footer *Premium Services* and insert the date and page number for notes and handouts. (Make sure there is no check mark in the Don't show on title slide option at the Header and Footer dialog box with the Slide tab selected.)
   c. Display Slide 2 in Normal view and then key the speaker note **Refer participants to the sample transaction**.

d. Display Slide 5 in Normal view and then key the speaker note **Discuss budget impact due to increased hours**.
   e. Change the background color for all slides. (Make sure you choose a complementary color.)
4. Save the presentation again with the same name (Revised Enhanced Services Pres).
5. Run the presentation.
6. Print Slides 2 and 5 as notes pages.
7. Close Revised Enhanced Services Pres.

Assessment 5

1. Presentations can be run using PowerPoint or on a computer without PowerPoint installed. This might be useful in a situation where you travel to different locations giving a presentation and not all locations have PowerPoint available. PowerPoint contains a Pack and Go Wizard that walks you through the steps of preparing a presentation to be run on a different computer. This process is referred to as "packing" and "unpacking." Use the PowerPoint Help feature to learn how to pack and then unpack a PowerPoint presentation.
2. Prepare a memo to your instructor in Word using one of the memo templates that explains the steps to pack and unpack a presentation. Save the memo and name it Word Ch 2, SA 05. Print and then close Word Ch 2, SA 05.
3. In PowerPoint, use the Pack and Go Wizard (this feature must be installed) to pack the Edited Trends Presentation. Save the packed presentation on your data disk.

Note: Make a copy in the root folder of your disk of the following presentations that you will need for chapter 3:

   Benefits Presentation (created in chapter 2, assessment 1)
   Edited Trends Presentation (created in chapter 2, assessment 3)
   Enhanced Services Presentation (created in chapter 2, exercise 4)
   Networking Presentation (created in chapter 1, exercise 6)
   Newsletter Presentation (created in chapter 1, assessment 3)

Chapter 03C

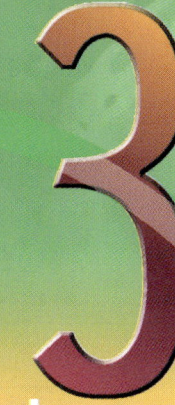

Adding Animation to Presentations

PERFORMANCE OBJECTIVES

Upon successful completion of chapter 3, you will be able to:
- Add animation effects to slides.
- Add a build to slides.
- Insert clip art images in a presentation.
- Size and scale clip art images.
- Create a watermark.
- Create a table in a slide.
- Link slides in a presentation to a Web site.
- Link slides in a presentation with Word documents.
- Link slides within the same presentation.
- Import text from Word into a presentation.
- Change a slide autolayout.
- Collect and paste multiple items.
- Publish a presentation to the Web.
- Preview a Web page presentation.
- Send a presentation via e-mail.

To add visual appeal and interest to a presentation, add animation effects, such as having an element fly into a slide, drive into a slide, or display as a camera effect. You also can have body text appear one step at a time during a slide show. Add impact to a presentation by inserting clip art images representing the text in the slide. Create hyperlinks from a slide to a site on the Internet. Use action buttons to link slides in a presentation to documents in other programs or slides within the same presentation. All of these topics will be covered in this chapter along with how to copy and paste data from a Word document into a slide in a PowerPoint presentation.

Adding Animation Effects to a Presentation

With options from the Animation Effects toolbar, you can add a variety of animation effects. To display animation choices, open a presentation, select the specific object within a slide to which you want the animation added, and then click the Animation Effects button on the Formatting toolbar. This causes the Animation Effects toolbar to display. Figure 3.1 describes the buttons on this toolbar.

Animation Effects

figure 3.1
Animation Effects Toolbar Buttons

Click this button	Named	To do this during a slide show
	Animate Title	Drop slide title from top of slide
	Animate Slide Text	Have body text appear one step at a time
	Drive-In Effect	Make selected text or object fly in from the right along with the sound of a car
	Flying Effect	Have selected text or object fly in from the left with a whoosh sound
	Camera Effect	Have selected text or object appear as if a camera shutter was opened
	Flash Once	Make selected text or object flash once after last build
	Laser Text Effect	Make selected text or object fly in from top right accompanied by the sound of a laser (If text is selected, it appears one character at a time.)
	Typewriter Text Effect	Make selected text or object appear one character at a time accompanied by the sound of a typewriter
	Reverse Text Order Effect	Make selected text appear from bottom up
	Drop-In Text Effect	Make selected object drop in from top of slide; text drops in one word at a time
	Animation Order	Select order in which selected text or object appears
	Custom Animation	Add or change animation effects
	Animation Preview	Display a miniature slide showing a preview of the animation effect(s)

CORE
P-104

Chapter Three

Many of the buttons on the Animation Effects toolbar are dimmed until text, an object, or an object box has been selected. To use the buttons on the Animation Effects toolbar, open a presentation, and then display a slide in the Slide pane. Select the text or object to which you want the effect applied, click the Animation Effects button on the Formatting toolbar, and then click the desired button. Continue in this manner until all animation effects have been added to selected text or objects in each slide.

Hint: Enhance the impact of your presentation with animation effects.

(Before completing computer exercises, delete the Chapter 02C folder on your disk. Next, copy the Chapter 03C folder from the CD that accompanies this textbook to your disk. Instructions for copying and deleting a folder are printed on the inside of the back cover of this textbook.)

exercise 1

Adding Animation Effects to a Presentation

1. Open PowerPoint and then open Enhanced Services Presentation. (You created this presentation in chapter 2, exercise 4.)
2. Save the presentation with Save As in the Chapter 03C folder on your disk and name it Enhanced Pres with Animation.
3. Add animation effects to the text in each slide by completing the following steps:
   a. Change to the Slide view. (Make sure the first slide displays in the Slide pane.)
   b. With Slide 1 displayed, add a flying effect to the title by completing the following steps:
      1) Click anywhere in the title *McCormack Annuity Funds*.
      2) Click the Animation Effects button on the Formatting toolbar.
      3) Click the Flying Effect button on the Animation Effects toolbar.
   c. With Slide 1 still displayed, add a flying effect to the subtitle *Enhanced Services* by completing steps similar to those in steps 3b.
   d. Click the Next Slide button at the bottom of the vertical scroll bar to display Slide 2.
   e. Click anywhere in the title *Enhanced Services* and click the Animate Title button on the Animation Effects toolbar.
   f. Select the text *Set up future accumulations transfers* and click the Laser Text Effect button on the Animation Effects toolbar.
   g. Preview the animation effects for Slide 2 by clicking the Animation Preview button on the Animation Effects toolbar.
   h. Close the Animation Preview miniature slide by clicking the Close button (contains an X) located in the upper right corner of the slide miniature.

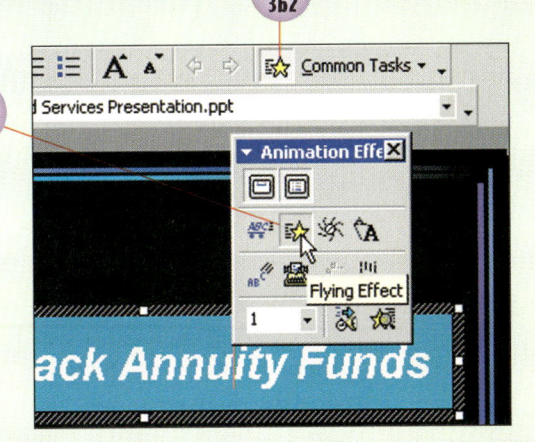

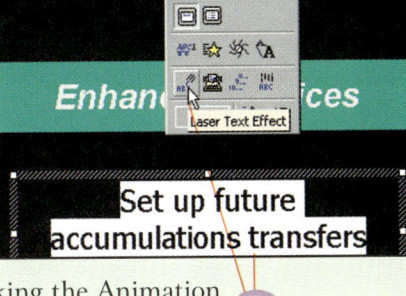

> i. Click the Next Slide button at the bottom of the vertical scroll bar to display Slide 3.
> j. Format the remaining slides (there are a total of six slides in this presentation) by completing steps similar to those in 3e and 3f.
> k. When all animation effects have been added to each slide, click the Close button on the Animation Effects toolbar. (This button is located in the upper right corner of the toolbar and contains an X.)
> 4. After formatting the last slide, change to the Slide Sorter view.
> 5. Click Slide 1.
> 6. Run the presentation by completing the following steps:
>   a. Click the Slide Show button on the View toolbar.
>   b. When the first slide displays (without the text), click the left mouse button. (This brings in the slide title.)
>   c. Click the left mouse button again. (This brings in the slide subtitle.)
>   d. Continue clicking the left mouse button to change slides and bring in text to each slide.
> 7. Save the presentation again with the same name (Enhanced Pres with Animation).
> 8. Close Enhanced Pres with Animation.

Adding a Build to Slides

With the buttons on the Animation Effects toolbar or a button on the Slide Sorter toolbar, you can display important points on a slide one point at a time. This is referred to as a *build technique*, which helps keep the audience's attention focused on the point being presented rather than reading ahead.

A build technique can be added to slides at the Slide Sorter view with the Slide Transition Effects button on the Slide Sorter toolbar. The Slide Sorter toolbar displays below the Standard toolbar. To add a build effect to a slide or slides, select the slide or slides, and then click the down-pointing triangle that displays at the right side of the Slide Transition Effects button. From the drop-down menu that displays, click the desired transition effect.

Slide Transition Effects

Custom Animation

With options from the Custom Animation dialog box with the Effects tab selected as shown in figure 3.2, you can customize a build. To display this dialog box, open a presentation, display the desired slide in the Slide pane, and then click the Animation Effects button on the Formatting toolbar. At the Animation Effects toolbar, click the Custom Animation button.

figure 3.2 Custom Animation Dialog Box with Effects Tab Selected

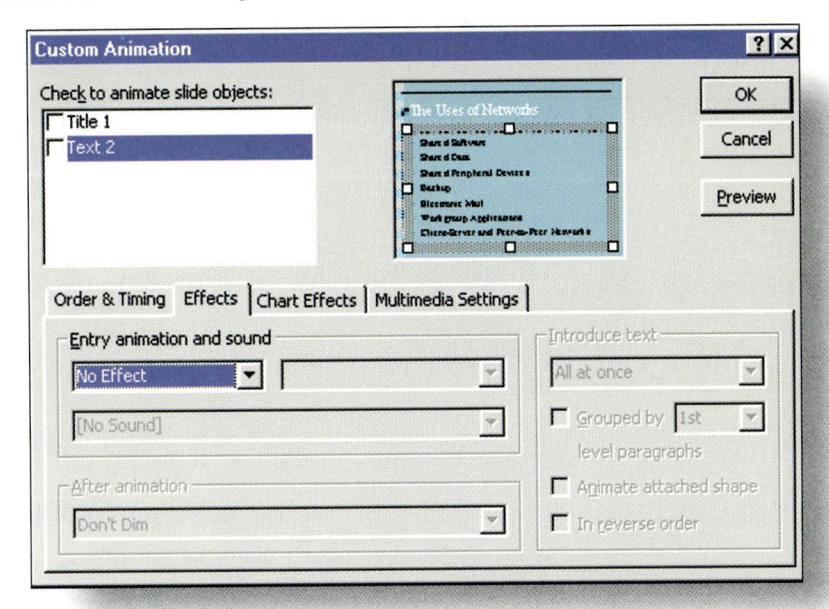

At the Custom Animation dialog box with the Order & Timing tab selected, specify the order that items display during a build with the Animation order option. With the Effects tab selected, in the Entry animation and sound section of the dialog box you can specify an animation effect such as flying, blinds, checkerboard, crawl, flash, or strip; and add sound such as a camera, laser, typewriter, or whoosh. With the After animation option, you can specify whether a previous build is dimmed when the next build is displayed. With options in the Introduce text section, you can specify that a build occurs all at once, by word, or by letter.

You were using a simple build technique in exercise 1—moving in individual objects within a slide. The build technique is very useful in slides containing more than one point. In exercise 2, you will be using the build technique on the Networking Presentation.

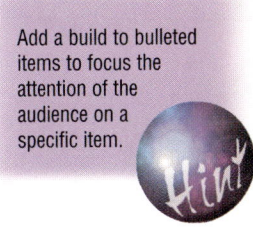

Hint: Add a build to bulleted items to focus the attention of the audience on a specific item.

exercise 2

Using the Build Technique for a Presentation

1. In PowerPoint, open Networking Presentation. (You created this presentation in chapter 1, exercise 6.)
2. Save the presentation with Save As in the Chapter 03C folder on your disk and name it Network Pres with Build.
3. Add a build effect to each point in the slides by completing the following steps:
   a. Change to the Slide view. (Make sure the first slide is displayed in the Slide pane.)
   b. With Slide 1 displayed in the Slide pane, add an animation effect to the title by completing the following steps:

1) Click anywhere in the title *NETWORKING*.
2) Click the Animation Effects button on the Formatting toolbar.
3) Click the Animate Title button on the Animation Effects toolbar.

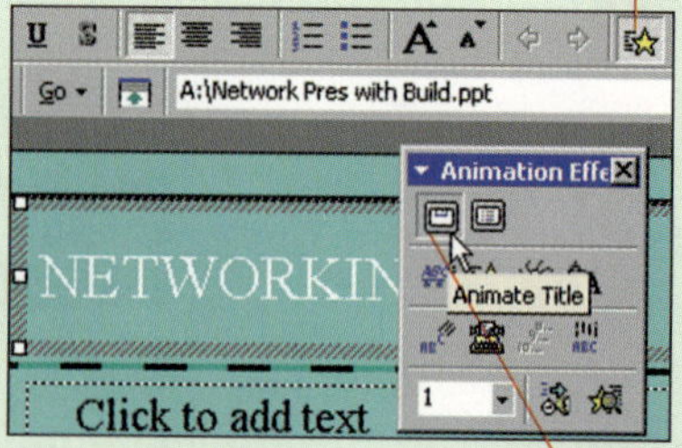

c. Click the Next Slide button at the bottom of the vertical scroll bar. (This displays Slide 2.)

d. With Slide 2 displayed in the Slide pane, add the Animate Title effect to the title *The Uses of Networks* by completing steps similar to those in steps 3b1 and 3b3.

e. With Slide 2 still displayed, add a build technique to the bulleted items on the slide by completing the following steps:
   1) Click once in the bulleted text. (You do not need to select all the text—the insertion point just needs to be positioned in the text object box.)
   2) Click the Custom Animation button on the Animation Effects toolbar.
   3) At the Custom Animation dialog box with the Effects tab selected, click the down-pointing triangle at the right of the first text box in the Entry animation and sound section (contains the text *No Effect*) and then click *Checkerboard* at the drop-down list. 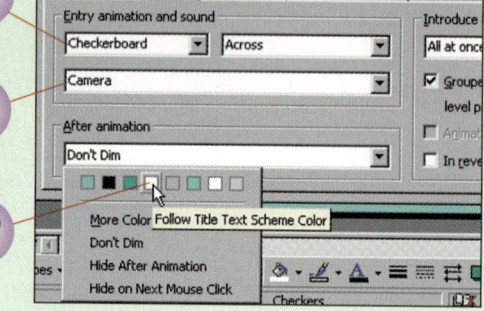
   4) Click the down-pointing triangle at the right of the text box containing the *[No Sound]* text and click *Camera* at the pop-up list.
   5) Click the down-pointing triangle to the right of the After animation text box containing the text *Don't Dim* and click the first white color.
   6) Click OK to close the Custom Animation dialog box.

f. Click the Next Slide button at the bottom of the vertical scroll bar to display Slide 3.

g. With Slide 3 displayed, animate the title *Layouts and Topologies* by completing steps similar to those in 3b1 and 3b3.

h. With Slide 3 still displayed, add a build technique to the bulleted items on the slide by completing the following steps:
   1) Click once in the bulleted text.
   2) Click the Custom Animation button on the Animation Effects toolbar.
   3) At the Custom Animation dialog box with the Effects tab selected, click the down-pointing triangle at the right of the first text box in the Entry animation and sound section, and then click *Checkerboard* at the drop-down list. 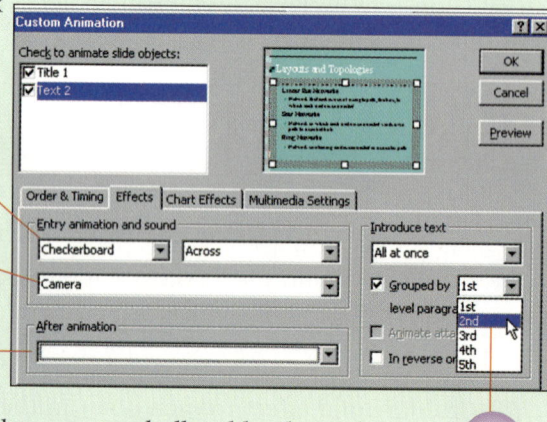
   4) Click the down-pointing triangle at the right side of the Grouped by level paragraphs option (contains the text *1st*) and click *2nd* at the drop-down list. (You choose *2nd* because there are two bulleted levels on this slide.)

Chapter Three

5) Click the down-pointing triangle at the right of the text box containing the *[No Sound]* text and then click *Camera* at the pop-up list.
6) Click the down-pointing triangle to the right of the After animation text box containing the text *Don't Dim* and click the first white color (Follow Title Text Scheme Color).
7) Click OK to close the Custom Animation dialog box.
   i. Format the remaining slide with the same title animation and build technique formatting. (Be sure to change the Grouped by level paragraphs option to *2nd*.)
   j. Click the Close button on the Animation Effects toolbar to remove it from the screen.
4. Display the presentation in Slide Sorter view and then click Slide 1.
5. Run the presentation by clicking the Slide Show button on the View toolbar. (Click the left mouse button to display the title and each bulleted item in the slides.)
6. Save the presentation again with the same name (Network Pres with Build).
7. Close Network Pres with Build.

Inserting Clip Art in a Presentation

Insert clip art images at the Insert ClipArt dialog box or the Microsoft Clip Gallery dialog box. (Both dialog boxes contain the same images.) Display the Insert ClipArt dialog box by clicking Insert, pointing to Picture, and then clicking Clip Art. Another method is to click the Insert Clip Art button on the Drawing toolbar. Display the Microsoft Clip Gallery dialog box by clicking Insert, clicking Object, and then double-clicking *Microsoft Clip Gallery*. Another method is to choose an autolayout that includes the image of a man's head and shoulders and then double-click the image.

> Not every slide needs a picture. Insert a picture in a slide only if it helps make a point.
>
> Insert ClipArt

Sizing and Scaling Images

Insert a clip art image in a slide and sizing handles display around the image. Use these sizing handles to increase or decrease the size of the image. Use the corner sizing handles to increase the height and width of the image at the same time. If you want to precisely control the size and scaling of an image, display the Format Picture dialog box with the Size tab selected. Display this dialog box by clicking the Format Picture button on the Picture toolbar. At the Format Picture dialog box, click the Size tab.

exercise 3

Inserting and Sizing a Clip Art Image in a PowerPoint Presentation

1. Open PowerPoint and then open Presentation 1, Ch 03. (This presentation is located in the *Presentations* folder on the CD that accompanies this textbook.)
2. Save the presentation with Save As in the Chapter 03C folder on your disk and name it PowerPoint C3, Ex 03.
3. Insert a clip art image in Slide 1 as shown in figure 3.3 by completing the following steps:
   a. Change to the Slide View and make sure Slide 1 is displayed.
   b. Click the Insert Clip Art button on the Drawing toolbar. (If the Drawing toolbar is not visible, click Insert, point to Picture, and then click Clip Art.)

c. At the Insert ClipArt dialog box, click in the Search for clips text box, key **medical**, and then press Enter. 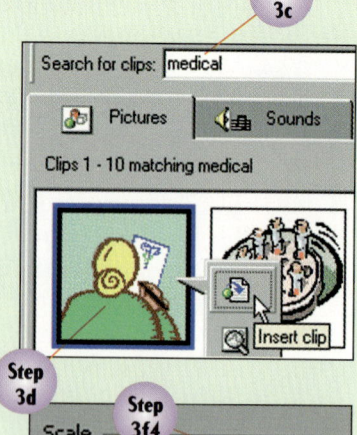
d. Click the image shown at the right and click the Insert clip button. If the image shown is not available choose another picture.
e. Close the Insert ClipArt dialog box.
f. Scale the image by completing the following steps:
   1) Make sure the clip art image is selected and the Picture toolbar displays. (If the Picture toolbar does not display, right-click the image and then click Show Picture Toolbar at the shortcut menu.)
   2) Click the Format Picture button on the Picture toolbar.
   3) At the Format Picture dialog box, click the Size tab.
   4) At the Format Picture dialog box with the Size tab selected, click the up-pointing triangle at the right side of the Height text box in the Scale section until *150%* displays in the text box. 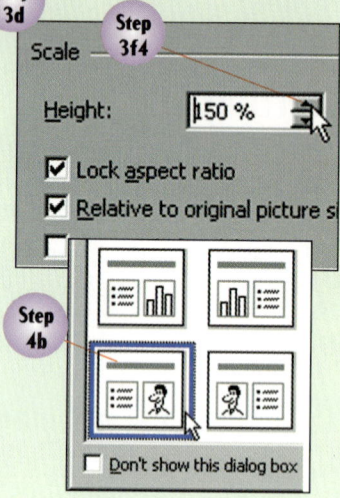
   5) Click OK to close the dialog box.
g. Move the image so it is positioned in the location shown in figure 3.3.
4. Create a new Slide 2 as shown in figure 3.4 by completing the following steps:
   a. Click the New Slide button on the Standard toolbar.
   b. At the New Slide dialog box, double-click the first autolayout in the third row (Text & Clip Art).
   c. At the slide, click in the text *Click to add title* and key **Times to Change Medical Plans**.
   d. Click the text *Click to add text* and then key the text after the first bullet as shown in figure 3.4.
   e. Press Shift + Enter and then press Enter.
   f. Key the text after the second bullet in figure 3.4.
   g. Continue keying the bulleted text shown in figure 3.4. (Separate the bulleted text by pressing Shift + Enter and then Enter.)
   h. Insert the clip art image by completing the following steps:
      1) Double-click the image of a man standing.
      2) At the Insert ClipArt dialog box, display the *Office* category.
      3) Click the image shown at the right and click the Insert clip button. 
      4) Close the Insert ClipArt dialog box.
   i. Size the image by completing the following steps:
      1) Make sure the clip art image is selected and the Picture toolbar displays. (If the Picture toolbar does not display, right-click the image and then click Show Picture Toolbar at the shortcut menu.)
      2) Click the Format Picture button on the Picture toolbar.
      3) At the Format Picture dialog box, click the Size tab.
      4) At the Format Picture dialog box with the Size tab selected, select the current measurement in the Height text box, and then key **2.8**. 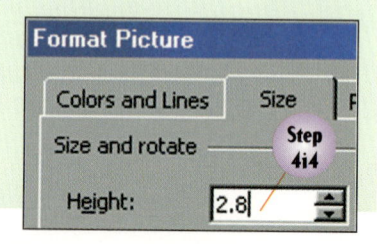
      5) Click OK to close the dialog box.

Chapter Three

j. If necessary, move the image so it is positioned as shown in figure 3.4.
5. Animate the slide titles and add a build to the slides containing bulleted text.
6. Run the presentation.
7. Save the presentation again with the same name (PowerPoint C3, Ex 03).
8. Print the presentation with two slides on a page.
9. Close PowerPoint C3, Ex 03.

figure 3.3

Exercise 3, Slide 1

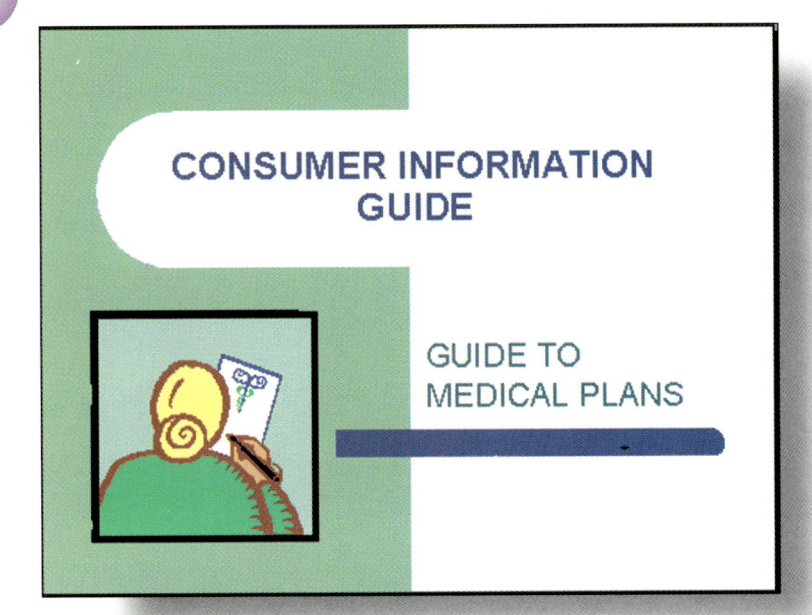

figure 3.4

Exercise 3, Slide 2

Inserting Images from a Disk

If you want the same clip art image on every slide, insert it on the Slide Master.

In exercise 3, you have inserted clip art images in a presentation from the Insert ClipArt dialog box. You can also insert images from other sources such as a disk or folder. For example, in exercise 4 you will insert images in a PowerPoint presentation from the CD that accompanies this textbook.

To insert images from a different source, click Insert, point to Picture, and then click From File. This displays the Insert Picture dialog box shown in figure 3.5. At this dialog box, change to the folder or drive containing the image. Click the desired image name in the list box and then click the Insert button. (You can also just double-click the image name.) Move, size, and/or format the image in the same manner as clip art from the Microsoft Clip Gallery.

figure 3.5

Insert Picture Dialog Box

exercise 4

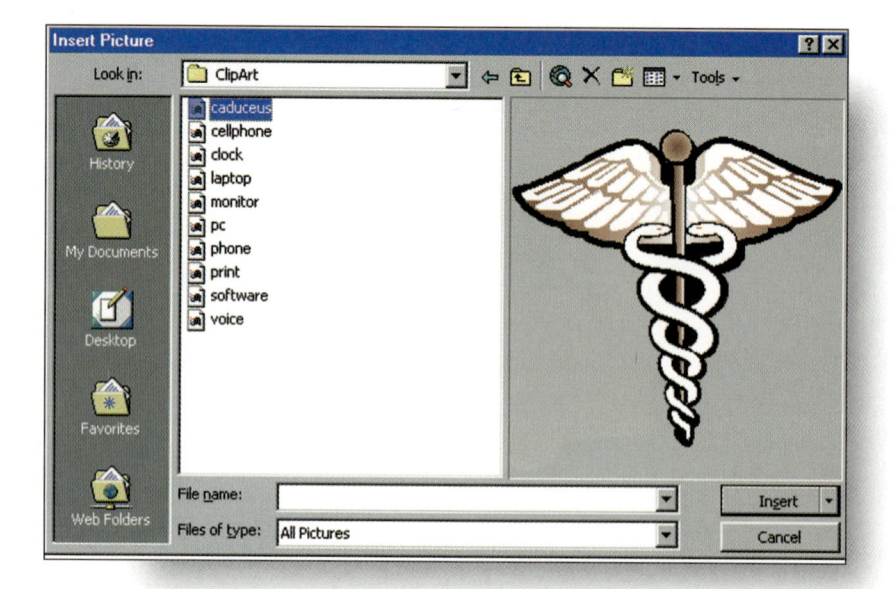

Inserting Images from a Disk into a PowerPoint Presentation

1. Open PowerPoint and then open Presentation 2, Ch 03. (This presentation is located in the *Presentations* folder on the CD that accompanies this textbook.)
2. Save the presentation with Save As in the Chapter 03C folder on your disk and name it PowerPoint C3, Ex 04.
3. Insert a clip art image in Slide 1 as shown in figure 3.6 by completing the following steps:
    a. Change to the Slide view with Slide 1 displayed.
    b. Display the Insert ClipArt dialog box.
    c. Display the *Communications* category.

      d. Click the telephone image shown in the slide in figure 3.6 and then click the Insert clip button.
      e. Close the Insert ClipArt dialog box.
4. Move and size the image so it displays as shown in figure 3.6.
5. Insert an image in Slide 2 as shown in figure 3.7 by completing the following steps:
      a. Click the Next Slide button to display Slide 2.
      b. Insert the CD that accompanies this textbook if you have removed it after step 1.
      c. Click Insert, point to Picture, and then click From File.
      d. At the Insert Picture dialog box, change to the drive where the CD is located.
      e. Double-click the *ClipArt* folder.
      f. Double-click *phone* in the list box.
6. Move and size the image so it displays as shown in figure 3.7.
7. Insert the image shown in figure 3.8 by completing the following steps:
      a. Click the Next Slide button to display Slide 3.
      b. Click Insert, point to Picture, and then click From File.
      c. At the Insert Picture dialog box, make sure the drive where the CD is located is selected, and *ClipArt* is the active folder.
      d. Double-click *cellphone* in the list box.
      e. Size and move the image so it is positioned in the slide as shown in figure 3.8.
8. Insert the clip art image named *voice* in Slide 4 as shown in figure 3.9 by completing steps similar to those in step 7.
9. Run the presentation.
10. Save the presentation again with the same name (PowerPoint C3, Ex 04).
11. Print the presentation with two slides on a page.
12. Close PowerPoint C3, Ex 04.

figure 3.6

Exercise 4, Slide 1

figure 3.7 *Exercise 4, Slide 2*

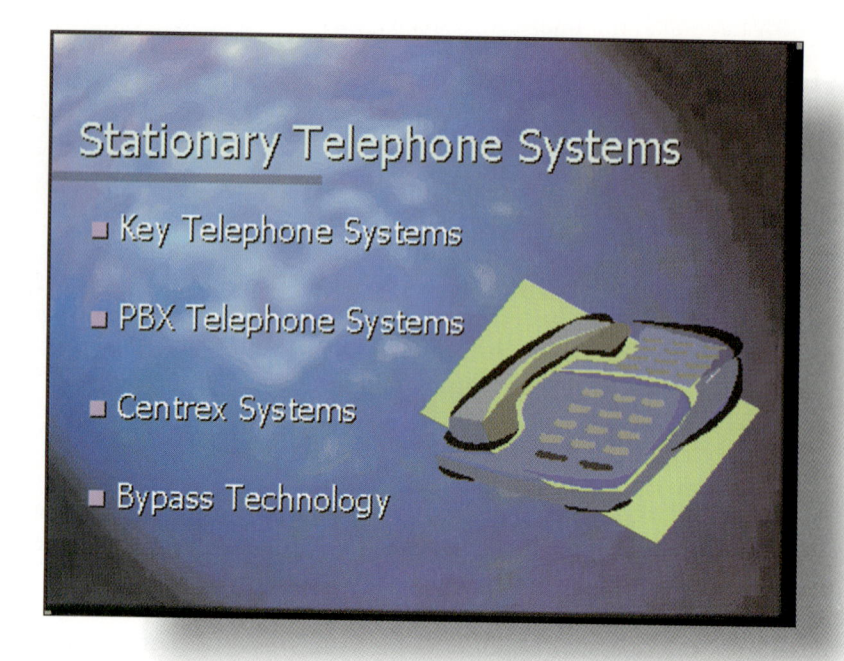

Stationary Telephone Systems
- Key Telephone Systems
- PBX Telephone Systems
- Centrex Systems
- Bypass Technology

figure 3.8 *Exercise 4, Slide 3*

Mobile Communication System
- Cellular Mobile Telephone System
- Mobile Telephone Systems
- Two-Way Radio
- Pagers

Chapter Three

figure 3.9   Exercise 4, Slide 4

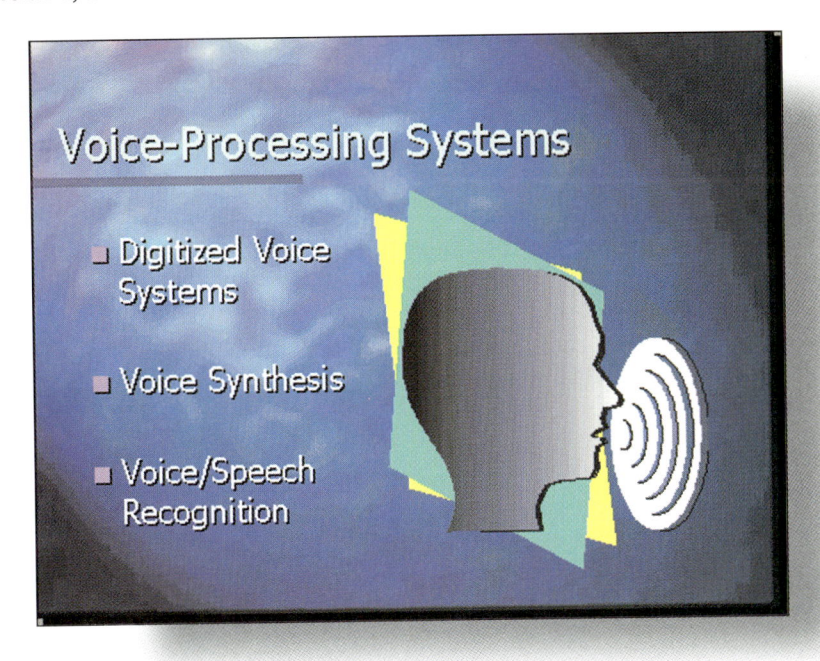

Recoloring Clip Art Images in PowerPoint

To recolor clip art images, click the Recolor Picture button on the Picture toolbar. The Recolor Picture dialog box will then display with options for changing the color of the various components of the clip art image. When you insert a Microsoft Windows Metafile (wmf) from the Clip Gallery, you might want to change the colors in the picture to coordinate with the color scheme of your presentation. If the picture that you inserted is a different file format such as bitmap (bmp), jpg, gif, or png image file, you will need to change its colors in an image editing program, such as Microsoft Photo Editor.

Recolor Picture

    In exercise 5, you will use the Recolor Picture dialog box to change the color of the phone.wmf picture you inserted on slide 1 in exercise 4.

exercise 5

Formatting a Clip Art Image in PowerPoint

1. Open PowerPoint C3, Ex 04.
2. Recolor the clip art image in slide 1 by completing the following steps:
   a. Display Slide 1 in Slide view.
   b. Click the clip art image to select it.
   c. If the Picture toolbar does not display, *right-click* the image, and then click Show Picture Toolbar at the shortcut menu.
   d. Click the Recolor Picture button on the Picture toolbar.

Step 2d

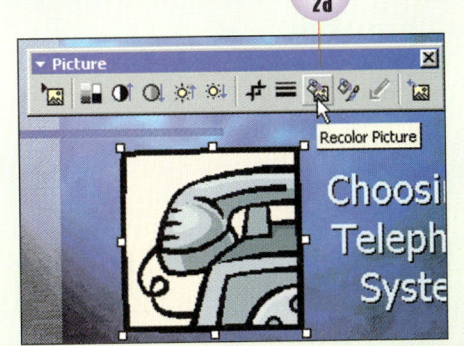

Adding Animation to Presentations

P-115

e. At the Recolor Picture dialog box, click the down-pointing triangle at the right side of the first button below the New section.
f. At the color palette that displays, click the dark blue color (third color from the left).
g. Scroll down to the end of the list box and then click the down-pointing triangle at the right side of the button containing the beige color (second button from the end of the list).
h. At the color palette that displays, click the light blue color (second color from the *right*).
i. Click OK to close the Recolor Picture dialog box.

3. Save the presentation with the same name (PowerPoint C3, Ex 04).
4. Print only slide 1.
5. Close PowerPoint C3, Ex 04.
6. Delete PowerPoint C3, Ex 04. (Check with your instructor before deleting this presentation.)

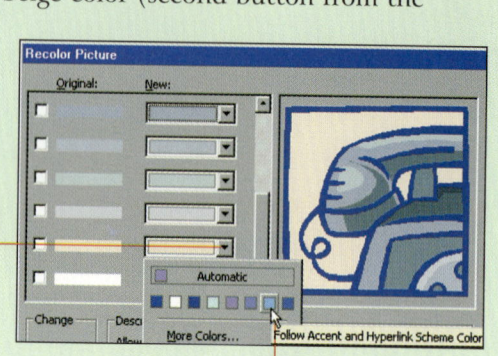

Creating Watermarks

Image Control

Create a watermark in a PowerPoint presentation by clicking the Image Control button on the Picture toolbar and then clicking Watermark. Move the watermark image behind the text by clicking the Draw button on the Drawing toolbar, pointing to Order, and then clicking Send to Back. Use the brightness and contrast buttons on the Picture toolbar to increase or decrease the brightness and intensity of the image.

exercise 6

Creating a Watermark in a PowerPoint Slide

1. Open the presentation named History of Computers 1980s. (This presentation is located in the *Presentations* folder on the CD that accompanies this textbook.)
2. Save the presentation with Save As in the Chapter 03C folder on your disk and name it PowerPoint C3, Ex 06.
3. Create a watermark in Slide 1 as shown in figure 3.10 by completing the following steps:
   a. Display slide 1 in Slide view.
   b. Display the Insert ClipArt dialog box.
   c. Display the *Science and Technology* category.
   d. Click the clip art image shown at the right and click the Insert clip button.

e. Close the Insert ClipArt dialog box.
  f. Make sure the image is selected and the Picture toolbar displays. (If the Picture toolbar does not display, right-click the image and click Show Picture Toolbar.)
  g. Click the Image Control button on the Picture toolbar, and then click Watermark at the drop-down list.
  h. Click twice on the Less Brightness button on the Picture toolbar.
  i. Click the Draw button that displays at the left side of the Drawing toolbar, point to Order, and then click Send to Back.
  j. Move and size the watermark image so it displays as shown in figure 3.10.
4. Save the presentation again with the same name (PowerPoint C3, Ex 06).
5. Print slide 1 only and then close PowerPoint C3, Ex 06.
6. Delete PowerPoint C3, Ex 06. (Check with your instructor before deleting this presentation.)

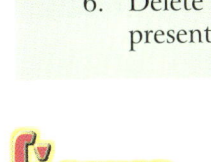

figure 3.10

Exercise 6

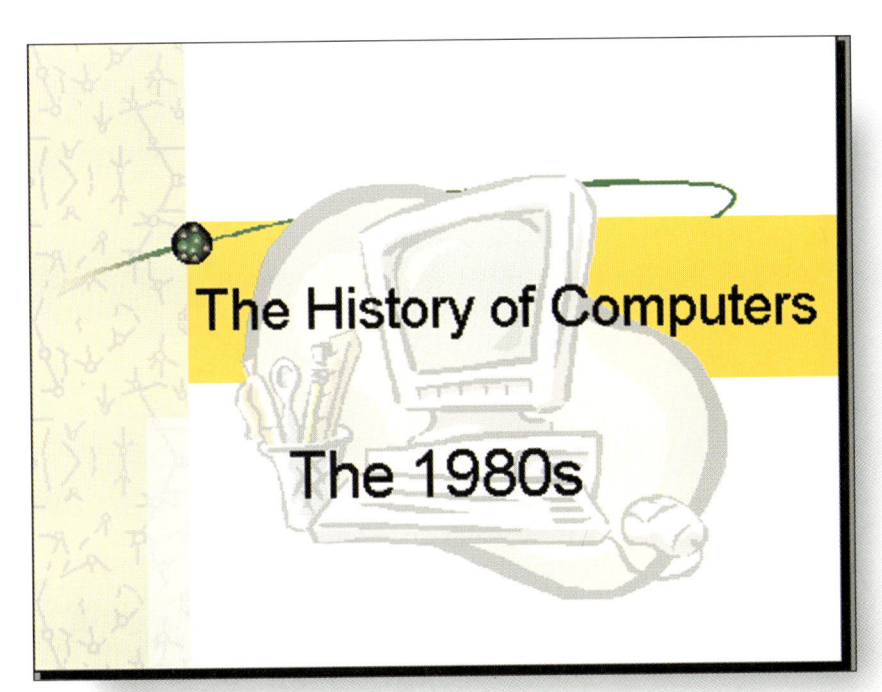

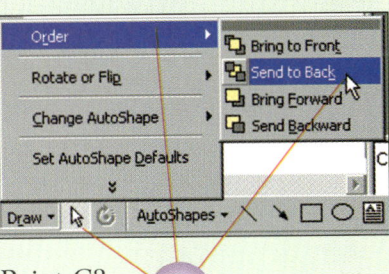

Adding Animation to Presentations

Creating a Table in a Slide

PowerPoint offers a variety of autolayouts. You have used several autolayouts including Title Slide, Bulleted List, Text & Clip Art, and Title Only. PowerPoint also includes the Table autolayout you can use to create a table in a PowerPoint presentation. To create a table in a slide, choose the Table autolayout at the New Slide dialog box, and then double-click the Table icon at the slide. At the Insert Table dialog box, specify the desired number of columns and rows and then click OK.

Format a table in a PowerPoint slide with buttons on the Tables and Borders toolbar. Display this toolbar by clicking the Tables and Borders button on the Standard toolbar. After formatting the table, double-click inside the first cell, and then key the text. Move the insertion point to the next cell by pressing the Tab key. (You can also click in the next cell.) Press Shift + Tab to move the insertion point to the previous cell.

exercise 7

Creating a Table in a Slide

1. Open PowerPoint C3, Ex 03.
2. Add the new slide shown in figure 3.11 by completing the following steps:
   a. Display Slide 4 in Slide view.
   b. Click the New Slide button.
   c. At the New Slide dialog box, double-click the Table autolayout (last autolayout in the top row). 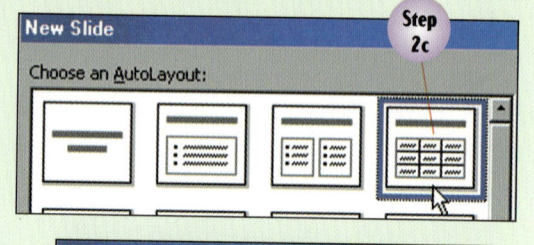
   d. At the slide, click in the text *Click to add title*, and then key **Information Resources**.
   e. Double-click the Table icon that displays in the middle of the slide.
   f. At the Insert Table dialog box, key **3**, press the Tab key, and then key **5**.
   g. Click OK to close the dialog box. 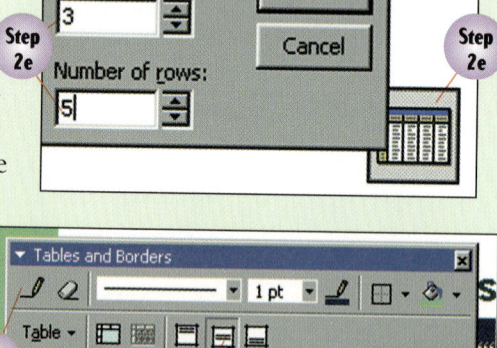
   h. Make sure the Tables and Borders toolbar displays. (If it does not, turn it on by clicking the Tables and Borders button the Standard toolbar.)
   i. Click the Draw Table button to deactivate the drawing tool.
   j. Select all the cells in the table and then click the Center Vertically button on the Tables and Borders toolbar. 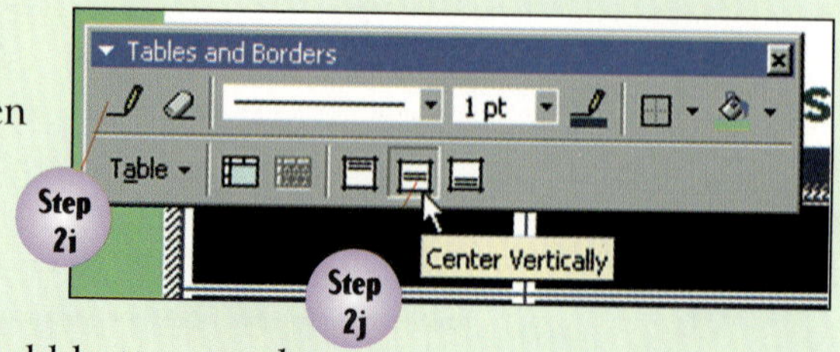
   k. Deselect the cells.
   l. Close the Tables and Borders toolbar.
   m. Select the first row of cells, click the Bold button on the Formatting toolbar, and then click the Center button.
   n. Click in the first cell and then key the text in each cell as shown in figure 3.11. (Press the Tab key to move to the next cell or press Shift + Tab to move to the previous cell.)

P-118

Chapter Three

3. Save the presentation again with the same name (PowerPoint C3, Ex 03).
4. Run the presentation.
5. Print all five slides on the same page.
6. Close PowerPoint C3, Ex 03.

figure 3.11

Exercise 7, Slide 5

Information Resources

Name	Region	Telephone
Jennifer Runez	Upper Peninsula	(360) 555-4300
Michael Brandt	Pierce County	(253) 555-3425
Lois Weinstein	Northwest	(206) 555-1255
Trevor Haydon	West Coast	(244) 555-0980

Creating Hyperlinks in a Presentation

In PowerPoint you can jump to the Internet from within PowerPoint, display Web sites, and search for specific information. To display the Web toolbar in PowerPoint, click View, point to Toolbars, and then click Web. You can also right click on any displayed toolbar and then click *Web* at the drop-down list. You may want to use the Internet to locate sites and research topics when designing and preparing a presentation. A presentation can also include hyperlinks that will connect to a specific Internet site while the presentation is running. Hyperlinks can also be created that link a slide in a presentation to another document, such as a Word document.

Creating Hyperlinks from a Slide to the Web

To create a hyperlink, from a slide in a presentation to a Web site, open the presentation where you want to create a link, and then display the specific slide in the Slide pane. Select the text to which you want to apply the hyperlink and

Hint: Make a Web page out of any presentation by clicking File and then Save as Web Page. At the Save As dialog box, key a name for the Web page presentation.

Hint: Consider inserting hyperlinks in your presentation to jump to interesting sites on the Internet that pertain to the presentation.

Insert Hyperlink

then click the Insert Hyperlink button on the Standard toolbar. At the Insert Hyperlink dialog box, key the URL in the Type the file or Web page name text box, and then click OK. When running a presentation containing a hyperlink, make sure you are connected to the Internet and then click the hyperlink.

exercise 8

Adding a Slide with Hyperlinks

1. Open Font Presentation. (This presentation is located in the *Presentations* folder on the CD that accompanies this textbook.)
2. Save the presentation with Save As in the Chapter 03C folder on your disk and name it Linked Font Pres.
3. Add a slide to the presentation and insert hyperlinks in the slide by completing the following steps:
   a. Change to the Slide view.
   b. Click the Next Slide button until Slide 4 displays. (Slide 4 is the last slide in the presentation.)
   c. Click the New Slide button on the Standard toolbar.
   d. At the New Slide dialog box, double-click the second autolayout (Bulleted List).
   e. With the new slide displayed, click the text *Click to add title* and key **Internet Typeface Resources**.
   f. Click the text *Click to add text* and key **Adobe**.
   g. Press Shift + Enter, press Enter, and then key **Monotype**.
   h. Press Shift + Enter, press Enter, and then key **Publish RGB**.
   i. Press Shift + Enter, press Enter, and then key **Will Harris-House**.
   j. Add a hyperlink to Adobe by completing the following steps:
      1) Select the text *Adobe*.
      2) Click the Insert Hyperlink button on the Standard toolbar.
      3) At the Insert Hyperlink dialog box, key **http://www.adobe.com** in the Type the file or Web page name text box, and then click OK. (The word Adobe displays underlined and in a different color.)
   k. Add a hyperlink to Monotype by completing steps similar to those in 3j. The Web address for Monotype is *http://www.monotype.com*.
   l. Add a hyperlink to *Publish RGB* by completing steps similar to those in 3j. The Web address for Publish RGB is *http://www.publish.com*.
   m. Add a hyperlink to *Will Harris-House* by completing steps similar to those in 3j. The Web address for Will Harris-House is *http://www.will-harris.com*.
4. Save the presentation again with the same name (Linked Font Pres).
5. Make sure you are connected to the Internet and run the presentation. When Slide 5 displays, click *Adobe* to jump to the Adobe home page. Scroll through this home page, click File, and then Close to close the Internet Explorer.
6. Jump to each of the other Web sites by clicking the hyperlink.
7. After running the presentation and viewing the Web sites, close Linked Font Pres.

Creating Hyperlinks from a Slide to a Word Document

In exercise 8, you created a hyperlink between a slide in PowerPoint and a location on the World Wide Web. A hyperlink can also be created that links a slide in PowerPoint to a document in another program such as Word. A link can be created at the Insert Hyperlink dialog box by specifying the document to which you want the slide linked or a link can be created with action buttons. To create a link between a slide and a Word document using action buttons, you would complete these steps:

1. Open the presentation to which you want a Word document linked.
2. Display the slide in Slide view that you want linked to a Word document.
3. Click the AutoShapes button on the Drawing toolbar located toward the bottom of the screen.
4. At the pop-up menu, point to Action Buttons. (This causes a palette of button choices to display.)
5. At the palette of button choices, drag the arrow pointer to the button named Action Button: Document (second button from the left in the bottom row), and then click the left mouse button.
6. Position the arrow pointer inside the slide, hold down the left mouse button, drag to create the button, and then release the mouse button.
7. At the Action Settings dialog box with the Mouse Click tab selected shown in figure 3.12, click in the white circle in front of the Hyperlink to option.
8. Click the down-pointing triangle at the right side of the Hyperlink to text box (displays with the words *Next Slide*). This causes a drop-down list to display.
9. At the drop-down list, click *Other File*.
10. At the Hyperlink to Other File dialog box, change to the folder where the desired document is located, and then double-click the document.
11. At the Action Settings dialog box, click OK.

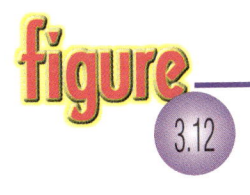

figure 3.12 Action Settings Dialog Box with Mouse Click Tab Selected

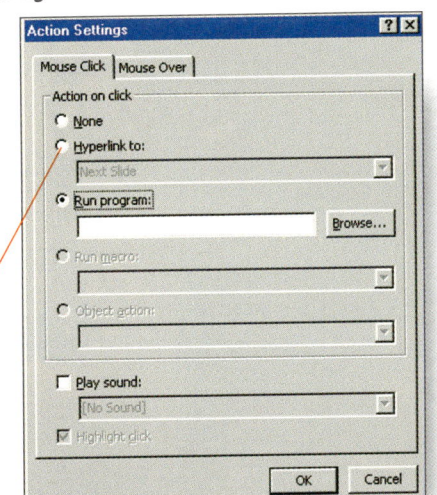

To create a hyperlink click the Hyperlink to option and then specify the location.

Once an action button has been inserted in a slide, you can click the button during the running of the presentation to display the linked document. After viewing the linked document, close the program containing the linked document and the slide redisplays. In exercise 9, you will create buttons on slides in the Font Presentation that link to Word documents.

exercise 9

Linking Word Documents to a PowerPoint Presentation

1. Open Font Presentation. (This presentation is located in the *Presentations* folder on the CD that accompanies this textbook.)
2. Save the presentation with Save As in the Chapter 03C folder on your disk and name it Font Pres, Action Buttons. 
3. Add a button linking Slide 2 with a Word document by completing the following steps:
   a. Display the presentation in Slide view and display Slide 2.
   b. Click the A<u>u</u>toShapes button on the Drawing toolbar located toward the bottom of the screen.
   c. At the pop-up menu, point to Ac<u>t</u>ion Buttons. (This causes a palette of button choices to display.)
   d. At the palette of button choices, point to the button named Action Button: Document (second button from the left in the bottom row), and then click the left mouse button. 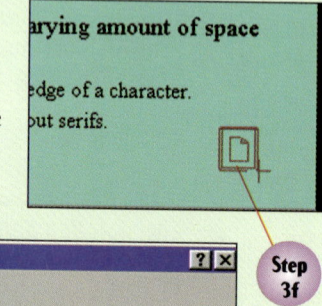
   e. Position the arrow pointer in the bottom right corner of the slide, hold down the left mouse button, drag to create the button (make the button about one-half inch in height and width), and then release the mouse button.
   f. At the Action Settings dialog box with the Mouse Click tab selected, click in the white circle in front of the <u>H</u>yperlink to option.
   g. Click the down-pointing triangle at the right side of the <u>H</u>yperlink to text box (displays with the words *Next Slide*).
   h. At the drop-down list that displays, click *Other File*. 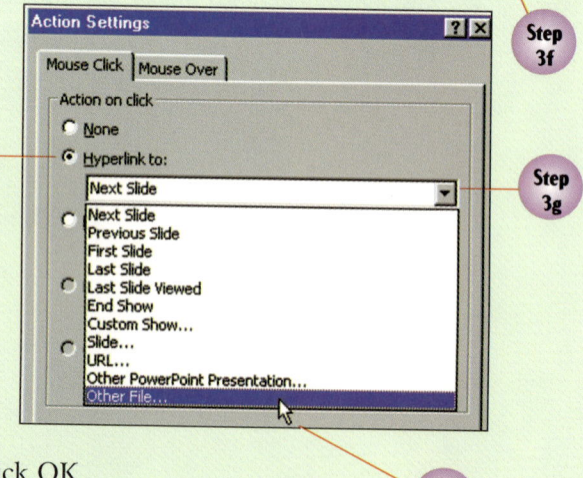
   i. At the Hyperlink to Other File dialog box, change to the Chapter 03C folder on your disk and then double-click the document named *Typeface Example*.
   j. At the Action Settings dialog box, click OK.
   k. Click outside the button to deselect it.

Chapter Three

4. Add a button linking Slide 3 to the Word document *Type Size Example* by completing steps similar to those in 3.
5. Add a button linking Slide 4 to the Word document *Type Style Example* by completing steps similar to those in 3.
6. Save the presentation again with the same name (Font Pres, Action Buttons).
7. Run the presentation. When Slide 2 displays, click the action button that displays in the lower right corner of the slide. (This displays the *Typeface Example* document in Word.)
8. After viewing the *Typeface Example* document, click File and the Exit.
9. Continue running the presentation and clicking the action buttons in Slides 3 and 4 to display the linked Word documents. (Be sure to click File and Exit after viewing each Word document.)
10. When the presentation is completed, close Font Pres, Action Buttons.

Linking Slides within a Presentation with Action Buttons

A slide in a PowerPoint presentation can be linked to a document in another program as you did in exercise 9. You can also link slides within the same presentation. Several methods are available for linking slides within the same presentation. One method is to insert a button that displays the "Home" slide (the first slide in the presentation) and also a button that returns to the last slide viewed. To do this, you would insert the action button named *Action Button: Home* in the slide you want linked to the beginning slide and insert the action button named *Action Button: Return* in the beginning slide.

exercise 10

Inserting Action Buttons to Link Slides in the Same Presentation

1. Open Newsletter Presentation. (You created this presentation in chapter 1, assessment 3.)
2. Save the presentation with Save As and name it Linked Newsletter Pres.
3. Add an action button to Slide 4 linking it to the beginning slide by completing the following steps:
   a. Display the presentation in Slide view and display Slide 4.
   b. Click the AutoShapes button on the Drawing toolbar.
   c. Point to Action Buttons.
   d. At the palette of button choices, point to the button named Action Button: Home (second button from the left in the top row) and click the left mouse button.

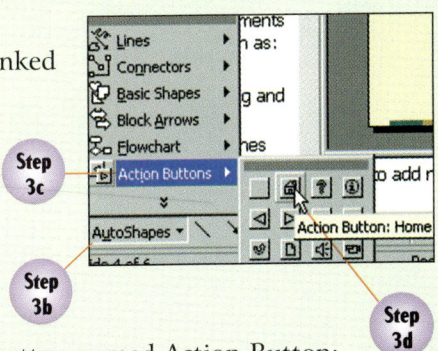

Adding Animation to Presentations P-123

e. Position the arrow pointer in the bottom right corner of the slide, hold down the left mouse button, drag to create the button (make the button about one-half inch in height and width), and then release the mouse button.
f. At the Action Settings dialog box, make sure the Hyperlink to option is selected and that *First Slide* displays in the text box.
g. Click OK to close the Action Settings dialog box.
h. At Slide 4, click outside the button to deselect it.

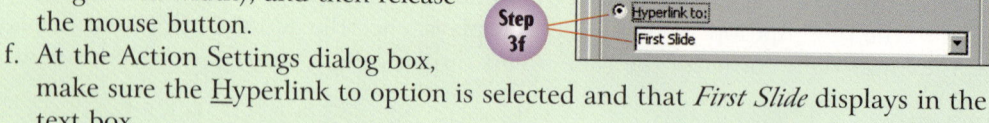

4. Add an action button to Slide 1 linking it to the last slide viewed by completing the following steps:
   a. Display Slide 1 in Slide view.
   b. Click the AutoShapes button on the Drawing toolbar.
   c. Point to Action Buttons.
   d. At the palette of button choices, point to the button named Action Button: Return (first button from the left in the bottom row) and click the left mouse button.
   e. Position the arrow pointer in the bottom right corner of the slide, hold down the left mouse button, drag to create the button (make the button about one-half inch in height and width), and then release the mouse button.
   f. At the Action Settings dialog box, make sure the Hyperlink to option is selected and that *Last Slide Viewed* displays in the text box.
   g. Click OK to close the Action Settings dialog box.
   h. At Slide 1, click outside the button to deselect it.

5. Save the presentation again with the same name (Linked Newsletter Pres).
6. Run the presentation. When Slide 4 displays, click the action button that displays in the lower right corner of the slide. (This displays Slide 1.)
7. After viewing Slide 1, click the action button that displays in the lower right corner of the slide. (This displays the last slide viewed—Slide 4.)
8. Continue running the presentation.
9. When the presentation is completed, close Linked Newsletter Pres.

Importing Text from Word

A variety of methods are available for sharing data between PowerPoint and other Office applications. In chapter 5 you will learn how to link and embed objects between applications. In this chapter, you will learn how to copy from one program to another by copying and pasting and by importing.

To copy and paste text between Word and PowerPoint, open the source document in Word and then open the destination presentation in PowerPoint.

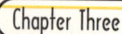

Chapter Three

Select the text in the Word document and then click the Copy button on the Standard toolbar. Make PowerPoint the active program, display the desired slide, and then click the Paste button on the Standard toolbar.

A Word document containing heading styles can be easily imported into a PowerPoint presentation. To do this, open the document, click File, point to Send To, and then click Microsoft PowerPoint. Paragraphs formatted with a Heading 1 style become the title of a new slide. Paragraphs formatted with a Heading 2 style become the first level of text, paragraphs formatted as a Heading 3 style become the second level of text, and so on. PowerPoint creates a presentation with the imported text using the Blank Presentation template. After importing the text into PowerPoint, apply the desired formatting, or apply a design template.

Changing the Autolayout

Text imported from Word into PowerPoint is inserted in a slide with a specific autolayout. In some cases, this autolayout is appropriate for the imported text. In other cases, you may need to change the autolayout. To do this, click the Common Tasks button on the Formatting toolbar and Slide Layout at the drop-down list. (You can also click Format and Slide Layout.) This displays the Slide Layout dialog box that contains the same autolayout choices as the New Slide dialog box.

(Note: If you are saving presentations in the Chapter 03C folder on your disk, consider deleting the following presentations before completing exercise 11: Enhanced Pres with Animation; Font Pres, Action Buttons; Linked Font Pres; Linked Newsletter Pres; Network Pres with Build; and PowerPoint C3, Ex 03.)

exercise 11

Importing Text from Word

1. Make sure PowerPoint is open and then open Word.
2. With Word the active program, open Word Outline 01.
3. Import the text (formatted with Heading 1 and Heading 2 styles) into PowerPoint by clicking File, pointing to Send To, and then clicking Microsoft PowerPoint.
4. Make PowerPoint the active program (this displays the imported text in a presentation created with the Blank Presentation template).
5. Change to the Title Slide autolayout for Slide 1 by completing the following steps:
    a. Display Slide 1 in Slide view.
    b. Click the Common Tasks button on the Formatting toolbar and then click Slide Layout at the drop-down list.
    c. At the Slide Layout dialog box, double-click the Title Slide autolayout (first autolayout from the left in the top row).
6. Apply the Factory design template to the presentation.
7. Make the following changes to the presentation:
    a. Increase the font size and line spacing of the bulleted text in Slides 2 through 4 so the bulleted lists are better spaced on the slides.
    b. Consider inserting an appropriate clip art image in one or two of the slides.
    c. Add a transition and sound of your choosing to each slide.
8. Save the presentation and name it Internet Presentation.

9. Run the presentation.
10. Print the presentation with all four slides on the same page.
11. Close Internet Presentation.
12. Make Word the active program and then close Word Outline 01.

Collecting and Pasting Multiple Items

As you learned in chapter 4, Office 2000 includes a new feature called *collecting and pasting* that you can use to collect up to 12 different items and then paste them in various locations. You can display the Clipboard toolbar by right-clicking an existing toolbar and then clicking *Clipboard*. Or, the Clipboard toolbar will display when you copy two consecutive items (without pasting an item). Copied data displays as an icon on the Clipboard toolbar.

To insert an item, position the insertion point in the desired location and then click the button on the Clipboard representing the item. Position the insertion point on a button and a ScreenTip displays with information about the item. If the item is text, the first 50 characters display. When all desired items are inserted, click the Clear Clipboard button to remove any remaining items.

Usually, if you copy any two items consecutively, the Clipboard toolbar automatically displays. If you close the Clipboard toolbar three times in a row without clicking a button on the toolbar, the Clipboard toolbar will no longer appear automatically. To display the Clipboard toolbar, right-click any currently displayed toolbar, and then click Clipboard. You can also click View, point to Toolbars, and then click Clipboard. When you display the Clipboard toolbar and then click a button on the toolbar, the count is reset, and from that point on the Clipboard toolbar appears automatically again.

exercise 12

Collecting Text in Word and Pasting it in a PowerPoint Slide

1. In PowerPoint, open Internet Presentation.
2. Create a new Slide 5 by completing the following steps:
    a. Display Slide 4 and then click the New Slide button on the Standard toolbar.
    b. At the New Slide dialog box, double-click the Bulleted List autolayout.
    c. Click the text *Click to add title* and then key **Internet Terminology**.
    d. Click the text *Click to add text* and then copy terms from Word and paste them into slides by completing the following steps:
       1) Open Word and then open Word Terms.
       2) Select the first term *(Information superhighway)* and its definition by triple-clicking with the mouse.
       3) With the term and definition selected, click the Copy button on the Standard toolbar.
       4) Select the second term *(TCP/IP)* and its definition and then click the Copy button. (This should display the Clipboard toolbar. If this toolbar does not display, right-click any currently displayed toolbar, and then click Clipboard.)

5) Select the third term *(ARPANet)* and its definition and then click the Copy button on the Clipboard toolbar.
6) Select the fourth term *(NSFNet)* and its definition and then click the Copy button on the Clipboard toolbar.
7) Click the button on the Taskbar representing the Internet Presentation.
8) Make sure the insertion point is positioned in the bulleted list placeholder and then click the button on the Clipboard toolbar representing the term *ARPANet*. (To find this button, use the ScreenTip.)
9) Click the button on the Clipboard representing the term *Information superhighway*.
3. Create a new Slide 6 by completing the following steps:
   a. Click the New Slide button on the Standard toolbar.
   b. At the New Slide dialog box, double-click the Bulleted List autolayout.
   c. Click the text *Click to add title* and then key **Internet Terminology**.
   d. Click the text *Click to add text* and then paste terms in the slide by completing the following steps:
      1) Make sure the insertion point is positioned in the bulleted list placeholder and then click the button on the Clipboard toolbar representing the term *NFSNet*.
      2) Click the button on the Clipboard representing the term *TCP/IP*.
4. Close the Clipboard toolbar.
5. Save the presentation again with the same name (Internet Presentation).
6. Print the six slides on one page.
7. Close Internet Presentation.
8. Make Word the active program, close Word Terms, and then exit Word.
9. Delete Internet Presentation. (Check with your instructor before deleting this presentation.)

Publishing a Presentation to the Web

Save a presentation as a Web page and PowerPoint will place a copy of the presentation in HTML format on the Web. You can run a presentation published to the Web in PowerPoint or run the presentation with Internet Explorer 4.0 or later. The same presentation can be published to different locations and you can publish the entire presentation, a single slide, or a range of slides.

To make a presentation available on the Internet, you need to contact an Internet service provider that will allocate space for the Web presentation. If you want to publish a presentation to a company intranet, you must have access to a Web server.

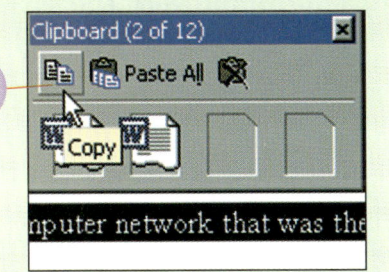

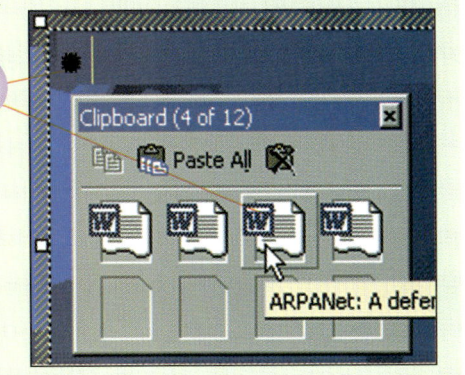

To save a presentation as a Web page, open the presentation, click File, and then click Save as Web Page. At the Save As dialog box, key the name in the File name text box. If you want to change the Web page title, click the Change Title button. At the Set Page Title dialog box, key a new title in the Page title text box, and then click OK. Click the Publish button at the Save As dialog box and the Publish as Web Page dialog box displays as shown in figure 3.13. At this dialog box, specify whether you want to publish the entire presentation or specific slides within the presentation, and specify the browser support such as Internet Explorer or Netscape Navigator. When all changes are made to the Publish as Web Page dialog box, click the Publish button.

figure 3.13 *Publish as Web Page Dialog Box*

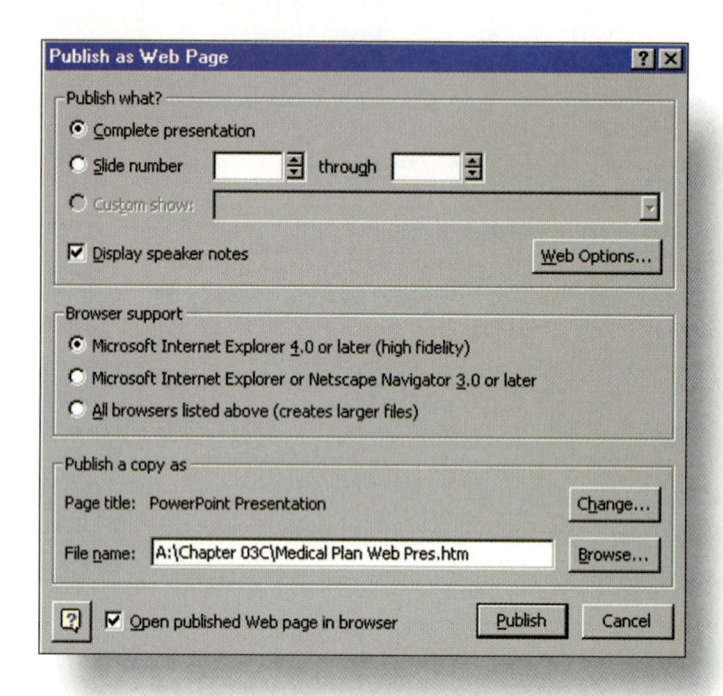

When you save a presentation as a Web page, a folder is created and Web page files are inserted in the folder. A Web page generally consists of a variety of items that are inserted in individual files. For example, each bullet image and clip art image or picture in a Web page is saved in a separate image file. Inserting all of these files into a folder makes it easier for you to take this information to another location. You can copy the contents of a Web page folder to another computer or onto a disk.

Previewing a Web Page

If you want to see how the presentation displays in your Web browser, view the presentation in Web Page Preview. To do this, open the presentation you have saved as a Web page, then click File and then click Web Page Preview. This displays the first slide in the Web browser as shown in figure 3.14. Figure 3.14 shows the Medical Plan Web Pres presentation in the Internet Explorer 5.0 Web browser. Your Web browser view may vary.

figure 3.14 Web Page Preview

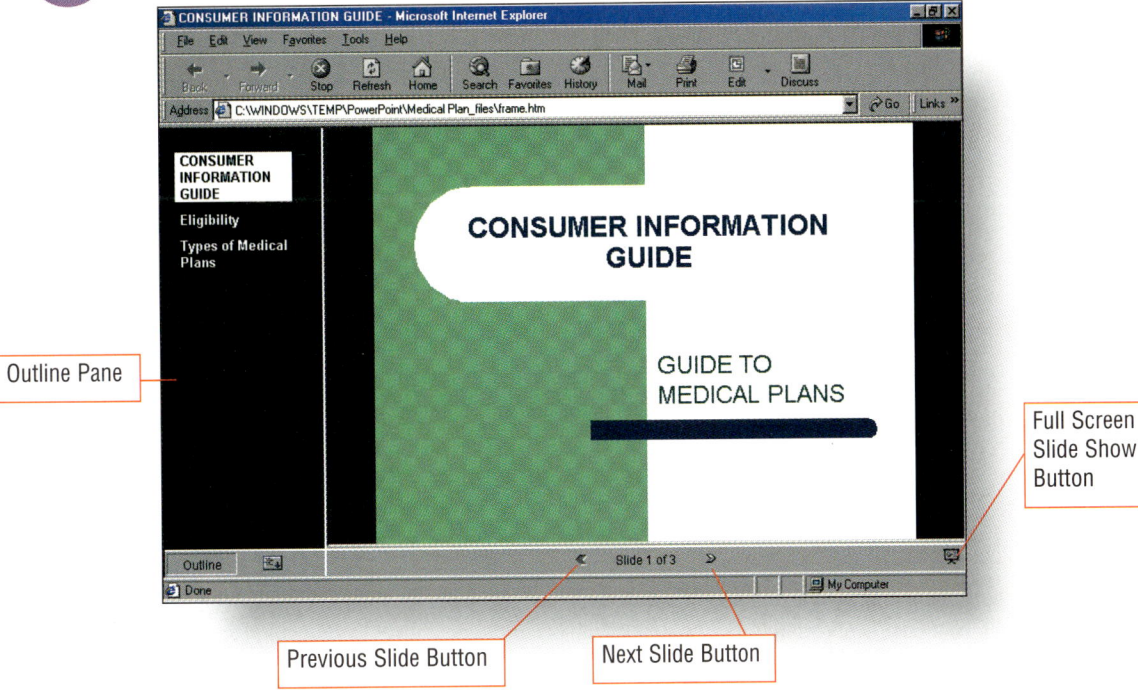

[Screenshot of Internet Explorer showing CONSUMER INFORMATION GUIDE presentation with labels: Outline Pane, Full Screen Slide Show Button, Previous Slide Button, Next Slide Button]

When you first display the presentation in Web Page Preview, you may need to click the Maximize button located in the upper right corner of the Web browser window. Scroll through the slides in the presentation by clicking the Next Slide button located towards the bottom of the browser window (see figure 3.14). Click the Previous Slide button to view the previous slide. The Outline pane displays at the left side of the browser. Move to various slides in the presentation by clicking the title of the desired slide in the Outline pane. If you want the slide to fill the entire screen, click the Full Screen Slide Show button located in the lower right corner of the browser window. Run the presentation as you would any other presentation.

exercise 13

Saving a Presentation as a Web Page and Previewing the Presentation

1. Open Presentation 1, Ch 03. (This presentation is located in the *Presentations* folder on the CD that accompanies this textbook.)
2. Save the presentation in the *Chapter 03C* folder on your disk with Save As and name it Medical Plan.
3. Save Medical Plan as a Web page by completing the following steps:
   a. Click File and Save as Web Page.
   b. At the Save As dialog box, key **Medical Plan Web Pres** in the File name text box.
   c. Click the Publish button.

Adding Animation to Presentations

d. At the Publish as Web Page dialog box, notice what browser is selected in the Browser support section, and then check with your instructor to determine if this is the proper browser.
   e. Click the Publish button.
4. Preview the presentation in your Web browser by completing the following steps:
   a. Click File and then Web Page Preview.
   b. When your presentation displays in your browser window, click the Maximize button located in the upper right corner of the browser window.
   c. Click *Eligibility* in the Outline pane. (This displays Slide 2.)
   d. Click *Types of Medical Plans* in the Outline pane. (This displays Slide 3.)
   e. Click twice on the Previous Slide button (located below the slide). (This displays Slide 1.)
   f. Run the presentation in the full screen by completing the following steps:
      1) Click the Full Screen Slide Show button located in the lower right corner of the browser window (see figure 3.14).
      2) Click the left mouse button to advance the slides.
      3) When the message *End of slide show, click to exit.* displays, click the left mouse button.
   g. Click File and then Close to close your Web browser.
5. Close the presentation.
6. Look at the folder and files created by PowerPoint for the Web presentation by completing the following steps:
   a. Display the Open dialog box with *Chapter 03C* on your disk the active folder.
   b. Double-click the *Medical Plan Web Pres_files* folder. (This was the folder created by PowerPoint.)
   c. Look at the files created by PowerPoint and then click the Up One Level button. (This returns you to the Chapter 03C folder.)
   d. Delete the Medical Plan Web Pres_files folder.
   e. Delete the Medical Plan Web Pres Web presentation document.
   f. Delete the Medical Plan presentation document.
   g. Close the Open dialog box.

Sending a Presentation via E-mail

E-mail

An individual slide within a presentation or the entire presentation can be sent via e-mail. To do this, click the E-mail button on the Standard toolbar. This displays a message asking if you want to send the entire presentation as an attachment or if you want to send the current slide as the message body. If you specify that you want to send the current slide as the message body, the E-mail header displays below the Formatting toolbar as shown in figure 3.15. At the e-mail header, key the name or e-mail address of the person who is to receive the slide, identify any people who are to receive a copy, establish a priority level, and then click the Send button.

When you send a slide as the message body, the slide is sent in HTML format. The person receiving the slide can view the slide in any e-mail program that can read e-mail messages in HTML format. The recipient does not need PowerPoint installed to view the slide.

figure 3.15 E-mail Header

E-mail Header

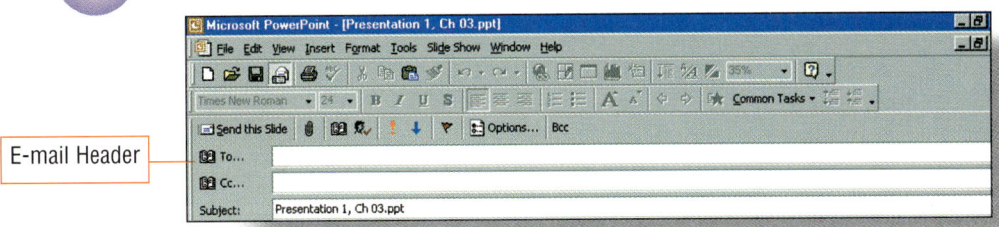

If you specify that you want to send the entire presentation as an attachment, a window displays where you can enter the name or e-mail address of the person who is to receive the attached presentation and additional information such as who is to receive copies and the priority level. To view a presentation you send as an e-mail attachment, the recipient needs to use PowerPoint.

In exercise 14, you will send a slide as an e-mail to your instructor. If your system is networked and your computer is not part of an intranet system, skip the step telling you to click the Send button.

exercise 14

Sending a Slide via E-Mail

(Note: Before completing this exercise, check to see if you can send e-mail messages. If you cannot, complete all the steps in the exercise except step 3e.)

1. Open Presentation 1, Ch 03. (This presentation is located in the *Presentations* folder on the CD that accompanies this textbook.)
2. Display Slide 2 in Normal view.
3. Send the slide as an e-mail message by completing the following steps:
   a. Click the E-mail button on the Standard toolbar.
   b. At the message asking if you want to send the entire presentation as an attachment or if you want to send the current slide as the message body, click *Send the current slide as the message body*.
   c. At the e-mail header, key your instructor's name or e-mail address in the To box.
   d. Click the Importance: High button.
   e. Click the Send this Slide button. (This step is optional.)
4. Close Presentation 1, Ch 03 without saving it.

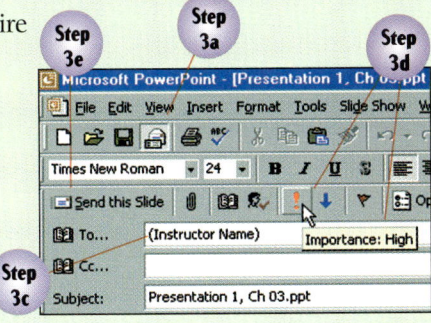

Adding Animation to Presentations

chapter summary

- Add animation effects to a slide with buttons on the Animation Effects toolbar. Display this toolbar by clicking the Animation Effects button on the Formatting toolbar. With buttons on the Animation Effects toolbar, effects can be applied to objects in slides, such as flying, camera, typewriter, laser, flash and sound effects.
- With options from the Animation Effects toolbar or a button on the Slide Sorter toolbar, important points on a slide can be presented one at a time. This is referred to as a build technique, which helps keep the audience's attention focused on the point being presented rather than reading ahead.
- Insert clip art images at the Insert ClipArt dialog box or the Microsoft Clip Gallery dialog box. A clip art image can also be inserted from another source such as a disk or folder.
- Size and scale clip art images with options at the Format Picture dialog box with the Size tab selected.
- Create a watermark in a slide using buttons on the Picture toolbar and Drawing toolbar.
- Use the Table autolayout to insert a table in a slide.
- A PowerPoint presentation can include hyperlinks that will connect to a specific Internet site while the presentation is running.
- Hyperlinks can be created that link a slide in a presentation to a document in another program. One method for linking a slide to a document in another program is to use action buttons. Action buttons are available from the AutoShapes button on the Drawing toolbar.
- Import a Word document into a PowerPoint presentation by opening the Word document, clicking File, pointing to Send To, and then clicking Microsoft PowerPoint.
- The autolayout on which a slide is based can be changed at the Slide Layout dialog box.
- Use the collecting and pasting feature to collect up to 12 different items and then paste them in various locations.
- Publish a presentation to the Web by clicking File and then Save as Web Page. At the Save As dialog box, key a name for the presentation. Click the Publish button, make any necessary changes at the Publish as Web Page dialog box, and then click the Publish button.
- When you save a presentation as a Web page, a folder is created and Web page files are inserted in the folder.
- Preview a presentation in your Web browser by clicking File and then Web Page Preview.
- An individual slide or an entire presentation can be sent via e-mail.
- Click the E-mail button on the Standard toolbar to display the e-mail header.

commands review

	Mouse/Keyboard
Display Animation Effects toolbar	Click Animation Effects button on Formatting toolbar
Display Custom Animation dialog box	Click Custom Animation button on the Animation Effects toolbar
Display Insert ClipArt dialog box	Click Insert, point to Picture, and then click Clip Art; or click the Insert Clip Art button on the Drawing toolbar; or double-click image in Text & Clip Art slide autolayout
Display the Format Picture dialog box	Click Format Picture button on Picture toolbar
Display Insert Picture dialog box	Click Insert, point to Picture, and then click From File
Display Hyperlink dialog box	Select text and click Insert Hyperlink button on Standard toolbar
Display Slide Layout dialog box	Click Common Tasks button on Formatting toolbar and then click Slide Layout; or click Format and then Slide Layout
Publish a presentation to a Web page	Click File, the Save as Web Page, key a name for the presentation, and then click Publish
Preview a Web page presentation	Click File and then Web Page Preview
Display e-mail header	Click E-mail button on Standard toolbar

thinking offline

Completion: In the space provided at the right, indicate the correct term, command, or symbol.

1. Click this button on the Animation Effects toolbar to drop a slide title from the top of the slide. — *animate title*
2. Click this button on the Animation Effects toolbar to have a selected text or object fly in from the left with a whoosh sound. — *flying effect*
3. This term refers to displaying important points on a slide one point at a time. — *build technique*
4. A build effect can be added to selected slides in the Slide Sorter view with this button on the Slide Sorter toolbar. — *slide transition effects*
5. One method for displaying the Insert ClipArt dialog box is to click the Insert Clip Art button on this toolbar. — *drawing*
6. Insert an image from a different source at this dialog box. — *insert picture*

7. Click this button on the Drawing toolbar to display a pop-up menu that contains the Action Buttons options. *AutoShapes* ~~Action Button~~

8. Insert this action button in a slide to display a document in another program when the button is clicked. *action button: document*

9. Insert this action button in a slide to display the beginning slide when the button is clicked. *action button: home*

10. Import a Word document into PowerPoint by clicking File, pointing to this option, and then clicking Microsoft PowerPoint. *Send to*

11. With the collecting and pasting feature, you can collect up to this number of items. *12*

12. To save a presentation as a Web page, open the presentation, click File, and then click this option. *Save as web page*

13. To see how a presentation saved as a Web page displays in your Web browser, view the presentation in this. *Web page preview*

Description: In exercises in this chapter, you have used three action buttons in presentations. Several other action buttons are available from the AutoShapes button on the Drawing toolbar. List at least three other action buttons (not the ones used in the exercises) that are available from the AutoShapes button and write an example of how the button could be used in a presentation.

1. First action button name: *sound*

   Example of how this button can be used in a presentation: _____

2. Second action button name: *movie*

   Example of how this button can be used in a presentation: _____

3. Third action button name: *hyperlink*

   Example of how this button can be used in a presentation: _____

Chapter Three

working hands-on

Assessment 1

1. Open Edited Trends Presentation. (You created this presentation in chapter 2, assessment 3.)
2. Save the presentation with Save As in the Chapter 03C folder on your disk and name it Animated Trends Presentation.
3. Add the following enhancements to the presentation:
    a. Display the master slide for Slide 1 and add a fill color of your choosing to the subtitle object box.
    b. Add a flying effect to the title of Slide 1.
    c. Add a flying effect to the title and subtitle of Slides 2 through 12.
4. Save the presentation again with the same name (Animated Trends Presentation).
5. Run the presentation.
6. Close Animated Trends Presentation.

Assessment 2

1. Open Benefits Presentation. (This presentation was created in chapter 2, assessment 1.)
2. Save the presentation with Save As in the Chapter 03C folder on your disk and name it Enhanced Benefits Presentation.
3. Make the following changes to the presentation:
    a. Add an animation effect to the title of slides 2 through 5 with the Animate Title button on the Animation Effects toolbar.
    b. Add a build technique to each bulleted paragraph in each slide. (Add a build technique that causes bulleted paragraphs to display one at a time and the previous bullet to dim. Also, consider adding a flying effect to the bulleted paragraphs.)
4. Save the presentation again with the same name (Enhanced Benefits Presentation).
5. Run the presentation.
6. Close Enhanced Benefits Presentation.

Assessment 3

1. Open Chart Presentation. (This presentation is located in the *Presentations* folder on the CD that accompanies this textbook.)
2. Save the presentation with Save As in the *Chapter 03C* folder on your disk and name it Animated, Linked Chart Pres.
3. Make the following changes to the presentation:
    a. Add a build technique to the bulleted paragraphs in Slides 3, 4, and 5.
    b. Add any additional animation features that will enhance the presentation.
    c. Insert the action button named Action Button: Document in Slide 2 that, when clicked, will display the Excel document named *Excel Chart Example*.
4. Save the presentation again with the same name (Animated, Linked Chart Pres).
5. Run the presentation. (Be sure to click the Action Button: Document button that displays in Slide 2. This will display the Excel document named Excel Chart Example.)
6. Print the five slides on one page.
7. Close Animated, Linked Chart Pres.

Assessment 4

1. Open PowerPoint and then open Presentation 3, Ch 03. (This presentation is located in the *Presentations* folder on the CD that accompanies this textbook.)
2. Save the presentation with Save As in the *Chapter 03C* folder on your disk and name it PowerPoint C3, SA 04.
3. Insert the following clip art images:
   a. Slide 1: Insert the image shown in figure 3.16 from the Clip Art folder on the CD that accompanies this textbook. The name of the image is *software*. Size and move the image so it displays as shown in figure 3.16.
   b. Slide 2: Insert the clip art image and recolor the image as shown in figure 3.17. (Find this image by displaying the Insert ClipArt dialog box, keying research in the Search for clips text box, and then pressing Enter.)
   c. Slide 3: Insert the clip art image and recolor the image as shown in figure 3.18. (Find this image by displaying the Insert ClipArt dialog box, keying time in the Search for clips text box, and then pressing Enter.)
4. Create a new Slide 4 as shown in figure 3.19. (Use the Table autolayout to create this slide.) Format and enter the text as shown in the figure.
5. Save the presentation again with the same name (PowerPoint C3, SA 04).
6. Print the presentation with three slides on a page. (Slides 5 and 6 will contain only a title. You will be inserting charts in these slides in assessment 5.)
7. Close PowerPoint C3, SA 04.

figure 3.16

Assessment 4, Slide 1

figure 3.17 *Assessment 4, Slide 2*

RESEARCH

- Survey of Customers
- Industry Direction
- Market Potential
- Technology Required

figure 3.18 *Assessment 4, Slide 3*

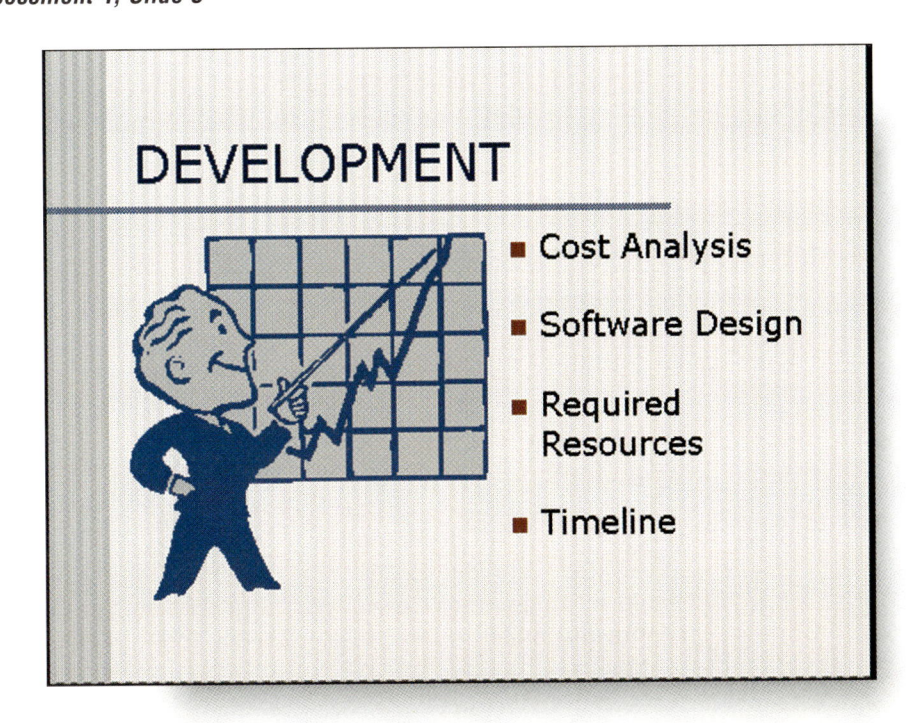

DEVELOPMENT

- Cost Analysis
- Software Design
- Required Resources
- Timeline

figure 3.19 Assessment 4, Slide 4

PROJECT TIMELINE

Task	Begin	End
Survey of Customers	February 1	April 30
Cost Analysis	March 1	March 15
Software Design	July 1	October 31

Assessment 5

1. Open Excel and PowerPoint.
2. With PowerPoint the active program, open PowerPoint C3, SA 04.
3. Copy an Excel chart into Slide 5 by completing the following steps:
   a. Display Slide 5 in Slide view.
   b. Make Excel the active program and open Excel Chart 01.
   c. Click the chart to select it.
   d. Click the Copy button on the Standard toolbar.
   e. Make PowerPoint the active program with Slide 5 displayed in Slide view.
   f. Click the Paste button on the Standard toolbar.
   g. Increase the size and move the chart so it is positioned as shown in figure 3.20.
   h. Make Excel the active program and then close Excel Chart 01 without saving the changes.
4. Copy the chart in Excel Chart 02 to Slide 6 by completing steps similar to those in step 3.
5. Make the following changes to the presentation:
   a. Add a transition to all slides in the presentation.
   b. Add an animation effect to the title of each slide with the Animate Title button on the Animation Effects toolbar.
   c. Add a build technique to each bulleted paragraph in Slide 2 and Slide 3. (Add a build technique that causes bulleted paragraphs to display one at a time and the previous bullet to dim. Also, consider adding a flying effect to the bulleted paragraphs.)

6. Run the presentation.
7. Print the presentation so three slides print on one page.
8. Save the presentation with the same name (PowerPoint C3, SA 04).
9. Close PowerPoint C3, SA 04 and exit PowerPoint.
10. With Excel the active program, close Excel Chart 02 without saving the changes and exit Excel.

figure 3.20 Assessment 5, Slide 5

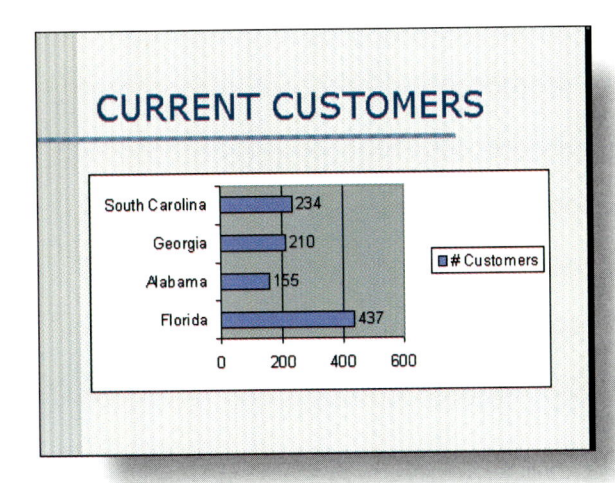

[Slide image: CURRENT CUSTOMERS bar chart showing # Customers — South Carolina 234, Georgia 210, Alabama 155, Florida 437]

Assessment 6

1. In some presentations in this chapter, you added sound effects to slide elements. You can also record a sound or comment on an individual slide and insert a CD audio track on a slide. Use PowerPoint's Help feature to learn to add sound effects and insert a CD track on a slide. Learn about any other methods for inserting sound in a presentation. Print the information you find.
2. Using the information, open Word and create a document describing what you have learned. You determine the formatting of the document.
3. Save the document and name it Word C3, SA 06.
4. Print and Close Word C3, SA 06.
5. If your computer system has a sound card and a microphone, consider adding sound to slides in a presentation.

Adding Animation to Presentations

Chapter 04C

Using WordArt and Creating Organizational Charts

PERFORMANCE OBJECTIVES

Upon successful completion of chapter 4, you will be able to:
- Enhance the visual appeal of PowerPoint presentations with text created in WordArt.
- Edit, size, move, shape, and customize WordArt.
- Draw and format objects in Word and Excel using buttons on the Drawing toolbar.
- Create an organizational chart in PowerPoint.
- Edit and customize an organizational chart.

Microsoft Office provides supplementary applications, including an application called WordArt that you can use to modify and conform text to a variety of shapes. With this application, create and add objects to a document, worksheet, or presentation. You can also use the WordArt application to create text in a variety of shapes and alignments and to add three-dimensional effects.

The MS Organization Chart 2.0 application is provided by Microsoft Office and is used to create an organizational chart. Customize an organizational chart with options at the Microsoft Organization Chart window. You will learn to create and customize organizational charts in PowerPoint in this chapter.

Using WordArt

With the WordArt application, you can distort or modify text to conform to a variety of shapes. This is useful for creating company logos and headings. With WordArt, you can change the font, style, and alignment of text. You can also use different fill patterns and colors, customize border lines, and add shadow and three-dimensional effects.

Hint: Use WordArt to create interesting text effects in a slide.

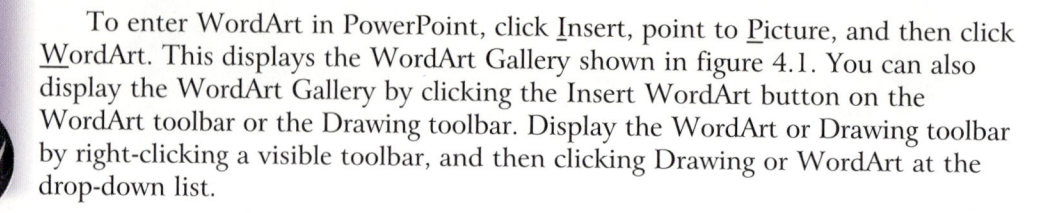

To enter WordArt in PowerPoint, click Insert, point to Picture, and then click WordArt. This displays the WordArt Gallery shown in figure 4.1. You can also display the WordArt Gallery by clicking the Insert WordArt button on the WordArt toolbar or the Drawing toolbar. Display the WordArt or Drawing toolbar by right-clicking a visible toolbar, and then clicking Drawing or WordArt at the drop-down list.

figure 4.1 WordArt Gallery

Insert WordArt

Double-click the desired WordArt option.

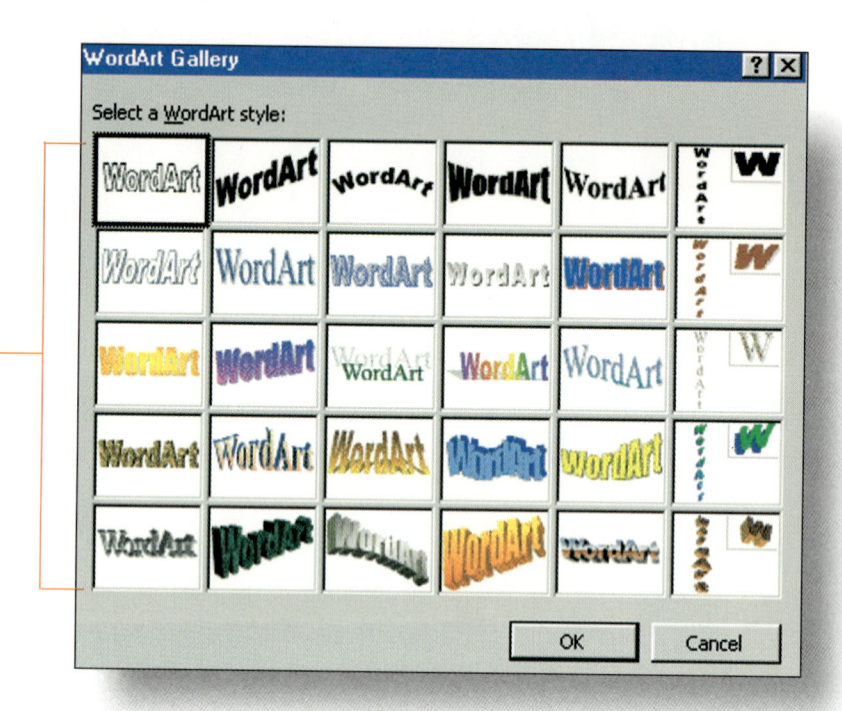

Entering Text

Hint: Exit WordArt by clicking in the slide outside the WordArt image.

Double-click a WordArt choice at the WordArt Gallery, and the Edit WordArt Text dialog box displays as shown in figure 4.2. At the Edit WordArt Text dialog box, the words *Your Text Here* are automatically selected in the Text box. Key the text in the text box and the original words are removed. Press the Enter key if you want to move the insertion point to the next line. After keying the desired text, click the OK button.

P-142 Chapter Four

figure 4.2 *Edit WordArt Text Dialog Box*

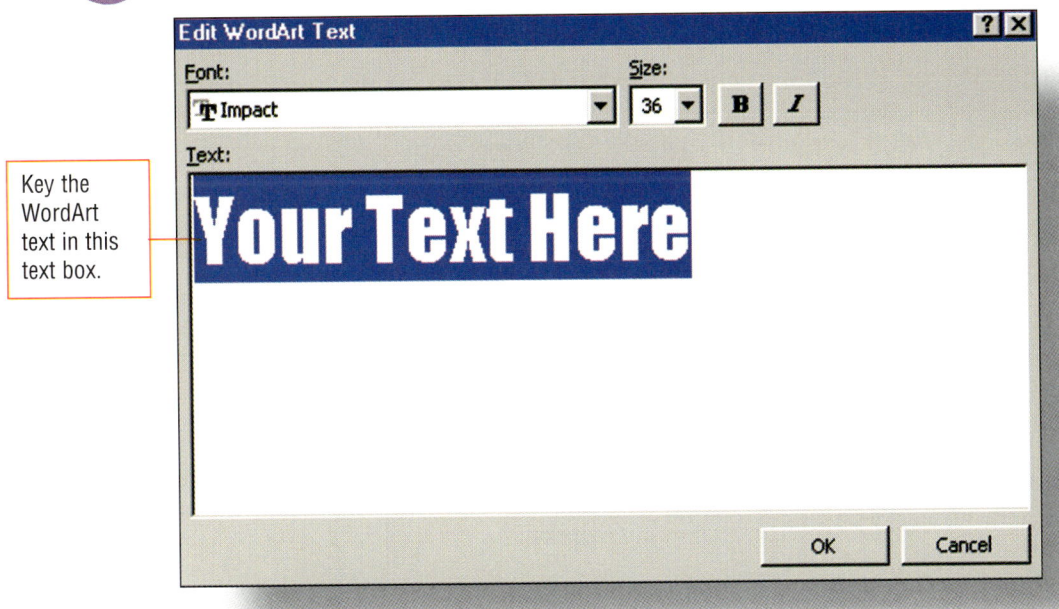

Key the WordArt text in this text box.

Sizing and Moving WordArt

WordArt text is inserted in the slide with the formatting selected at the WordArt Gallery. The WordArt text is surrounded by white sizing handles and the WordArt toolbar displays near the text. Use the white sizing handles to change the height and width of the WordArt text. Use the yellow diamond located at the bottom of the WordArt text to change the slant of the WordArt text. To do this, position the arrow pointer on the yellow diamond, hold down the left mouse button, drag to the left or right, and then release the mouse button. This moves the yellow diamond along the bottom of the WordArt and changes the slant of the WordArt text.

To move WordArt text, position the arrow pointer on any letter of the WordArt text until the arrow pointer displays with a four-headed arrow attached. Hold down the left mouse button, drag the outline of the WordArt text box to the desired position, and then release the mouse button.

When all changes have been made to the WordArt text, click outside the WordArt text box. This removes from the screen the white sizing handles, the yellow diamond, and the WordArt toolbar.

Hint: Use sizing handles to change the size of a WordArt object.

Changing the Font and Font Size

Edit a WordArt object by double-clicking the object.

The font for WordArt text will vary depending on the choice you make at the WordArt Gallery. You can change the font at the Edit WordArt Text dialog box with the Font option. To do this, click the down-pointing triangle at the right side of the Font text box. This causes a drop-down menu of font choices to display. Scroll through the list until the desired font is visible and click the desired font.

The font size can be changed by clicking the down-pointing triangle at the right side of the Size text box. This causes a drop-down menu of size options to display. Scroll through the list of sizes until the desired size is visible and click the size.

Delete a WordArt object by clicking the object to select it and then pressing the Delete key.

The Edit WordArt Text dialog box contains Bold and Italic buttons. Click the Bold button to apply bold formatting to the WordArt text and click the Italic button to apply italic formatting.

Customizing WordArt

WordArt Gallery

Edit Text

The WordArt toolbar, shown in figure 4.3, contains buttons for customizing the WordArt text. Click the Insert WordArt button and the WordArt Gallery shown in figure 4.1 displays. You can also display this gallery by clicking the WordArt Gallery button on the WordArt toolbar. Click the Edit Text button and the Edit WordArt Text dialog box displays.

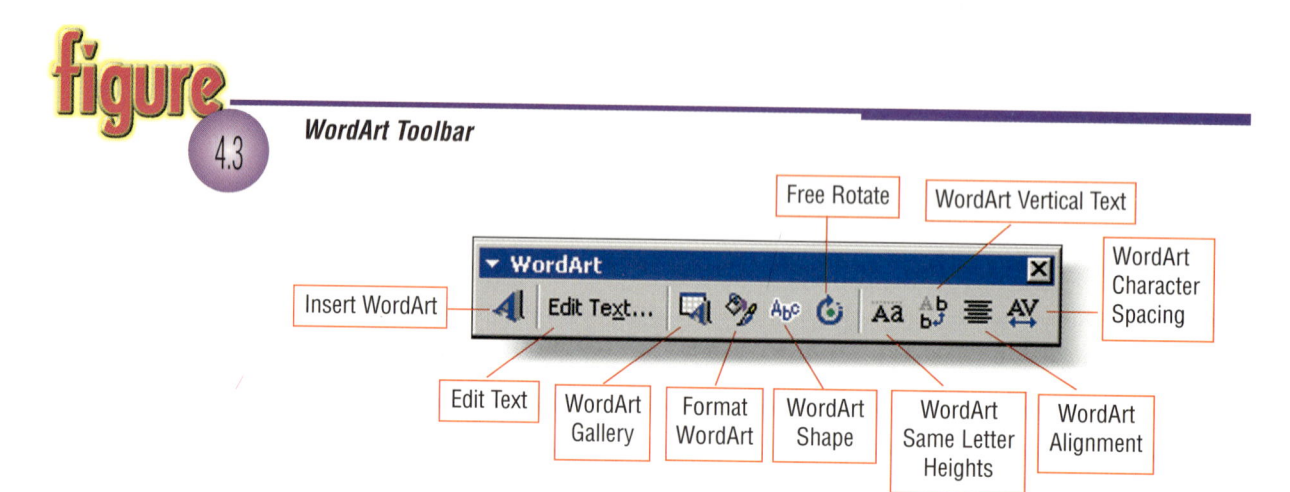

figure 4.3 WordArt Toolbar

[WordArt toolbar with labeled buttons: Insert WordArt, Edit Text, WordArt Gallery, Format WordArt, WordArt Shape, Free Rotate, WordArt Same Letter Heights, WordArt Vertical Text, WordArt Alignment, WordArt Character Spacing]

Customizing WordArt with Options at the Format WordArt Dialog Box

Format WordArt

Customize WordArt text at the Format WordArt dialog box shown in figure 4.4. To display this dialog box, click the Format WordArt button on the WordArt toolbar.

P-144 Chapter Four

figure 4.4 *Format WordArt Dialog Box with the Colors and Lines Tab Selected*

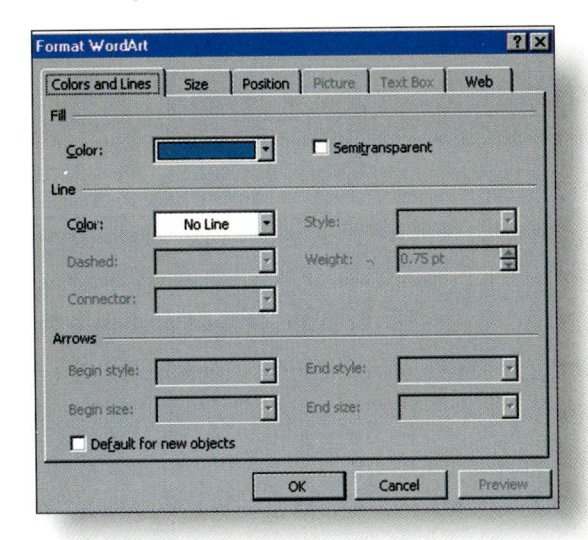

Change the color of the WordArt text and the line creating the text at the Format WordArt dialog box with the Colors and Lines tab selected. Click the Size tab and the dialog box displays options for changing the size and rotation of the WordArt text as well as the scale of the text. Specify the horizontal and vertical position of the WordArt on the slide with options in the Position tab. When all changes have been made to the Format WordArt dialog box, click the OK button. This removes the dialog box and applies the formatting to the WordArt text.

Changing Shapes

The WordArt Gallery contains a variety of predesigned WordArt options. Formatting is already applied to these gallery choices. You can, however, customize the gallery choices with buttons on the WordArt toolbar. Use options from the WordArt Shape button to customize the shape of WordArt text. Click the WordArt Shape button on the WordArt toolbar and a palette of shape choices displays as shown in figure 4.5.

figure 4.5
WordArt Shape Palette

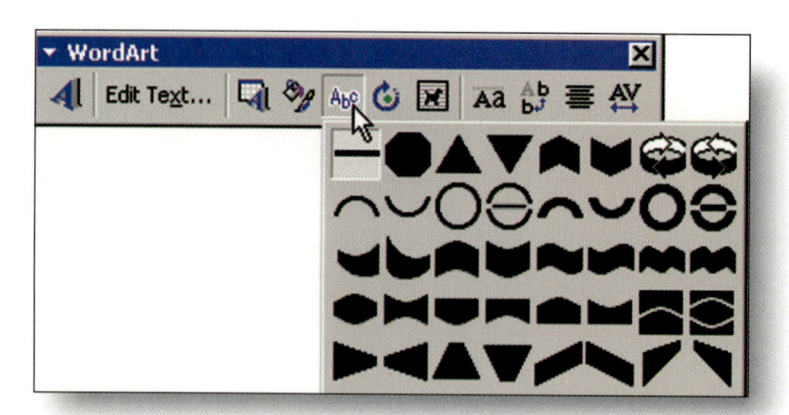

With the choices at the WordArt Shape palette, you can conform text to a variety of shapes. To select a shape, click the desired shape, and the WordArt text will conform to the selected shape. If you want to return text to the default shape, click the first shape in the first row.

(Before completing computer exercises, delete the Chapter 03C folder on your disk. Next, create the Chapter 04C folder. Instructions for deleting a folder are printed on the inside of the back cover of this textbook.)

exercise 1

Creating and Shaping WordArt Text in a PowerPoint Presentation

1. Open PowerPoint.
2. Create a new presentation by completing the following steps:
   a. At the blank PowerPoint screen, click File and New.
   b. At the New Presentation dialog box, click the Design Templates tab.
   c. Double-click *Sumi Painting* in the list box.
   d. At the New Slide dialog box, double-click the last autolayout in the third row (Blank).
   e. At the blank slide, insert text in WordArt by completing the following steps:
      1) Click the Insert, point to Picture, and then click WordArt.
      2) At the WordArt Gallery, double-click the second option from the *right* in the first row.
      3) At the Edit WordArt Text dialog box, key **Career Development**.

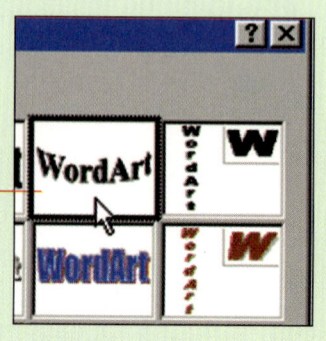

Step 2e2

Chapter Four

4) Click the OK button.
5) Change the shape of the WordArt text by completing the following steps:
    a) Click the WordArt Shape button on the WordArt toolbar.
    b) At the palette of shape choices, click the seventh shape from the left in the third row (Double Wave 1).
6) Change the size, location, and color of the WordArt text by completing the following steps:
    a) Click the Format WordArt button on the WordArt toolbar.
    b) At the Format WordArt dialog box with the Colors and Lines tab selected, click the down-pointing triangle to the right of the Color text box in the Fill section.
    c) At the color palette that displays, click the third color from the left in the top row.
    d) Click the Size tab.
    e) At the Format WordArt dialog box with the Size tab selected, select the current measurement in the Height text box, and then key **2**.
    f) Select the current measurement in the Width text box and key **7.5**.
    g) Click the Position tab.
    h) At the Format WordArt dialog box with the Position tab selected, select the current measurement in the Horizontal text box and key **1.5**.
    i) Select the current measurement in the Vertical text box and then key **3**.
    j) Click OK to close the dialog box.
7) Click outside the WordArt text (this deselects the WordArt text box).
f. Create Slide 2 by completing the following steps:
    1) Click the New Slide button.
    2) At the New Slide dialog box, double-click the first autolayout (Title Slide).
    3) Click the text *Click to add title* and key **Informational Interview**.
    4) Click the text *Click to add sub-title* and key **Step 1:**.
    5) Press Enter and key **Identify companies that you know employ workers in your career field.**

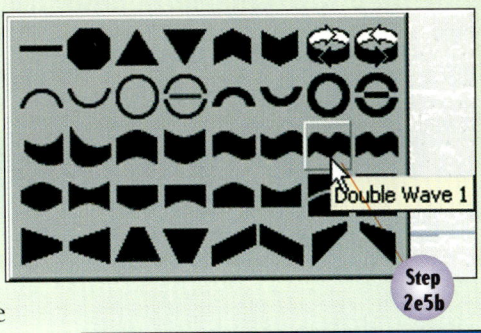

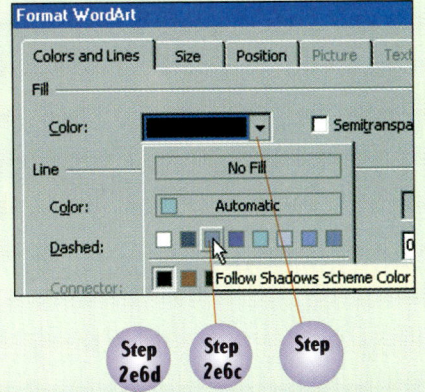

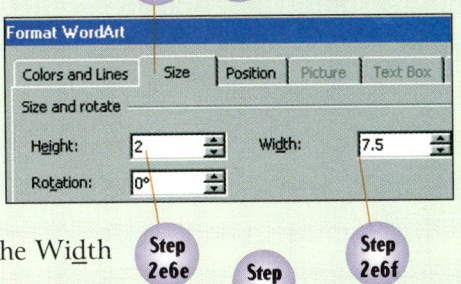

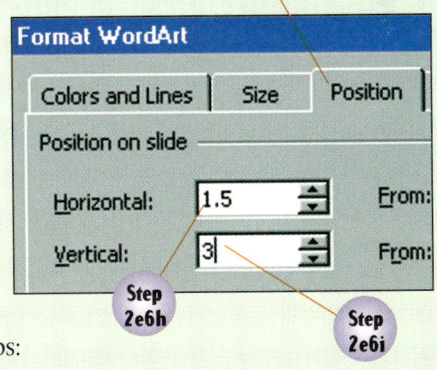

Using WordArt and Creating Organizational Charts

P-147

g. Create Slide 3 by following steps similar to those in step 2f except key the following text:

**Step 2:
Prepare a script.**

h. Create Slide 4 by following steps similar to those in step 2f except key the following text:

**Step 3:
Telephone the contact person and explain your reason for calling.**

i. Create Slide 5 by following steps similar to those in step 2f except key the following text:

**Step 4:
Arrive promptly in professional dress and greet your contact person sincerely.**

j. Create Slide 6 by following steps similar to those in step 2f except key the following text:

**Step 5:
Get down to business as soon as possible with your questions.**

k. Add a transition of your choosing to each slide.
3. Save the presentation in the Chapter 04C folder on your disk and name it PowerPoint C4, Ex 01.
4. Run the presentation.
5. Print the presentation so three slides fit on one page.
6. Close PowerPoint C4, Ex 01.

Customizing WordArt with Buttons on the Drawing Toolbar

The Drawing toolbar offers a variety of buttons with options for customizing WordArt. For example, you can change the letter color, line color, line style, add a shadow, and add a three-dimensional effect. To display the Drawing toolbar shown in figure 4.6, click View, point to Toolbars, and then click Drawing. You can also position the arrow pointer on any visible toolbar, click the *right* mouse button, and then click Drawing at the drop-down menu. Figure 4.6 identifies several buttons on the Drawing toolbar that can be used to create and then customize WordArt text.

figure 4.6

Drawing Toolbar

Fill Color | Line Color

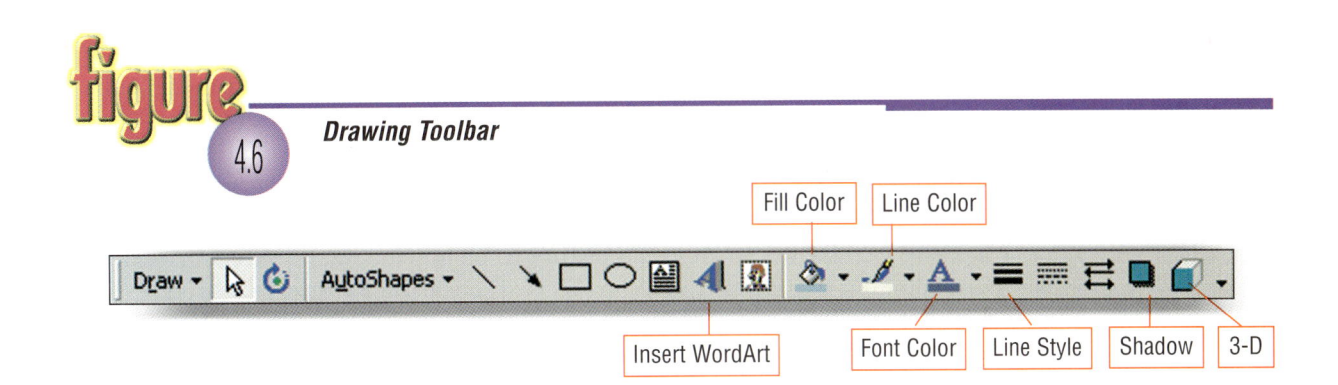

Insert WordArt | Font Color | Line Style | Shadow | 3-D

Adding Fill Shading or Color

With the Fill Color button on the Drawing toolbar, shading or color can be added to WordArt text. Click the Fill Color button and the WordArt text will be filled with the fill color displayed on the Fill Color button. If you want to choose a different color, click the down-pointing triangle at the right side of the Fill Color button. This causes a palette of color choices to display. At this palette, click the desired fill color.

Fill Color

The Fill Color palette also includes two options—More Fill Colors and Fill Effects. Click the More Fill Colors option and the Colors dialog box shown in figure 4.7 displays. At this dialog box, click the desired color in the Colors section, and then click OK.

figure 4.7

Colors Dialog Box with Standard Tab Selected

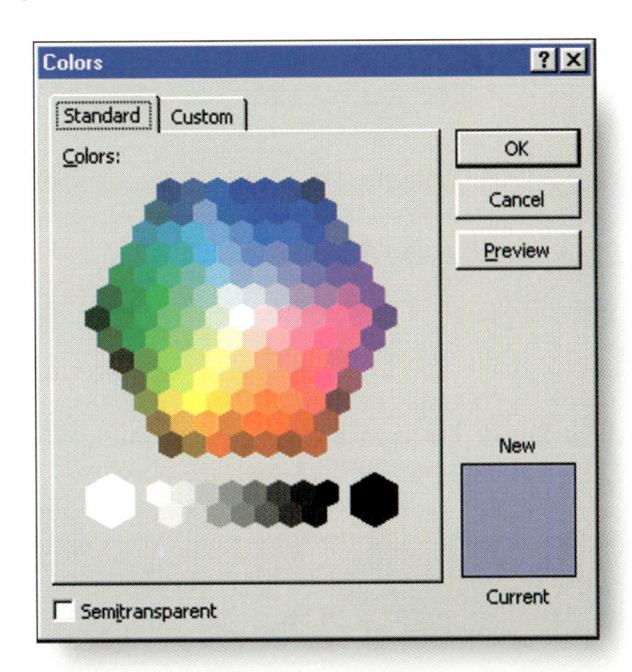

Using WordArt and Creating Organizational Charts

P-149

Click the other option at the Fill Color palette, Fill Effects, and the Fill Effects dialog box with the Gradient tab selected displays as shown in figure 4.8. At the dialog box with the Gradient tab selected, you can specify how many colors you want used in the gradient. You can also specify the style of gradient such as horizontal, vertical, diagonal, from the corner, or from the center The options at this dialog box will vary depending on the WordArt selected.

Click the Texture tab to choose a texture to be applied to the WordArt text. If you want to add a pattern to the WordArt text, click the Pattern tab. After making the desired choices at the dialog box, click OK.

figure 4.8 Fill Effects Dialog Box with Gradient Tab Selected

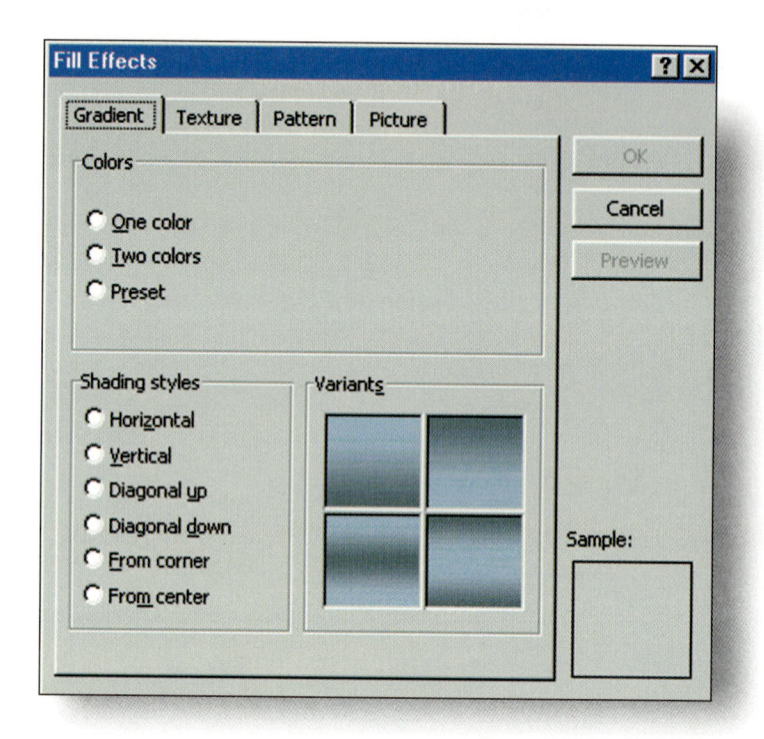

Changing Line and Font Color

Line Color

WordArt text is surrounded by a border line. The color of this line can be changed with the Line Color button on the Drawing toolbar. Click the Line Color button and the line color of the WordArt text changes to the color displayed on the button. If you want to choose a different color, click the down-pointing triangle at the right side of the Line Color button. This causes a palette of color choices to display. At this palette, click the desired color.

The Line Color palette also includes two options—More Line Colors and Patterned Lines. Click the More Line Colors option and the Colors dialog box shown in figure 4.7 displays. Click the Patterned Lines option and the Patterned Lines dialog box shown in figure 4.9 displays. Choose a pattern and a foreground and/or background color for the object at this dialog box.

figure 4.9
Patterned Lines Dialog Box

In some situations, you may want to remove the line around WordArt text. To do this, click the down-pointing triangle at the right side of the Line Color button, and then click *No Line* at the color palette.

Change the WordArt font color by clicking the Font Color button on the Drawing toolbar. At the color palette that displays, click the desired color. Click the More Colors option at the palette and the Colors dialog box displays as shown in figure 4.7.

Changing Line Style

The WordArt text line can be changed with options from the Line Style button on the Drawing toolbar. To change the line style, click the Line Style button, and then click the desired line style at the pop-up menu that displays.

Adding Shadow and 3-D Effects

Click the Shadow button on the Drawing toolbar and a palette of shadow options displays. Click the desired option or click the Shadow Settings option and a Shadow Settings toolbar displays. This toolbar contains buttons for turning shadows off or on and buttons for nudging the shadow up, down, left, or right.

If you want to add a three-dimensional look to an object, select the object, and then click the 3-D button on the Drawing toolbar. This displays a palette of three-dimensional choices as well as a 3-D Settings option. Click this option and the 3-D Settings toolbar displays. This toolbar contains buttons for turning 3-D on or off and changing the tilt, depth, direction, and light source.

Font Color

Line Style

Shadow

3-D

Using WordArt and Creating Organizational Charts P-151

exercise 2

Customize WordArt Text

1. Open PowerPoint C4, Ex 01.
2. Save the presentation with Save As and name it PowerPoint C4, Ex 02.
3. Change to Slide view and make sure the Drawing toolbar is displayed. (If it is not, click View, point to Toolbars, and then click Drawing.)
4. Change the font color and line style of the WordArt text in Slide 1 by completing the following steps:
   a. Display Slide 1 in Slide View.
   b. Position the arrow pointer on any letter of the WordArt text, *Career Development*, until the arrow pointer displays with a four-headed arrow attached, and then click the left mouse button. (This selects the WordArt text and also displays the WordArt toolbar.)
   c. Customize the WordArt text by completing the following steps:
      1) Click the down-pointing triangle at the right side of the Fill Color button on the Drawing toolbar.
      2) At the palette of color choices that displays, click the light purple color (sixth color from the left in the top row).
      3) Click the Line Style button on the Drawing toolbar.
      4) At the pop-up menu that displays, click the *3 pt* line.
      5) Click the down-pointing triangle at the right side of the Line Color button.
      6) At the pop-up menu that displays, click the second color from the left in the top row.
   d. Click outside the WordArt text box to deselect it. 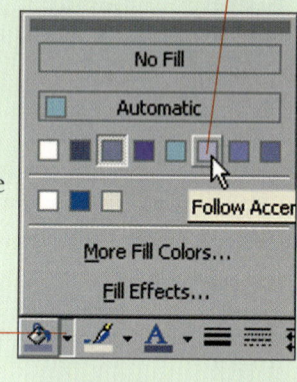 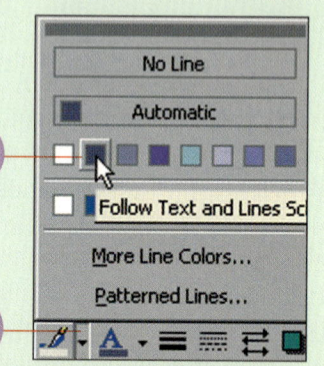
5. Change the color of the text in slides 2 through 6 by completing the following steps:
   a. Display Slide 2.
   b. Change to the Title Master View.
   c. Click anywhere in the text *Click to edit Master title style*.
   d. Click the down-pointing triangle at the right side of the Font Color button.
   e. At the pop-up menu that displays, click the More Font Colors button.
   f. At the Colors dialog box with the Standard tab selected, click a dark blue-gray color of your choosing.
   g. Click OK to close the dialog box.
   h. Click anywhere in the text *Click to edit Master subtitle style*.
   i. Click the down-pointing triangle at the right side of the Font Color button.

P-152 Chapter Four

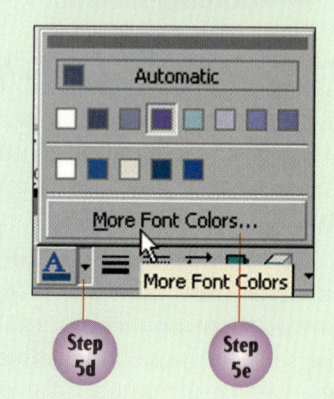

j. At the pop-up menu that displays, click the maroon color (fourth color from the left in the top row).
k. Click the Slide View button to display Slide 2.
6. Insert a new slide at the end of the presentation and create and customize a WordArt object on the slide by completing the following steps:
   a. Display slide 6 in Slide View.
   b. Click the New Slide button on the Standard toolbar and select the Blank slide autolayout.
   c. Insert text in WordArt on the new slide by completing the following steps:
      1) Click the Insert WordArt button on the Drawing toolbar.
      2) At the WordArt Gallery, double-click the second option from the right in the first row.
      3) At the Edit WordArt Text dialog box, key **Remember to thank** (press Enter) **the Contact Person**, and then click OK.
   d. Change the size of the WordArt text to 4-inches in height by 7.5-inches in width.
   e. Position the WordArt object in the center of the slide by positioning the pointer inside the WordArt object until the pointer displays with the four-headed arrow attached to it, and then drag the object to the center of the slide horizontally and vertically.
   f. Change the shape of the WordArt text object to *Chevron Up* (fifth shape from the left in the first row of the WordArt shape palette).
   g. Change the fill color, line style, and line color of the WordArt object by completing steps similar to those in 4c.
   h. Add a Shadow effect and adjust the Shadow Settings by completing the following steps:
      1) Click the Shadow button on the Drawing toolbar.
      2) Click the second button from the left in the first row of shadow styles (Shadow Style 2).
      3) Click the Shadow button and click Shadow Settings.
      4) Click the Nudge Shadow Down button five times (third button from the left in the Shadow Settings toolbar).
      5) Click the Nudge Shadow Left button three times (fourth button from the left in the Shadow Settings toolbar).
      6) Close the Shadow Settings toolbar.
7. Save the presentation again with the same name (PowerPoint C4, Ex 02).
8. Print the presentation so four slides fit on one page.
9. Close PowerPoint C4, Ex 02.

Creating an Organizational Chart

Another application provided by the Microsoft Office suite is MS Organization Chart 2.0. This application can be used in Word, Excel, or PowerPoint to create an organizational chart like the one shown in figure 4.11. You will be creating this organizational chart in exercise 3.

To create an organizational chart, display the slide you want to create it on, and then click Insert and then Object. At the Object dialog box, double-click *MS Organization Chart 2.0* in the Object type box. This displays the Microsoft Organization Chart window shown in figure 4.10.

You can also choose an autolayout containing an organizational chart icon. To display the Microsoft Organization Chart window, double-click the organizational chart icon.

figure 4.10 *Microsoft Organization Chart Window*

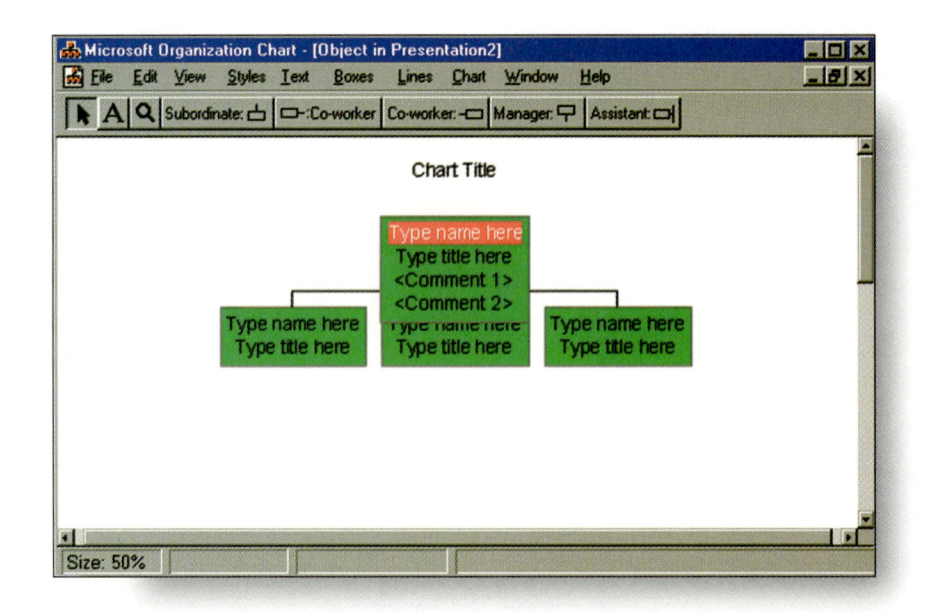

Keying Information in an Organizational Chart

At the Microsoft Organization Chart window, select *Chart Title* and then key a name for the chart. To enter information in a box, click the box, and then key the information. When you click a box, the entire box is selected. When you begin keying text, however, the text appears in the position where *Type name here* displays. Also, when you begin keying text, two additional options display at the bottom of the box: *<Comment 1>* and *<Comment 2>*. Key the text for the name and then press Enter. This selects *Type title here*. Key a title and then press Enter if you are keying more information in the box, or, click the next box. To deselect a box, click anywhere in the chart outside the box, or press the Esc key (located in the upper left corner of the keyboard).

When you click another box or close the Microsoft Organization Chart window, any options that were not chosen are removed from the box. For example, if you do not key text where *<Comment 1>* and *<Comment 2>* display in the box, they are removed from the box.

When all desired information is keyed in the chart, update the chart by clicking File and Update *(presentation name)*. Close the Microsoft Organization Chart window by clicking File and then Exit and Return to *(presentation name)*. The chart is inserted in the presentation on the active slide and the chart is also selected.

Sizing and Moving an Organizational Chart

Change the size of an organizational chart using sizing handles. To display sizing handles, select the organizational chart. If you want to move an organizational chart, position the arrow pointer on the selected organizational chart, hold down the left mouse button, drag the outline of the chart to the desired position, and then release the mouse button.

> **Hint:** Use sizing handles to change the size of an organizational chart.

exercise 3

Creating an Organizational Chart in Word

1. At the PowerPoint screen, click File, then New, and then select Blank Presentation in the General tab of the New Presentation dialog box.
2. Select the Blank slide autolayout in the New Slide dialog box and then create the organizational chart shown in figure 4.11 by completing the following steps:
   a. Click Insert and then Object.
   b. At the Insert Object dialog box, double-click *MS Organization Chart 2.0*. (You will need to scroll down the list to see this program.)

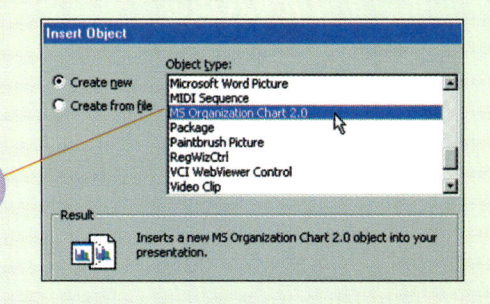

Step 2b

Using WordArt and Creating Organizational Charts

    c. At the Microsoft Organization Chart window (shown in figure 4.10), click the Maximize button that displays at the right side of the Microsoft Organization Chart title bar.
    d. Select the words *Chart Title* and key **Bethel Manufacturing**.
    e. Press Enter and key **Executive Officers**.
    f. Click the top middle box. (This selects the box.)
    g. Key **Raye Lawson**.
    h. Press Enter and key **President**.
    i. Click the box at the far left side of the next row. (This selects the box.)
    j. Key **Kenneth Erskine**.
    k. Press Enter and key **Vice President**.
    l. Press Enter and key **Financial Services**.
    m. Click the middle box. (This selects the box.)
    n. Key **Melissa Ingram-Hoyt**.
    o. Press Enter and key **Vice President**.
    p. Press Enter and key **Human Resources**.
    q. Click the box at the right side. (This selects the box.)
    r. Key **Dale Stein**.
    s. Press Enter and key **Vice President**.
    t. Press Enter and key **Plant Operations**.
3. Update the chart by clicking <u>F</u>ile and <u>U</u>pdate Presentation3 (your presentation number may vary).
4. Close the Microsoft Organization Chart window by clicking <u>F</u>ile and then E<u>x</u>it and Return to Presentation (your presentation number may vary).
5. Increase the width and height of the chart and move the chart by completing the following steps:
    a. With the chart selected, position the arrow pointer on the middle sizing handle at the right side until it turns into a double-headed arrow pointing left and right.
    b. Hold down the left mouse button, drag the outline to the right approximately 2 inches and then release the mouse button.
    c. Position the arrow pointer on the middle sizing handle at the bottom of the chart until it turns into a double-headed arrow pointing up and down.
    d. Hold down the left mouse button, drag down the outline approximately 1 inch and release the mouse button.
    e. With the chart still selected, drag the chart to the middle of the slide.
6. Save the organizational chart in the Chapter 04C folder on your disk and name it PowerPoint C4, Ex 03.
7. Print and close PowerPoint C4, Ex 03.

figure 4.11 Exercise 3

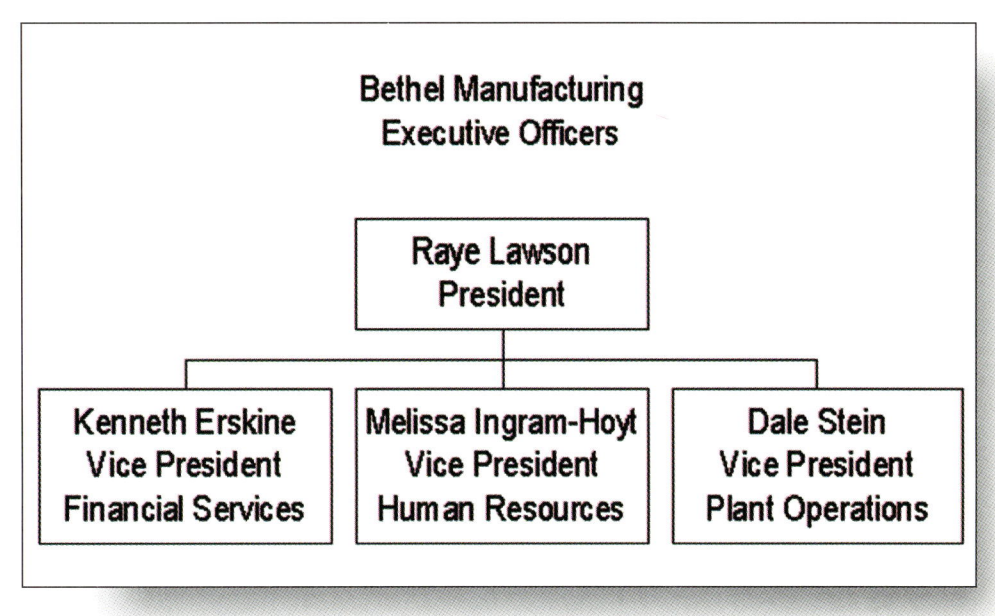

```
                    Bethel Manufacturing
                     Executive Officers

                         Raye Lawson
                          President

        ┌────────────────────┼────────────────────┐
   Kenneth Erskine      Melissa Ingram-Hoyt      Dale Stein
   Vice President         Vice President       Vice President
  Financial Services     Human Resources      Plant Operations
```

Editing an Existing Organizational Chart

Editing an existing organizational chart is similar to editing other Microsoft features. To edit an existing chart, position the arrow pointer anywhere in the chart, and then double-click the left mouse button. This displays the chart in the Microsoft Organization Chart window.

To edit an organizational chart, double-click the chart.

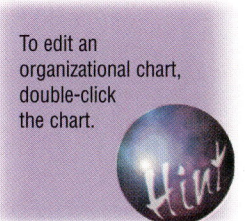

Adding Boxes to an Organizational Chart

The Microsoft Organization Chart window displays with a toolbar below the menu bar. Buttons on this toolbar can be used to add boxes to an organizational chart. For example, to add a box for an assistant director below a director's box, you would click the Subordinate button on the toolbar, click the director's box (this adds the new box and selects the box), and then key the information. The buttons on the toolbar contain an icon of the box that helps illustrate where the box will appear in the organizational chart. For example, if you want to add a box above another box, click the Manager button on the toolbar.

A box can be removed from a chart with the Clear option from the Edit drop-down menu. To remove a box, click the box, click Edit, and then click Clear.

exercise 4

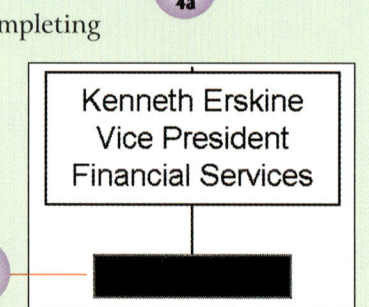

Adding Boxes to an Organizational Chart

1. Open PowerPoint C4, Ex 03.
2. Save the presentation with Save As and name it PowerPoint, C4, Ex 04.
3. Add a box above the President box by completing the following steps:
   a. Double-click the organizational chart. (This displays the chart in the Microsoft Organization Chart window. If necessary, maximize the organizational chart window.)
   b. Click the Manager button on the toolbar.
   c. Click the President box (contains the name *Raye Lawson*). (This inserts a box above the President box and also selects the new box.)
   d. Key **Aubrey Knowles** in the new box that displays above the President box.
   e. Press Enter and key **Chief Executive Officer**.
4. Add a box below the box for Kenneth Erskine by completing the following steps:
   a. Click the Subordinate button on the toolbar.
   b. Click the box containing the name *Kenneth Erskine*.
   c. Key **William Keeley** in the new box that displays below the box for Kenneth Erskine.
   d. Press Enter and then key **Director**.
   e. Press Enter and then key **Financial Services**.
5. Add a box below the box for Melissa Ingram-Hoyt by completing steps similar to those in step 4. Key the following information in the new box:
   > **Dean Howell**
   > **Director**
   > **Human Resources**
6. Add a box below the box for Dale Stein by completing steps similar to those in step 4. Key the following information in the new box:
   > **Jennifer Fleming**
   > **Director**
   > **Plant Operations**
7. Update the chart by clicking File and Update PowerPoint C4, Ex 04.
8. Close the organizational chart by clicking File, Exit and Return to PowerPoint C4, Ex 04.
9. Save the presentation again with the same name PowerPoint C4, Ex 04.
10. Print and close PowerPoint C4, Ex 04.

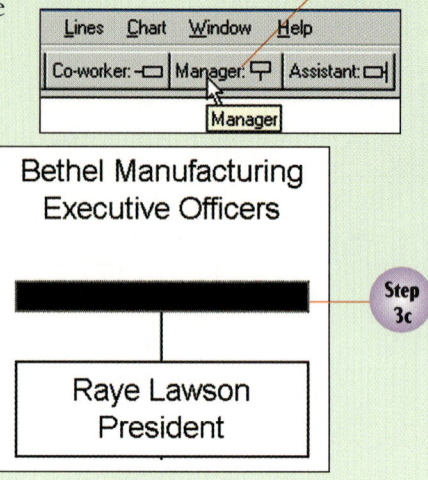

Customizing an Organizational Chart

With options on the Organizational Chart menu bar, you can customize a chart. Customizing can include adding color to a box or the chart background, changing the font of text in a box, changing the border of a box, adding a shadow to a box, and changing the alignment of text in a box.

Click the Text option on the Organizational Chart menu bar and a drop-down menu displays with the following options: Font, Color, Left, Right, and Center. Click the Font option and the Font dialog box displays where you can change the font, the font style, and the font size. Use the Color option if you want to change the text color in a box. The default alignment of text in a box is Center. This can be changed to Left or Right at the Text drop-down menu.

Click the Boxes option on the Organizational Chart menu bar and a drop-down menu displays with the following options: Color, Shadow, Border Style, Border Color, and Border Line Style. Choose the Color option to change the color of the box. Add a shadow to the box with the Shadow option. With the last three options at the Boxes drop-down menu, you can change the border style, border color, and border line style of a box.

With the options from the Lines drop-down menu, you can change the line thickness, style, and color of a line that connects boxes. To use the Lines options, you must first select the line connecting boxes that you want to change. To do this, position the arrow pointer on the desired line, and then click the left mouse button. This will change the display of the line to a dotted line.

Use the Chart option on the Microsoft Organization Chart menu bar to change the background color of the entire chart.

If you want to customize more than one box at a time, you can select multiple boxes. To do this, hold down the Shift key while clicking the desired boxes. If you want to select all boxes in an organizational chart, press Ctrl + A. If you select all boxes, the lines connecting the boxes are also selected.

Changing the View in an Organizational Chart

When the Microsoft Organization Chart window is open, the default display is the actual size of the chart. This can be changed with options at the View drop-down menu. The View drop-down menu contains the following options: Size to Window, 50% of Actual, Actual Size, 200% of Actual, and Show Draw Tools. With the first four options, you can specify how much of the chart you want displayed. If you click the last option, Show Draw Tools, four buttons display at the right side of the Microsoft Organization Chart toolbar. With these buttons, you can draw horizontal and vertical lines, diagonal lines, auxiliary lines, and rectangles.

exercise 5

Creating Organizational Charts using an Autolayout

1. Open Presentation 1, Ch 04. (This presentation is located in the *Presentations* folder on the CD that accompanies this text.)
2. Save the presentation with Save As in the Chapter 04C folder on your disk and name it PowerPoint C4, Ex 05.
3. Create an organizational chart in Slide 5 by completing the following steps:
    a. Display Slide 5 in Slide view.
    b. Double-click the organizational chart icon.
    c. At the Microsoft Organization Chart window, click the Manager button on the toolbar.

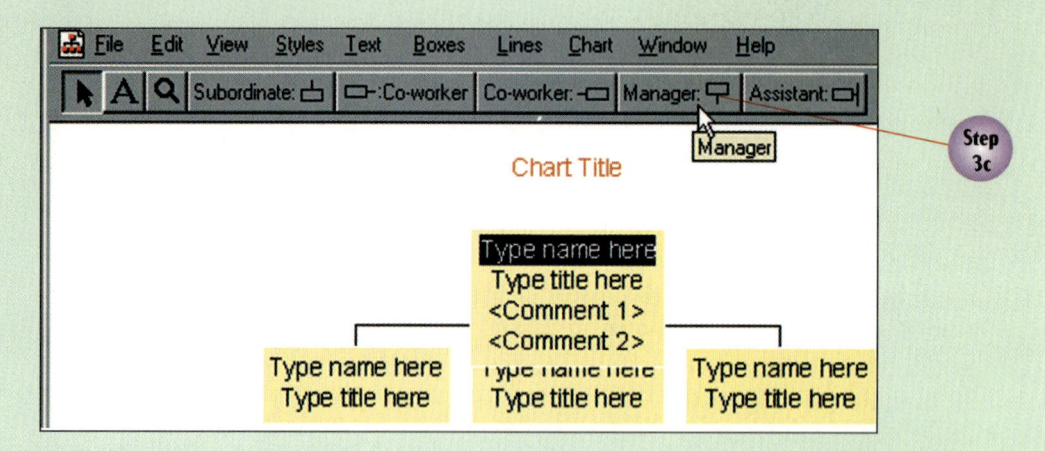

    Step 3c

    d. Click the first box in the chart. (This adds a new box above the original first box.)
    e. Key **Michael Cruz**, press Enter, and then key **President**.
    f. Click the box immediately below the Michael Cruz box. (You may need to first click outside the box to make the second box visible.)
    g. Key **Cassandra Dodd**, press Enter, and then key **Vice President**.
    h. Click the box at the left side of the chart.
    i. Key **Harley Gleason**, press Enter, and then key **Director**. Press Enter again and key **Production**.
    j. Click the box immediately to the right of the Harley Gleason box.
    k. Key **Bonnie Cavali**, press Enter, and then key **Director**. Press Enter again and key **Personnel**.
    l. Click the box immediately to the right of the Bonnie Cavali box.
    m. Key **Teddy Arneson**, press Enter, and key **Director**. Press Enter again and key **Finances**.
    n. Click File and Update PowerPoint C4, Ex 05.
    o. Click File and Exit and Return to PowerPoint C4, Ex 05.
4. Save the presentation again with the same name (PowerPoint C4, Ex 05).
5. Print all five slides on one page.
6. Close PowerPoint C4, Ex 05.

exercise 6

Customizing Organizational Charts in a PowerPoint Presentation

1. Open PowerPoint C4, Ex 05.
2. Save the presentation with Save As and name it PowerPoint C4, Ex 06.
3. Make the following changes to the presentation:
   a. Display Slide 3 in Slide View.
   b. Change the box color and text font of the organizational chart by completing the following steps:
      1) Double-click the chart. (This displays the Microsoft Organization Chart window.)
      2) Press Ctrl + A to select all boxes in the organizational chart.
      3) Click Boxes and Color.
      4) At the Color dialog box, click the gold color (fifth from the left in the top row).
      5) Click OK to close the Color dialog box.
      6) With the boxes still selected, click Text and Font.
      7) At the Font dialog box, click Times New Roman in the Font list box (you will need to scroll down the list), and click Bold in the Font style list box.
      8) Click OK to close the Font dialog box.
      9) Click File and Update PowerPoint C4, Ex 06.
      10) Click File, Exit and Return to PowerPoint C4, Ex 06. 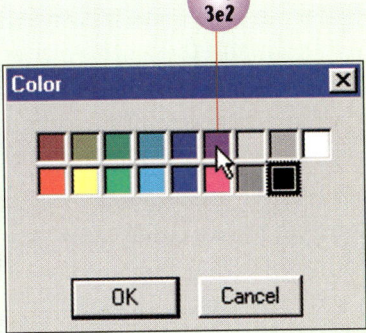
   c. Display Slide 4 and make the changes described in step 3b.
   d. Display Slide 5 and make the changes described in step 3b.
   e. Add a transition of your choosing to each slide.
4. Run the presentation.
5. Save the presentation again with the same name (PowerPoint C4, Ex 06).
6. Print all five slides on one page.
7. Close PowerPoint C4, Ex 06.

chapter summary

- With the WordArt application, you can distort or modify text to conform to a variety of shapes. With WordArt, you can change the font, size, and alignment of text. You can also add fill color, line color, change the line style, and add shadow and three-dimensional effects.
- Display the WordArt Gallery by clicking Insert, pointing to Picture, and then clicking WordArt or clicking the Insert WordArt button on the Drawing toolbar.
- Select an option at the WordArt Gallery by double-clicking the desired option.
- After an option at the WordArt Gallery is selected, the Edit WordArt Text dialog box displays.

- Use the white sizing handles around WordArt text to change the size.
- Move WordArt text by positioning the arrow pointer on any letter until it displays with a four-headed arrow, hold down the left mouse button, move the outline of the WordArt box to the desired position, and then release the mouse button.
- Specify a font and font size for WordArt at the Edit WordArt Text dialog box.
- Customize WordArt text with buttons on the WordArt toolbar.
- Create and customize WordArt with buttons on the Drawing toolbar.
- Draw and format objects in Word and Excel using buttons on the Drawing toolbar.
- Use the Microsoft Organization Chart 2.0 application to create an organizational chart in Word, Excel, or PowerPoint.
- One method for displaying the Microsoft Organization Chart window is to click Insert, Object, and then double-click *MS Organization Chart 2.0*. You can also enter the chart window by choosing an autolayout containing an organizational chart icon.
- Change the size of an organizational chart by selecting the chart and using the sizing handles that display around the chart.
- To move an organizational chart, select the chart, and then drag it with the mouse.
- To edit an existing organizational chart, double-click the chart. (This displays the chart in the Microsoft Organization Chart window.)
- Use buttons on the Organizational Chart toolbar to add boxes to an organizational chart.
- Remove a box from an organizational chart by selecting the box, clicking Edit, and then clicking Clear.
- Customize an organizational chart with options on the Organization Chart menu bar. Customizing can include adding color to boxes or the chart background, changing the font of the text in a box, changing the box border, adding shadow, and changing the alignment of text within a box.
- To customize more than one box at a time, hold down the Shift key and click the desired boxes. To customize all boxes in a chart at the same time, select all boxes by pressing Ctrl + A.
- An organizational chart is displayed in actual size in the Microsoft Organization Chart window. This can be changed with options at the View drop-down menu.

commands review

	Mouse/Keyboard
WordArt Gallery	Click Insert, point to Picture, and then click WordArt; or click the Insert WordArt button on the Drawing toolbar
Format WordArt dialog box	Click the Format WordArt button on WordArt toolbar
WordArt shape palette	Click the WordArt Shape button on WordArt toolbar
Drawing toolbar	Click View, point to Toolbars, and then click Drawing; or position arrow pointer on toolbar, click *right* mouse button, and click Drawing

Colors dialog box	Click down-pointing triangle at right side of Fill Color button and click More Fill Colors
Fill Effects dialog box	Click down-pointing triangle at right side of Fill Color button and click Fill Effects
Patterned Lines dialog box	Click down-pointing triangle at right side of Line Color button and click Patterned Lines
Microsoft Organization Chart 2.0	Click Insert, Object, and then double-click MS Organization Chart 2.0, or on a slide, double-click organizational chart icon
Edit organizational chart	Double-click organizational chart

thinking offline

Completion: In the space provided at the right, indicate the correct term, command, or number.

1. Click Insert, point to Picture, and then click WordArt and this displays on the screen. — *word art gallery*
2. Key WordArt text at this dialog box. — *edit wordart text*
3. Click this button on the WordArt toolbar to display a palette of shape options. — *word art shape*
4. Click this button on the Drawing toolbar to change the color of WordArt text. — *fill color*
5. Double-click this option in the Object dialog box to display the Microsoft Organization Chart window. — *organization chart 2.0*
6. To select more than one box in the Microsoft Organization Chart window, hold down this key while clicking the desired boxes. — *shift*
7. Press these keys to select all boxes in the Microsoft Organization Chart window. — *ctrl + A*
8. To delete a box from an organizational chart, select the box, click Edit, and then click this option. — *clear*
9. To add a box below another box in an organizational chart, click this button on the Organizational Chart toolbar. — *subordinate*
10. Click this button on the Organizational Chart toolbar to add a box above an existing box. — *manager*
11. Use this option on the Organization Chart menu bar to change the background color of the entire chart. — *boxes/chart*

12. In the space provided below, list the steps you would complete to change the text color to red and add a shadow to existing WordArt text.

___

___

___

13. In the space provided below, list the steps you would complete to change the color of all boxes in an existing organizational chart to blue and change the background color to gray.

___

___

___

working hands-on

Assessment 1

1. Open Presentation 1, Ch 04. (This presentation is located in the Presentations folder on the CD that accompanies this textbook.)
2. Save the presentation with Save As in the Chapter 04C folder on your disk and name it PowerPoint C4, SA 01.
3. Display slide 1 in Slide View.
4. Select the title placeholder and delete it. To do this, position the mouse pointer anywhere over the title text and click the left mouse button. Position the pointer along the border of the selected placeholder and click the left mouse button again (this removes the insertion point from within the placeholder). Press Delete.
5. Select the subtitle placeholder and delete it.
6. Change the autolayout for slide 1 by completing the following steps:
    a. Click Format, and click Slide Layout.
    b. At the Slide Layout dialog box, double-click the Blank side autolayout.
7. Create the title **International Securities** as a WordArt text object as shown in figure 4.12 with the following specifications:
    a. Select the first option in the fourth row at the WordArt Gallery.
    b. Change the font to Times New Roman.
    c. Change the shape to Deflate (second option from the left in the fourth row of shapes at the WordArt Shape palette).
    d. Set the height to 2 inches and the width to 7.5 inches.
    e. Set the horizontal position to 1.25 inches and the vertical position to 2 inches.
8. Create the subtitle **Corporate Restructuring** as a WordArt text object as shown in figure 4.12 with the following specifications:
    a. Select the third option from the left in the first row at the WordArt Gallery.
    b. Change the font to Tahoma.

c. Change the shape to Plain Text (first option from the left in the first row of shapes at the WordArt Shape palette).
   d. Change the fill color to orange (fourth color from the left at the fill color palette).
   e. Change the line style to ⁄ point.
   f. Size and position the WordArt text object as shown in figure 4.12.
9. Save the revised presentation with the same name (PowerPoint C4, SA 01).
10. Print Slide 1 only.
11. Close PowerPoint C4, SA 01.

figure 4.12 *Assessment 1*

Assessment 2

1. Create an organizational chart at a new presentation screen, with the title Production Department, and then key the following information in the organizational chart boxes in the order displayed: *(Hint: To remove the third box provided by Microsoft Organization Chart, select the unneeded box, and then click Edit and Clear.)*

   Harley Gleason
   Director

   Jenna Steiner
   Assistant Director

   Robert Lyons   **Cheri Koesel**
   Plant Manager   **Production Manager**

2. Make the following changes to the organizational chart:
   a. Add color to all boxes in the chart. (You determine the color.)
   b. Change the font of the text in the boxes. (You determine the font.)
   c. Add a background color to the chart. (You determine the color.)
3. After creating the organizational chart, select and move the chart to the middle of the slide.
4. Save the organizational chart and name it PowerPoint C4, SA 02.
5. Print and then close PowerPoint C4, SA 02.

Assessment 3

1. Open Presentation 2, Ch 04. (This presentation is located in the *Presentations* folder on the CD that accompanies this textbook.)
2. Save the presentation with Save As in the *Chapter 04C* folder on your disk and name it PowerPoint C4, SA 03.
3. Display Slide 1 in Slide view and then use WordArt to create a title with the following specifications:
   a. At the WordArt Gallery, choose the fourth option from the left in the third row.
   b. At the Edit WordArt Text dialog box, key **RAINBOW ARTWORKS**.
   c. Change the shape of the WordArt text to Arch Up (Pour) (fifth option from the left in the second row).
   d. Display the Format WordArt dialog box with the Size tab selected and change the Height to *8* and the Width to *8*.
   e. Display the Format WordArt dialog box with the Position tab selected and change the Horizontal option to *1* and the Vertical option to *2.4*.
4. Create a new Slide 5 with the following specifications:
   a. Choose the third autolayout from the left in the second row (Organization Chart) at the New Slide dialog box.
   b. Key the title **AGENCY STRUCTURE** and create an organizational chart with the following information:

   Monica Chun
   Director

   Liam Randall
   Assistant Director

   Josephine Piper   **Leska Winters**   **Rudy Serosky**
   Artistic Designer   **Program Coordinator**   **Education Director**

   c. Center the organizational chart on the slide.
   d. Add transitions of your choosing to the slides.
5. Save the presentation using the same name (PowerPoint C4, SA 03).
6. Run the presentation.
7. Print the five slides on one page.
8. Close PowerPoint C4, SA 03.

Chapter Four

Assessment 4

1. Open PowerPoint C4, SA 03.
2. Make the following changes to the organizational chart in Slide 5:
   a. Change the color of all boxes in the organizational chart to gold.
   b. Change the font of the text in the boxes to Tahoma bold.
3. Save the presentation with the same name (PowerPoint C4, SA 03).
4. Print all five slides on one page.
5. Close PowerPoint C4, SA 03.

Assessment 5

1. Open PowerPoint C4, SA 02.
2. Use the Help feature in Microsoft Organization Chart 2.0 to learn about chart styles by completing the following steps:
   a. Double-click the organizational chart. (This displays the chart in the Microsoft Organization Chart window.)
   b. Click Help on the Microsoft Organization Chart menu bar.
   c. At the drop-down menu, click Index.
   d. At the Microsoft Organization Chart Help dialog box, click *Menu commands and icons*.
   e. At the next help screen, click *Styles menu*.
   f. At the next help screen, read and then print the information.
   g. Click *Rearranging boxes*.
   h. At the next help screen, read and then print the information.
   i. Exit Help.
3. Make the following changes to the organizational chart:
   a. Click one of the Co-worker buttons on the Organization Chart toolbar.
   b. Click the box containing the name Robert Lyons.
   c. Key **Sondra Jamison** in the new box.
   d. Press Enter and key **Quality Control Manager**.
   e. Click the Co-worker button on the Organization Chart toolbar.
   f. Click the box containing the name Cheri Koesel.
   g. Key **Lloyd Harris** in the new box.
   h. Press Enter and key **Materials Manager**.
4. Change the organizational style of the bottom four boxes by completing the following steps:
   a. Select the bottom four boxes in the organizational chart. (To do this, hold down the Shift key while clicking each of the four boxes.)
   b. Click Styles.
   c. At the drop-down menu that displays, click the last group in the first row.
5. Update the organizational chart and then exit and return to the presentation.
6. Save the presentation again with the same name (PowerPoint C4, SA 02).
7. Print and close PowerPoint C4, SA 02.

Chapter 05C

Linking and Embedding Objects and Replacing Fonts

PERFORMANCE OBJECTIVES

Upon successful completion of chapter 5, you will be able to:
- Link an Excel chart to a presentation.
- Edit a linked object.
- Embed an Excel worksheet in a presentation.
- Embed and edit a Word table in a presentation.
- Replace fonts in a presentation.
- Create a new presentation from existing slides.

Microsoft Office is a suite that allows integration, which is the combining of data from two or more programs into one document. Integration can occur by copying and pasting data between programs. Copying and pasting information between programs is fairly easy but it has some drawbacks. For example, if you continually update an Excel worksheet that you had copied to a PowerPoint presentation, you would need to copy and paste the edited worksheet each time a change is made. This is because the changes you make to the Excel worksheet are not reflected in the presentation. If you are copying and pasting an object between programs, you need to remember the program in which you created the object. To edit the object, you would need to open the original program or application.

Microsoft Office offers two options for overcoming the drawbacks of copying and pasting. With the programs in Microsoft Office, you can create something in one program and then share it with another program. For example, you can create a worksheet in Excel and then share it with a PowerPoint presentation. This type of sharing is referred to as object linking and embedding (OLE—pronounced oh-LAY).

An object created in one program can be linked or embedded in another program. The program containing the object is called the *source* and the program the object is linked to or embedded in is called the *destination*. An object can be a table, workbook, chart, picture, text, or any other type of information you create.

There is a difference between linking and embedding. When an object is linked, the object exists in the source program but not as a separate object in the destination program. The destination program contains only a code that identifies the name and location of the source program, file, and the location in the file.

When an object is embedded, it resides in both the source and the destination programs. The difference between embedding and just copying and pasting an object from one program to another is that embedding an object makes the source application tools available for editing. Embedding causes an OLE code to be inserted in the file that points to the source application. If a change is made to an embedded file at either the source program or the destination program, the change is not reflected in the other program. For example, if you make a change to a worksheet in Excel and that worksheet is embedded in a PowerPoint presentation, the worksheet in the PowerPoint presentation is not changed. However, if you edit the worksheet that is embedded in the PowerPoint presentation, the Excel tools will be available for editing.

The size of a file in the destination program containing a linked object does not increase. This is because the object does not reside in the file in the destination program. An embedded object in a file in the destination program will increase the file size. This is because the embedded object becomes a part of the file in the destination program.

Deciding whether to link or embed an object depends on how the information in the object is to be used. For example, if you want to insert an Excel worksheet into a PowerPoint presentation that contains information you do not need to update, consider embedding or simply copying the worksheet into the PowerPoint presentation. If the object you are copying will be continually updated and you want the updates to appear in the destination program, then link the object.

> **Hint:** Linking provides a more direct connection between data in two programs than embedding.

> **Hint:** Linking does not increase the size of the document in the destination program.

Linking Objects

As mentioned earlier, when an object is linked, there is only the one object, so changes made to the object will be reflected in the source as well as the destination program. By default, Microsoft Office updates a link automatically. This means that a link is updated whenever you open the destination program or you edit the linked object in the destination program. The steps to link an object between programs are basically the same regardless of the program or application. For example, to link an Excel worksheet to a PowerPoint presentation, you would follow these basic steps:

> **Hint:** Linking is one way of attaching data from one document to another.

1. Make sure both PowerPoint presentation and Excel are open.
2. With Excel the active program, open the workbook containing the worksheet you want to link to the PowerPoint presentation.
3. Select the cells in the worksheet you want to link to PowerPoint.
4. Click the Copy button on the Standard toolbar, or click Edit and then Copy.
5. Make PowerPoint the active program. (To do this, click the button on the Taskbar representing PowerPoint.)
6. Open the PowerPoint presentation where you want to insert the worksheet cells.

Chapter Five

7. Move the insertion point to the slide where you want the worksheet cells inserted.
8. Click Edit and then Paste Special and the Paste Special dialog box displays as shown in figure 5.1.
9. At the Paste Special dialog box, choose the necessary object in the As list box, and then click Paste link.
10. Click OK to close the dialog box.

figure 5.1
Paste Special Dialog Box

To link an object, click the type of object in the As list box and also click Paste link.

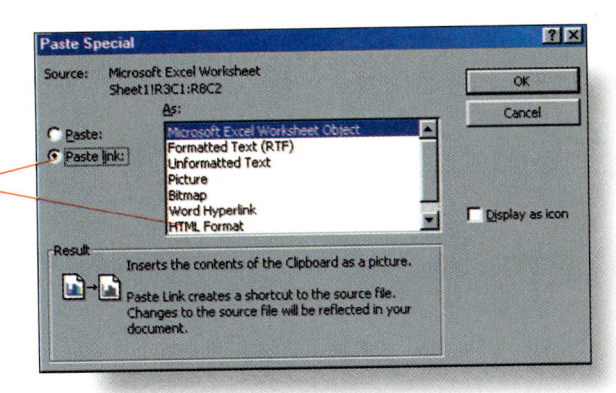

A link is updated when a file is opened or printed. If you want to update information in a linked object, make the changes in the object at the source program. For example, if you want to edit an Excel worksheet that is linked to a PowerPoint presentation, edit the worksheet in Excel. Any changes made to the Excel worksheet will be reflected in the linked presentation in PowerPoint.

When embedding or linking objects to a presentation, consider the data and what impact you want it to have on the audience. A table or worksheet may be difficult to read when presented in a slide. For this reason, consider linking or embedding a chart into a presentation rather than a table or worksheet. A chart provides a visual display of information and has more of an impact on the audience.

(Before completing computer exercises, delete the Chapter 04C folder on your disk. Next, copy the Chapter 05C folder from the CD that accompanies this textbook to your disk. Instructions for copying and deleting a folder are printed on the inside of the back cover of this textbook.)

> **Hint:** When data in a source file changes, the data in the destination file is updated. This is referred to as a *dynamic data exchange*.

> **Hint:** A chart in PowerPoint will provide a more visual display of data than a table or worksheet.

Linking and Embedding Objects and Replacing Fonts

exercise 1

Linking Charts to a PowerPoint Presentation

1. Open Excel and then PowerPoint.
2. Open the presentation named Presentation 1, Ch 05. (This presentation is located in the *Presentations* folder on the CD that accompanies this textbook.)
3. Save the presentation with Save As in the *Chapter 05C* folder on your disk and name it PowerPoint C5, Ex 01.
4. Change to the Slide view and make Slide 2 the active slide.
5. Make Excel the active program and then open Excel Worksheet 23.
6. Save the Excel worksheet with Save As and name it Excel C5, Slide 2.
7. Link the chart in the worksheet to Slide 2 of the presentation by completing the following steps:
    a. Click once in the chart area to select it. (Click just inside the chart border. Make sure you do not select a specific chart element.)
    b. Click the Copy button on the Standard toolbar.
    c. Make PowerPoint the active program. (This should display PowerPoint C5, Ex 01 with Slide 2 the active slide.)
    d. Click Edit and then Paste Special.
    e. At the Paste Special dialog box, make sure *Microsoft Excel Chart Object* displays in the As list box, and then click Paste link.
    f. Click OK to close the dialog box.
    g. Increase the size of the chart in the slide by dragging the white sizing handles that display around the chart. Increase the size of the chart so it fills a good portion of the bottom part of the slide.
    h. Save the presentation again with the same name (PowerPoint C5, Ex 01).
8. Make Excel the active program and then close Excel C5, Slide 2.
9. Open Excel Worksheet 24.
10. Save the worksheet with Save As and name it Excel C5, Slide 3.
11. Link the chart in the worksheet to Slide 3 by completing steps similar to those in step 7.
12. Save the presentation again with the same name (PowerPoint C5, Ex 01).
13. Print the slides as a handout with all slides on one page. (The fourth slide will be blank, except for the title. You will be inserting a chart in this slide in exercise 3.)
14. Close the presentation and then exit PowerPoint.
15. With Excel the active program, close Excel C5, Slide 3, and then exit Excel.

As you have learned about linking, the advantage to linking over just copying and pasting is that you can change information in the object at the source program and the change will also occur in the object in the destination program. In exercise 2, you will make changes to information in the Excel charts, and this will update the charts in the PowerPoint presentation.

exercise 2

Changing Data in Linked Charts

1. Open PowerPoint and Excel.
2. With Excel the active program, open Excel C5, Slide 2.
3. Make the following changes to the data in the cells in the worksheet:
   a. Change B2 from 18% to 10%.
   b. Change B3 from 28% to 20%.
4. Save the worksheet again with the same name (Excel C5, Slide 2).
5. Close Excel C5, Slide 2.
6. Open Excel C5, Slide 3.
7. Make the following changes to the data in the cells in the worksheet:
   a. Change B2 from 13% to 17%.
   b. Change B3 from 9% to 4%.
   c. Change B6 from 15% to 19%.
8. Save the worksheet again with the same name (Excel C5, Slide 3).
9. Close Excel C5, Slide 3.
10. Make PowerPoint the active program.
11. Open PowerPoint C5, Ex 01.
12. At the question asking if you want to update links, click OK.
13. Save the presentation with the same name (PowerPoint C5, Ex 01).
14. Print the slides as a handout with all slides on one page. (The fourth slide will be blank except for the title. You will be inserting a chart in this slide in exercise 3.)
15. Close PowerPoint C5, Ex 01.
16. Exit PowerPoint and then exit Excel.

	A	B
1		Percentage
2	1995	10%
3	1996	20%
4	1997	30%
5	1998	5%
6	1999	12%

Step 3

	A	B
1		Percentage
2	1995	17%
3	1996	4%
4	1997	18%
5	1998	4%
6	1999	19%

Step 7

After printing the table and the presentation, notice that some of the bars in the charts in Slide 2 and Slide 3 reflect the changes made to the charts in Excel.

A table or chart created in Word can be linked to a PowerPoint presentation just as an Excel chart can be linked. The steps for linking a Word table or chart are basically the same as linking an Excel chart.

Embedding Objects

An object in a file in the source program can be embedded in a file in the destination program. When an object is embedded, the object resides in the file in the destination program. This is different from linking the object, which inserts

> **Hint:** If you take a file containing an embedded object to another computer, make sure that computer contains the necessary application before trying to edit the embedded object.

only a code in the file in the destination program, not the entire object. If a change is made to the embedded object at the source program, the change is not made to the object in the destination program. Since the object is actually inserted in the file in the destination program, it is a separate object from the original object.

Since an embedded object is not automatically updated as a linked object is, the only advantage to embedding rather than simply copying and pasting is that you can edit an embedded object using the tools of the program or application in which the object was created.

Given that embedded objects are edited within the source program, it is important to remember that the source program must reside on the computer when the file is opened for editing. If you are preparing a presentation that will be edited on another computer, you may want to check before embedding any objects to verify that the other computer has the same programs.

Complete the following steps to embed an object from one program to another:

1. Open both applications and open both files needed for the integration.
2. Activate the source program.
3. Select the content for the source object.
4. Copy the selected object using the Copy button on the toolbar, the Copy option on the Edit menu, or the Copy option from the shortcut menu.
5. Activate the destination program.
6. Move to the location where you want the object inserted.
7. Select Edit, then Paste Special to open the Paste Special dialog box.
8. Select the source of the object in the As list box, click OK.

Editing an Embedded Object

> **Hint:** To edit an embedded object, open the file containing the object, and then double-click the object.

An object that has been embedded can be edited in the destination program using the tools of the source program. You do not need to return to the source program, to edit the object.

To edit an object in the destination program, open the destination program, open the file containing the embedded object, and then double-click the object. This causes the tools for the source program to display. This will display the Menu bar and Standard and Formatting toolbars at the top of the screen for the source program. Make any changes as required then click outside the embedded object to return the menu and toolbars to the destination program.

Chapter Five

exercise 3

Embedding and Editing a Chart in a PowerPoint Presentation

1. Open PowerPoint and open PowerPoint C5, Ex 01. (At the message asking if you want to update the link, click OK.)
2. Save the presentation with Save As and name it PowerPoint C5, Ex 03.
3. Change to Slide View and make Slide 4 the active slide.
4. Open Excel and then open Excel Worksheet 25.
5. Save the worksheet with Save As and name it Excel C5, Ex 03.
6. Embed the chart in Slide 4 of the presentation by completing the following steps:
    a. Click once in the chart area to select the chart.
    b. Click the Copy button on the Standard toolbar.
    c. Make PowerPoint the active program. (This should display PowerPoint C5, Ex 03 with Slide 4 the active slide.)
    d. Click Edit and Paste Special.
    e. At the Paste Special dialog box, make sure *Microsoft Excel Chart Object* is selected in the As list box, and then click OK.
7. Increase the size of the chart in the slide by dragging the white sizing handles that display around the worksheet.
8. Save the presentation with the same name (PowerPoint C5, Ex 03).
9. Print the slides as a handout with all slides on one page.
10. Edit data in the embedded chart by completing the following steps:
    a. In PowerPoint with Slide 4 the active slide, double-click the chart. (This displays the chart with Excel editing tools available.)
    b. Click the Sheet1 tab located toward the bottom of the chart. (This displays the worksheet with the data in cells along with the chart.)
    c. Make the following changes to the data in the cells in the worksheet:
        1) Change B3 from *21%* to *12%*.
        2) Change B5 from *7%* to *15%*.
    d. Click the Chart1 tab. (This returns the display to the chart.)
    e. Click once outside the chart to remove the Excel editing tools.
11. Save the presentation again with the same name (PowerPoint C5, Ex 03).
12. Print the presentation so all slides fit on one page.
13. Close the presentation and then exit PowerPoint.
14. With Excel the active program, save and then close Excel C5, Ex 03.
15. Exit Excel.

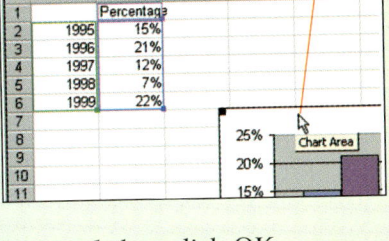

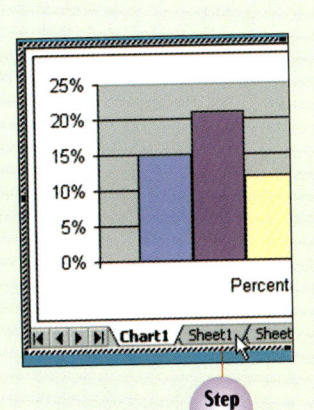

Linking and Embedding Objects and Replacing Fonts

P-175

exercise 4

Embedding a Word Table in a PowerPoint Presentation

1. Open PowerPoint and open PowerPoint C5, Ex 03.
2. Save the presentation with Save As and name it PowerPoint C5, Ex 04.
3. Open Word, and open Word Foreign Equities.
4. Select all of the text within the table below the title and opening paragraph.
5. Click the Copy button on the toolbar.
6. Make PowerPoint the active program.
7. With PowerPoint C5, Ex 04 the active presentation, embed the Word table in a new slide by completing the following steps:
   a. Display Slide 4 in Slide view.
   b. Click the New Slide button on the toolbar, select the Title Only layout in the New Slide dialog box.
   c. Key **FOREIGN EQUITIES MARKET** as the slide title (the title will wrap).
   d. Click Edit, and Paste Special.
   e. In the Paste Special dialog box, select *Microsoft Word Document Object* in the As list box, and click OK.
   f. Display the Drawing toolbar if it is not visible, then click the down-pointing arrow to the right of the Fill Color button.
   g. Select the pale blue color (fourth from left).
   h. Deselect the table.
8. Edit the embedded table to remove the borders and increase the row height by completing the following steps:
   a. Double-click the embedded table.
   b. Select all of the cells within the table.
   c. Click the down-pointing triangle to the right of the Borders button on the Formatting toolbar.
   d. Select No Border from the drop-down palette.
   e. Click Table, select Table Properties, and then click the Row tab in the Table Properties dialog box.
   f. Click the Specify height check box, and key enter **0.5** in the text box.
   g. Click OK to close the Table Properties dialog box.
   h. Click outside the table to deselect it.

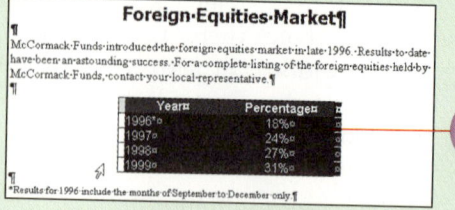

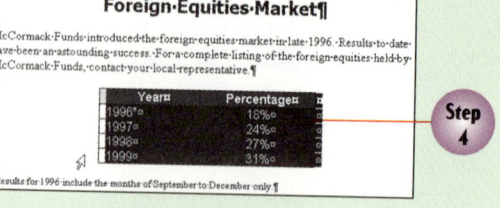

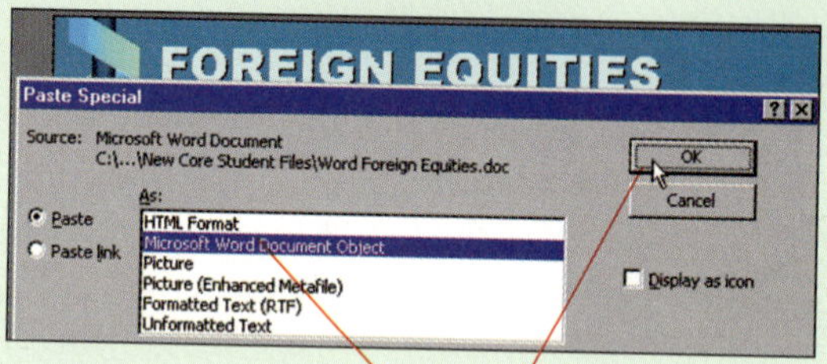

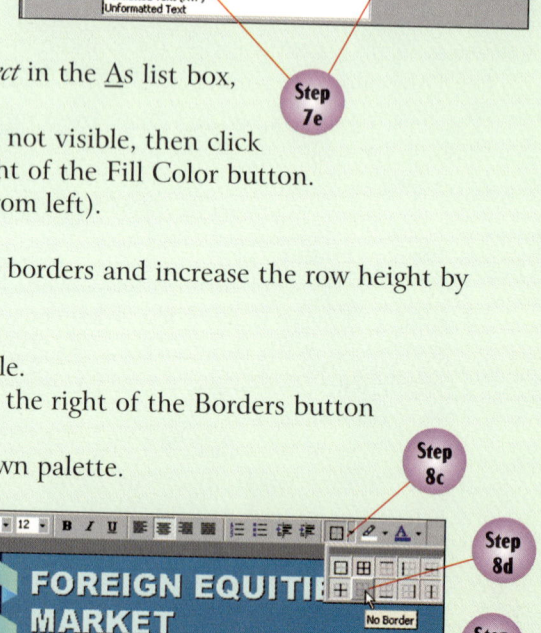

> i. Use the sizing handles to resize the table as large as possible without distorting the text.
> 9. Print Slide 5 only.
> 10. Save the revised presentation with the same name (PowerPoint C5, Ex 04).
> 11. Close PowerPoint C5, Ex 04 and exit PowerPoint.
> 12. Exit Word.

Replace Fonts

In chapter 2, you used the Replace feature to find and replace text automatically within slides in a presentation. PowerPoint includes another replace feature that searches through a presentation for a font and replaces it with another font. Click Format and select Replace Fonts. The Replace Font dialog box opens as shown in figure 5.2. Select the font you want to find from the Replace drop-down list, the font you want to change it to in the With drop-down list, and then click Replace.

figure 5.2 *Replace Font Dialog Box*

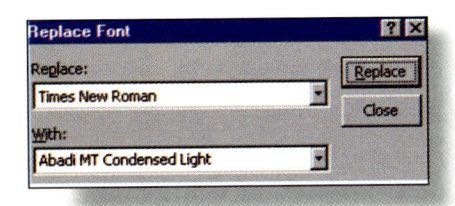

exercise 5

Replacing Fonts in a Presentation

1. Open PowerPoint and open PowerPoint C5, Ex 04.
2. Save the presentation with Save As and name it PowerPoint C5, Ex 05.
3. Change the font used throughout the presentation for the slide titles by completing the following steps:
   a. Display the presentation in Slide Sorter View.
   b. Click Format and Replace Fonts.
   c. Make sure the Replace text box displays *Arial Black*. If not, click the down-pointing triangle to the right of the Replace text box, and then select *Arial Black* from the drop-down list.
   d. Click the down-pointing triangle to the right of the With text box and select *Times New Roman* from the drop-down list.
   e. Click Replace.

f. Close the Replace Font dialog box.
4. Save the revised presentation with the same name (PowerPoint C5, Ex 05).
5. Print the entire presentation as Handouts with 4 slides per page.
6. Close PowerPoint C5, Ex 05.

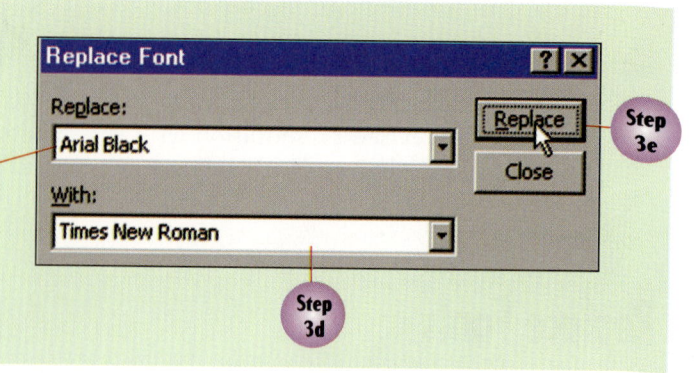

Create a New Presentation from Existing Slides

If you have slides in an existing presentation file that you would like to use in a new presentation file, consider copying the slides from the existing presentation to avoid duplicating your efforts. To do this, start the new presentation file. When you reach the point in the presentation where you want to insert the slides from another presentation, complete the following steps to copy the slides:

1. Click Insert, and click Slides from Files to display the Slide Finder dialog box shown in figure 5.3.
2. Click Browse, and navigate to the presentation file to copy the slide(s) from.
3. In the Select slides section of the Slide Finder dialog box, click to select the slide(s) you want to copy. If you are copying more than one slide, hold Shift while clicking the slides. A horizontal scroll bar displays along the bottom of the Select slides section to display slides beyond the first three in the file.
4. Click Insert. To copy an entire presentation, click Insert All.

figure 5.3

Slide Finder Dialog Box

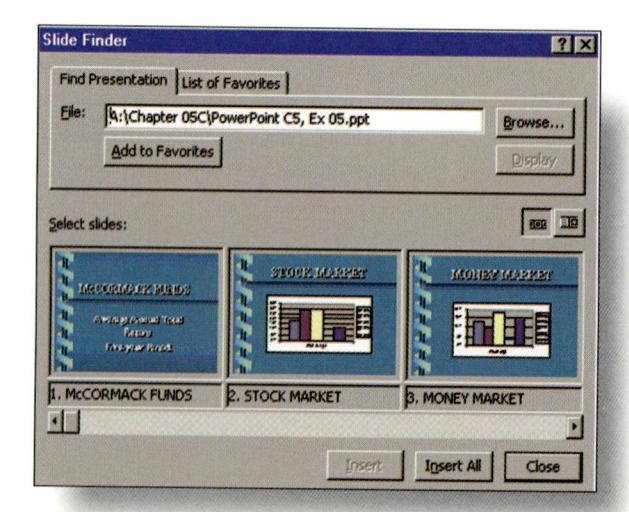

The inserted slides take on the design template of the destination presentation. If you have a slide in a presentation file that you will be copying into other presentations often, click the Add to Favorites button in the Slide Finder dialog box to add the presentation filename to the List of Favorites tab.

exercise 6

Creating a New Presentation from Existing Slides

1. At a blank PowerPoint presentation click File, click New, and then select the *Fireball* template design.
2. Select the Title Slide autolayout and key the following text as the slide title and subtitle:
   MCCORMACK FUNDS
   Annual Shareholders Meeting
3. Insert three slides from an existing presentation by completing the following steps:
   a. Click Insert, and Slides from Files.
   b. Click Browse, and double-click the presentation named PowerPoint C5, Ex 05 in the Browse dialog box.
   c. Click to select slide 2 in the Select slides section.
   d. Hold down the Shift key and click to select Slide 3.
   e. Click the right scroll arrow on the horizontal scroll bar to display Slide 4, and hold down the shift key and select slide 4.
   f. Click Insert.
   g. Close the Slide Finder dialog box.
4. Display the presentation in Slide Sorter View.
5. Save the presentation in the Chapter 05C folder on your disk and name it PowerPoint C5, Ex 06.
6. Print the entire presentation so that all slides will fit on one page.
7. Close PowerPoint C5, Ex 06 and then exit PowerPoint.

chapter summary

➤ An object created in one program can be linked to another program. The program containing the object is called the source and the program the object is linked to is called the destination.

➤ A linked object exists in the source program but not as a separate object in the destination program. The destination program contains only a code that identifies the name and location of the source program, document, and the location in the document.

➤ To link an object, copy the object in the source program, and then paste it in the destination program by clicking Edit and then Paste Special. At the Paste Special dialog box, click Paste link.

➤ Edit a document containing a linked object in the source program. Any changes made will be reflected in the destination program.

- An embedded object resides in the source program as well as the destination program. If a change is made to the embedded object at the source program, the change is not made to the object in the destination program.
- An embedded object can be edited using the tools of the source program. To edit an object in the destination program, double-click the object, which causes the tools for the source program to display.
- Use the Replace Fonts feature to instruct PowerPoint to automatically find all occurrences of a font and replace it with another font.
- Display the Slide Finder dialog box to copy slides from an existing presentation into a new presentation.

commands review

	Mouse
Link object	Select object; click Copy button on Standard toolbar; make destination program active; activate slide; click Edit, Paste Special; at Paste Special dialog box, click desired object in As list box, click Paste link, and then click OK
Embed object	Select object; click Copy button on Standard toolbar; make destination program active; activate slide; click Edit, Paste Special; at Paste Special dialog box and click desired object in As list box; click OK
Edit embedded object	In destination program, double-click object
Replace Font dialog box	Click Format and Replace Fonts
Slide Finder dialog box	Click Insert and Slides from Files

thinking offline

Completion: In the space provided at the right, indicate the correct term, symbol, or command.

1. The program containing the original linked object is referred to as this.
2. The program an object is linked to is referred to as this.
3. To link an object, click the Paste link option at this dialog box.
4. If you want to update information in a linked object, make changes to the object at this program.
5. Use this in a presentation instead of a table or worksheet because it provides a visual display of information and has more of an impact on the audience.
6. When this is done to an object, only a code is inserted in the file in the destination program.
7. If this has been done to an object in a file, the object can be edited in the destination program using the tools of the source program.

Chapter Five

8. The Replace Fonts feature is accessed from this option on the Menu bar. _____
9. Selecting Insert, Slides from Files will cause this dialog box to open. _____

In the space provided below the situation, indicate which of the following procedures you would choose: copy and paste, copy and link, or copy and embed.

10. **Situation:** You travel to various companies showing a PowerPoint presentation to prospective customers. The presentation includes several charts showing information such as quarterly sales figures, production figures, and projected sales. These charts are updated quarterly. Which of the three procedures would you use for including the charts in the presentation? Why?

_____
_____

working hands-on

Assessment 1

1. Open PowerPoint and then open PowerPoint C5, Ex 03. At the message asking if you want links updated, click OK. (You must have completed exercises 1 and 3 in this chapter before completing this assessment.)
2. Save the presentation with Save As and name it PowerPoint C5, SA 01.
3. Add a new slide to the presentation (the new slide will be Slide 5) with the following specifications:
   a. At the New Slide dialog box, double-click the third autolayout format from the left in the third row (Title Only).
   b. Key the title **GLOBAL EQUITIES.**
   c. Click the Center button on the Formatting toolbar to center the title in the object box.
   d. Select the title *GLOBAL EQUITIES* and change the font size to 54 points.
4. Open Excel and then open Excel Worksheet 26.
5. Save the worksheet with Save As and name it Excel C5, Slide 5.
6. Copy the chart and link it to Slide 5 in PowerPoint C5, SA 01. Increase the size of the chart so it fills most of the bottom part of the slide.
7. Save the presentation again with the same name (PowerPoint C5, SA 01).
8. Add another new slide to the presentation (the new slide will be Slide 6) with the following specifications:
   a. At the New Slide dialog box, double-click the third autolayout format from the left in the third row (Title Only).
   b. Key the title **SOCIAL CHOICE.**
   c. Click the Center button on the Formatting toolbar to center the title in the object box.
   d. Select the title *SOCIAL CHOICE* and change the font size to 54 points.
   e. Open Excel Worksheet 27.
   f. Save the worksheet with Save As and name it Excel C5, Slide 6.
   g. Copy the chart and link it to Slide 6 in PowerPoint C5, SA 01. Increase the size of the chart so it fills most of the bottom part of the slide.
9. Save the presentation again with the same name (PowerPoint C5, SA 01).
10. Print the slides as a handout with six slides per page.

Linking and Embedding Objects and Replacing Fonts

11. Close the PowerPoint C5, SA 01.
12. Make Excel the active program, close Excel C5, Slide 6, and then close Excel C5, Slide 5.

Assessment 2

1. Make sure PowerPoint and Excel are open.
2. With Excel the active program, open Excel C5, Slide 5.
3. Make the following changes to the data in the cells in the worksheet:
   a. Change B2 from *5%* to *12%*.
   b. Change B4 from *10%* to *15%*.
   c. Change B6 from *8%* to *17%*.
4. Save the worksheet again with the same name (Excel C5, Slide 5).
5. Close Excel C5, Slide 5.
6. Open Excel C5, Slide 6.
7. Make the following changes to the data in the cells in the worksheet:
   a. Change B3 from *3%* to *11%*.
   b. Change B4 from *7%* to *15%*.
8. Save the worksheet again with the same name (Excel C5, Slide 6).
9. Close Excel C5, Slide 6.
10. Make PowerPoint the active program.
11. Open PowerPoint C5, SA 01. (At the message asking if you want to update the links, click OK.)
12. Print the slides as a handout with six slides per page.
13. Save and then close PowerPoint C5, SA 01.
14. Exit PowerPoint and then exit Excel.

Assessment 3

1. Open PowerPoint and start a new presentation using the Neon Frame design template.
2. Select the Title Slide autolayout, and key the following text as the slide title and subtitle:
   McCormack Funds
   Equity Investment Workshop
3. Copy Slides 2 and 5 from PowerPoint C5, SA 01 into the new presentation.
4. Use the Replace Fonts feature to replace the *Tahoma* font with *Garamond*. If the Garamond font is not available on your system, choose Times New Roman.
5. Display the Slide Master, and bold the title placeholder.
6. Insert, size, and position an appropriate clip art image to slide 1.
7. Save the presentation in the Chapter 05C folder on your disk and name it PowerPoint C5, SA 03.
8. Print the presentation with 3 slides per page.
9. Close PowerPoint C5, SA 03.

Assessment 4

1. With PowerPoint the active program, use the Help feature to learn how to break a link. *(Hint: Use the Office Assistant and ask the question "How do I break a link?")* After finding, reading, and printing the information on breaking links, complete the following steps:
   a. Open PowerPoint C5, SA 01 and break the link the presentation contains with Excel C5, Slide 6.
   b. Open Excel, and open Excel C5, Slide 6.
   c. Make the following changes to the worksheet:
      1) Change B3 from *11%* to *8%*.
      2) Change B4 from *15%* to *20%*.
   d. Save and print Excel C5, Slide 6.
   e. Exit Excel.
   f. With PowerPoint C5, SA 01 open, check that the changes made to Excel C5, Slide 6 were not reflected in the presentation.
   g. Save and print PowerPoint C5, SA 01.
2. Exit PowerPoint.

Performance Assessments

PPT CPA

CORE LEVEL

ASSESSING CORE PROFICIENCIES

In this book, you have learned to create, print, save, close, open, view, run, edit, and format a PowerPoint presentation. You also learned how to add animation, build, add sound effects in a presentation, and insert hyperlinks. In addition to creating and formatting PowerPoint presentations, you learned how to insert WordArt and organizational charts in a PowerPoint slide; and copy and and embed or copy and link objects from one program to another.

(Before completing Performance Assessments, delete the Chapter 05C folder on your disk. Next, copy the PPT CPA folder from the CD that accompanies this textbook to your disk. Instructions for copying and deleting a folder are printed on the inside of the back cover of this textbook.)

Assessment 1

1. Create a presentation with the text shown in figure C1.1. You determine the design template and the autolayout. Add the following enhancements:
   a. Transitions
   b. Builds
   c. Sound and/or fill color.
2. After creating the presentation, save it in the PPT CPA folder on your disk and name it Concepts Presentation.
3. Print the slides in Concepts Presentation on two pages.
4. Run and then close Concepts Presentation.

Slide 1	Title	=	TELECOMMUNICATIONS TECHNOLOGY
	Subtitle	=	Concepts of Technology
Slide 2	Title	=	ENCODING
	Bullets	=	• Common Devices
			- 35 mm Camera
			- Television
			- Mouse
Slide 3	Title	=	ENCODING
	Bullets	=	• System Applications

Figure C1.1 • Assessment 1 (continues)

			- Broadcast Radio
			- Telephone
			- Broadcast Television
			- Automation Systems
Slide 4	Title	=	TRANSMITTING
	Bullets	=	• Common Devices
			- Optical Fibers
			- Amplifiers
			- Transmitting Antenna
Slide 5	Title	=	RECEIVING
	Bullets	=	• Common Devices
			- Television Antenna
			- Tuner
			- Satellite Dish
Slide 6	Title	=	STORING
	Bullets	=	• System Applications
			- Television
			- Computer Systems
			- Telephone
			- Automation Systems

Figure C1.1 • Assessment 1

Assessment 2

1. Open Concepts Presentation.
2. Create a new Slide 7 by completing the following steps:
    a. Display Slide 6 and click the New Slide button.
    b. At the New Slide dialog box, double-click the Bulleted List autolayout.
    c. Click the text *Click to add title* and key **APPLICATIONS**.
    d. Click the text *Click to add text* and copy text from Word and paste the text into Slide 7 by completing the following steps:
        1) Open Word and file Word Concepts 01.
        2) Select *RECEIVING,* and the paragraph below it, and then click the Copy button.
        3) Select *STORING,* and the paragraph below it, and then click the Copy button. (Make sure the Clipboard toolbar displays.)
        4) Select *TRANSMITTING,* and the paragraph below it, and then click the Copy button.
        5) Click the button on the Taskbar representing the Concepts Presentation.
        6) Make sure the insertion point is positioned in the bulleted list placeholder in Slide 7 and click the button on the Clipboard toolbar containing the heading *TRANSMITTING.*
        7) Click the button on the Clipboard containing the heading *RECEIVING.*
        8) Click the Clear Clipboard button on the Clipboard toolbar and close the toolbar.
3. Insert the footer *Concepts Presentation* and the current date and slide number so they will print on note pages.
4. Save the presentation again with the same name (Concepts Presentation).
5. Print Slides 1 and 7 as notes pages then close Concepts Presentation.
6. Make Word the active program, close Word Concepts 01, and then exit Word.

Assessment 3

1. Make sure PowerPoint is open. Open Word, and open Word Outline 03.
2. Import the text into PowerPoint.
3. Make PowerPoint the active program.
4. Make the following changes to the presentation:
   a. Change to the Title Slide autolayout for Slide 2.
   b. Change to the Title Slide autolayout for Slide 3.
   c. Apply a design template of your choosing.
   d. Insert a clip art image related to "software" in Slide 5.
   e. Check each slide and make any formatting changes to enhance the appearance of the slide.
   f. Add transitions and builds to the slides in the presentation.
   g. Create the following hyperlinks for the text in Slide 6:
      Apple Computer   =   http://www.apple.com
      Blizzard Entertainment =   http://www.blizzard.com
      id Software   =   http://www.idsoftware.com
      Microsoft Corporation =   http://www.microsoft.com
   h. Insert the action button named Action: Home at the bottom of Slide 3, Slide 4, and Slide 5.
   i. Insert the action button named Action Button: Return at the bottom of Slide 1.
5. Save the presentation in the PPT CPA folder on your disk and name it Apex Presentation.
6. Run the presentation. (When all text has displayed in Slide 3, click the Home action button. After viewing Slide 1, click the Return action button. Continue in this manner until all slides have been viewed.)
7. Print all six slides on one page and then close Apex Presentation.
8. Exit Word.

Assessment 4

1. Open Apex Presentation.
2. Make the following changes to the presentation:
   a. Delete the action button that displays in slides 1, 3, 4, and 5.
   b. Display Slide 1 in Slide view and change to the Slide Master view.
   c. Change the first level bullet to a character bullet in a different color and increase the bullet size (you determine the character, the color, and the size).
   d. Make at least one other change to the Slide Master (suggestions include changing the font, font color, adding a fill color, and so on).
   e. Insert a new Slide 1 with the Blank autolayout.
   f. Insert WordArt in Slide 1 that contains the company name *Apex Cyberware*. You determine the formatting and shape of the WordArt text.
   g. Display Slide 5 in Normal view and add the speaker note *Include specific timeline on hiring new personnel*.
   h. Display Slide 6 in Normal view and add the speaker note *Specify the percentage of business for each category*.
   i. Insert the current date and slide number on all slides in the presentation.
3. Run the presentation.
4. Print four slides per page. (The first page will contain four slides and the second page will contain three slides.)
5. Print slides 5 and 6 as note pages.
6. Save the presentation again with the same name (Apex Presentation).
7. Close Apex Presentation.

Assessment 5

1. Create a new presentation with the following specifications:
   a. Use a design template provided by PowerPoint.
   b. Create the first slide with the following specifications:
      1) Use the last autolayout at the New Slide dialog box (Blank).
      2) Use WordArt to create the text *International Securities*. (You determine the shape and formatting of the WordArt text.)
   c. Create the second slide with the following specifications:
      1) Use the first autolayout at the New Slide dialog box (Title Slide).
      2) Key **2001 SALES MEETING** as the title.
      3) Key **European Division** as the subtitle.
   d. Create the third slide with the following specifications:
      1) Use the third autolayout from the left in the third row at the New Slide dialog box (Title Only).
      2) Key **REGIONAL SALES** as the title.
      3) Open Excel and then Open Excel Worksheet 28. Save the worksheet with Save As and name it PPT CPA Worksheet 28. Embed PPT CPA Worksheet 28 in Slide 3.
      4) Increase the size of the chart so it better fills the slide.
   e. Create the fourth slide with the following specifications:
      1) Use the second autolayout in the first row at the New Slide dialog box (Bulleted List).
      2) Key **2002 GOALS** as the title.
      3) Key the following as the bulleted items:
         - **Increase product sales by 15 percent.**
         - **Open a branch office in Spain.**
         - **Hire one manager and two additional account managers.**
         - **Decrease production costs by 6 percent.**
   f. Create the fifth slide with the following specifications:
      1) Use the Table autolayout (last autolayout in the top row at the New Slide dialog box).
      2) Key **HIRING TIMELINE** as the title.
      3) Key the following text in the cells in the table. (You determine the formatting of the cells.)

Task	Date
Advertise positions	03/01/01 - 04/30/01
Review resumes	05/15/01 - 06/01/01
Perform interviews	06/15/01 - 07/15/01
Hire personnel	08/01/01

   g. Create the sixth slide with the following specifications:
      1) Use the third autolayout from the left in the third row at the New Slide dialog box (Title Only).
      2) Key **PRODUCTION EXPENSES** as the title.
      3) Make Excel the active program. Open Excel Worksheet 29 and then save the worksheet with Save As and name it PPT CPA Worksheet 29. Copy and then link PPT CPA Worksheet 29 into Slide 6.
      4) Increase the size of the pie chart so it better fills the slide. (Be sure to maintain the integrity of the chart.)
   h. Create the seventh slide with the following specifications:
      1) Choose the third autolayout from the left in the second row at the New Slide dialog box (Organization Chart).

2) Key the title **OFFICE STRUCTURE** as the title and create the following text in the organizational chart boxes:

Ricardo Miraflores
Manager

Miguel Tumbes
Assistant Manager

Audrina Chorrillos   **Hector Palencia**
Account Manager   Account Manager

2. Add the following enhancements to the presentation:
   a. Add a transition of your choosing to each slide.
   b. Add a build technique to the bulleted items in Slide 4.
3. Save the presentation and name it PowerPoint CPA 05.
4. Run the presentation.
5. Print the slides as a handout with four slides per page. (The first page will contain four slides and the second page will contain three slides.)
6. Close PowerPoint CPA 05.
7. Exit Excel.

Assessment 6

1. Open Excel and then open PPT CPA Worksheet 29.
2. Make the following changes:
   a. B2: Change *38%* to *41%*.
   b. B3: Change *35%* to *32%*.
   c. B4: Change *18%* to *21%*.
   d. B5: Change *9%* to *6%*.
3. Save the worksheet again with the same name (PPT CPA Worksheet 29).
4. Print and close PPT CPA Worksheet 29.
5. Make PowerPoint the active program and open PowerPoint CPA 05. (At the question asking if you want to update the link, click OK.)
6. Make the following changes to the embedded worksheet in Slide 3:
   a. C2: Change *2,678,450* to *2,857,300*.
   b. C3: Change *1,753,405* to *1,598,970*.
   c. C5: Change *2,315,600* to *2,095,170*.
7. Save the presentation with the same name (PowerPoint CPA 05).
8. Print the slides as a handout with all slides on one page.
9. Close PowerPoint CPA 05.

WRITING ACTIVITIES

The following activities give you the opportunity to practice your writing skills along with demonstrating an understanding of some of the important PowerPoint features you have mastered in this textbook. Use correct grammar, appropriate word choices, and clear sentence structure.

Activity 1

1. Print the document named Key Life Health Plan in Word. Looking at the printing of this document, create a presentation in PowerPoint that presents the main points of the plan. (Use bullets in the presentation.) Add a transition and build to the slides.
2. Save the presentation and name it Key Life Presentation.
3. Run Key Life Presentation.
4. Print the slides as handouts with six slides per page.
5. Close Key Life Presentation.
6. Exit Word.

Activity 2

1. Open Word and then open, print, and then close Key Life Corporation.
2. Using the information in the Key Life Corporation document, create an organizational chart in a PowerPoint slide with the following specifications:
   a. Include an appropriate title.
   b. Change box and text color.
   c. Add a background color.
3. Save the organizational chart and name it PowerPoint CPA, Act 02.
4. Print and close PowerPoint CPA, Act 02.
5. Exit Word.

Activity 3

1. Using PowerPoint's Help feature, find and print information on how to save a presentation to the Web.
2. Create a memo in Word to your instructor describing how to save a presentation to the Web and include the specific steps for doing this.
3. Save the document and name it Word CPA, Act 03.
4. Print and then close Word CPA, Act 03.

INTERNET ACTIVITY

Make sure you are connected to the Internet and then explore the Time Magazine Web site at http://www.time.com. Discover the following information for the site:

- magazine categories e.g., *Time Daily, Magazine, Community*, and so on.)
- the type of information presented in each category
- services available
- information on how to subscribe

Using the information you discovered about the Time Magazine Web site, create a PowerPoint presentation that presents the information in a clear, concise, and logical manner. Add formatting and enhancements to the presentation to make it more interesting. Include a hyperlink in one of the slides to the Time Magazine Web site. When the presentation is completed, save it and name it Time Mag Presentation. Run, print, and then close the presentation.

Index

Action buttons: inserting to link slides in same presentation, 123-124
Action Settings dialog box, 122, 124
  with Mouse Click Tab selected, 121
Alignment
  changing text, in box, 159
  changing with WordArt, 141
  of objects, 76
Animation: adding to presentations, 103-131
Animation effects, 7
  commands review for, 133
Animation Effects toolbar: buttons on, 103, 104, 105
Apply Design Template dialog box, 81, 82
Arrow button, 66
Audience: for presentation, 4
AutoContent Wizard, 4, 5
  planning presentation with, 19-20
Autolayout, 118
  changing, 125
  creating organization chart using, 160
Autolayout format: placeholders in, 9
Autoshape: text wrapped in, 72
AutoShapes
  creating, 68
  creating, grouping, aligning, distributing, 76-77
Auxiliary lines: drawing, 159

Back button, 37
Background color: changing in chart, 159
Background dialog box, 80
Backgrounds: for slides, 78
Black and white
  overheads, 3
  printing presentation in, 15
Blank presentation: creating, then applying design template, 83
Bold button: in WordArt, 144
Border: changing, 159
Boxes
  adding to organization chart, 157-158
  changing/adding borders or shadow to, 159
Build technique, 106
  adding to slides, 106-107
  for presentation, 107-109
Bulleted List autolayout, 86, 118
Bulleted list placeholder, 9
Bulleted text: creating in slide, 62
Bullets
  changing, 86-87, 88
  formatting with, 86-89
  for speaker notes, 91
Bullets and Numbering dialog box

  with Bulleted tab selected, 86
  with Numbers tab selected, 87
Charts
  changing data in linked, 173
  embedding/editing in PowerPoint presentation, 175
  linking to PowerPoint presentation, 172-173
  placeholder, 9. *See also* Organization charts
Circles, 66
ClipArt dialog box, 109
Clip art images, 7, 40, 103
  formatting in PowerPoint, 115
  inserting/sizing in PowerPoint presentation, 109-111
  in Web page, 128
Clip art in presentations, 109-117
  formatting clip art images in PowerPoint, 115-16
  images inserted from disk, 112-113
  sizing and scaling images, 109-111
  watermark creation, 116-117
Clip art placeholder, 9
Clipboard toolbar, 126, 127
Clip Gallery: Microsoft Windows Metafile inserted from, 115
Close button, 37
Closing: presentations, 16
Collecting and pasting: multiple items, 126-127
Color
  adding to WordArt text, 149-150
  bullet, 86
  changing to box or chart background, 159
  changing with WordArt, 145
  for clip art images, 115
  for fonts, 150-151
  formatting slide color scheme, 78-79
  line or fill, 69
  with WordArt, 141, 148
Color Scheme dialog box, 78
  with Custom tab selected, 80
  with Standard Tab selected, 79
Colors dialog box, 79, 151
  with Standard tab selected, 149
Color transparencies, 3
Commands: for controlling slide show, 22
Copy button, 52, 54, 55
Copying
  objects, 69
  slides, 52
  slides from existing presentation, 178
  text in slides, 55
Copying and pasting
  drawbacks with, 169
  text between Word and PowerPoint, 124-125

vs. embedding, 170
Custom Animation dialog box, 106
  with Effects Tab selected, 107
Customizing
  bullets, 86
  formatting in presentation, 63
  organizational charts, 159
  organizational charts in PowerPoint presentation, 161
  placeholders, 66
  slide color scheme, 81. *See also* Editing; Formatting
Customizing WordArt, 144-148
  changing shapes, 145-148
  with options at Format WordArt dialog box, 144-145
  text, 152-153
Customizing WordArt with buttons on Drawing toolbar, 148-153
  adding fill shading or color, 149-150
  adding shadow and 3-D effects, 151
  changing line and font color, 150-151
  changing line style, 151
Cut button, 54, 55

Data: changing in linked charts, 173
Dates
  inserting into presentations, 90
  in notes and handouts, 92
Deleting
  objects, 69
  presentations, 36
  slides, 51
Demote button: on Formatting toolbar, 33
Design template
  applying after creating blank presentation, 83
  changing, 81, 82
Design templates, 60
  color changes in, 78
  for transparencies, 83
Design Templates tab, 9
Destination program, 169, 170
  editing embedded object in, 174
  embedding objects in, 173
Detect and Repair dialog box, 40
Diagonal lines: drawing, 159
Disk: images inserted from, 112-113
Draw button, 75
  distributing and aligning objects with, 76
  grouping objects with, 75
  rotating objects with, 75
Drawing
  lines, 66
  objects, 68
Drawing toolbar, 66
  Draw button on, 116
  Fill Color button on, 149
  Font Color button on, 151

formatting with buttons on, 66
Line color button on, 150
Line Style button on, 151
in PowerPoint window, 7
Shadow button on, 151
WordArt button on, 142
Drawing toolbar buttons, 66-67
Drop-down menus: expanding, 15

Editing
commands review for, 95
embedded objects, 174
and embedding, 170
images, 115. See also Customizing; Formatting; Text
Editing slides, 49-60
completing spellcheck, 57
copying slides, 52
finding and replacing text, 50-51
inserting and deleting slides, 51
inserting and deleting text, 50
rearranging object boxes, 55
rearranging slides, 55
rearranging text, 54-55
using buttons on Standard toolbar, 55
Edit WordArt Text dialog box, 142, 143, 144
Effect text box, 26
Elevator: on vertical scroll bar, 7, 21
E-mail: presentation sent via, 130-131
E-mail header, 131
Embedded objects: editing, 174
Embedding
and editing chart in PowerPoint presentation, 175
objects, 173-175
vs. linking, 170
Word table in PowerPoint presentation, 176-177. See also Links and linking
Excel
MS Organization Chart 2.0 used in, 154
worksheets, 169
Expand All button, 34

Fill Color button, 69
Fill Effects dialog box: with Gradient tab selected, 150
Fill patterns: with WordArt, 141
Fill shading: adding to WordArt text, 149-150
Find and replace feature: for text in slides, 50
Find Dialog box, 51
First rank options, 15
Folders
creating, 16
images inserted from, 112
Web page files inserted in, 128
Font color
changing, 60
changing in WordArt text, 150-151
Font dialog box, 159
Fonts
for autolayout formats, 33

changing, 60, 159
changing in WordArt, 141, 144
replacing, 177
Font size: changing in WordArt, 144
Footers. See Headers and footers
Format AutoShape dialog box, 73
Format Painter: formatting with, 83
Format Painter button: on Standard toolbar, 83
Format Picture dialog box, 109
Formatting
with bullets and numbers, 86-89
with buttons on Drawing toolbar, 66
clip art images in PowerPoint, 115-116
commands review for, 95
with Format Painter, 83
with master slide, 63-66
objects, 69
presentations, 60-91
slide color scheme, 78-81
slides, 4
speaker notes, 91. See also Customizing; Editing
Formatting toolbar, 60, 130
Animation Effects button on, 105
buttons on, 61
Common Tasks button on, 125
Demote button on, 33
in PowerPoint Window, 5, 6
Format WordArt dialog box
with colors and lines tab selected, 145
customizing WordArt at, 144-145
Forward button, 37
Free form lines, 66
Full Screen Slide Show button, 129

Gradient: specifying in WordArt, 150
Grayscale: printing presentation in, 15
Grayscale Preview button, 15
on Standard toolbar, 18

Handouts, 4
header, footer, and date inserted in, 92-93
inserting headers and/or footers in, 91
printing those selected at Print dialog box, 12
Header and Footer dialog box, 89
with Slide Tab selected, 89
Headers and footers
inserting in notes/handouts, 91
inserting in presentation, 89-90
Heading styles: importing into, from Word document to PowerPoint presentation, 125
Height/width of text: changing with WordArt, 143
Help: from AutoContent Wizard, 19-20
Help Dialog box: using, 37-39
Help feature: using, 36-41
Help files, 40
Horizontal lines: drawing, 159

Horizontal scroll bar: in PowerPoint window, 7
HTML format: presentation saved in, on Web, 127
Hyperlinks, 7, 38, 103
creating from slide to Word document, 121-122
creating in presentation, 119-120
slides added with, 120
from slide to Web, 119-120. See also Links and linking

Images
brightness/intensity of, 116
inserting from disk, 112-113
sizing and scaling, 109-111. See also Clip art images; Color
Importing: text from Word, 124-127
Insert Hyperlink dialog box, 120
Inserting: slides, 51
Insert Picture dialog box, 112
Insert Table dialog box, 118
Integration: defined, 169
Internet: hyperlinks on, 119. See also Internet Explorer, 128
Internet Explorer 4.0, 127
Internet Explorer 5.0, 128
Intranet: presentation published to, 127
Italic button: WordArt, 144

Line
with arrowheads, 66
changing in organization charts, 159
changing in WordArt text, 150-151
creating new, 62
Line button, 66
Line color: with WordArt, 148
Line Color button, 69, 150
Line Spacing dialog box, 62
Line style: in WordArt, 148, 151
Line Style button, 151
Links and linking
charts to PowerPoint presentation, 172-173
objects, 170-171
vs. embedding, 170
updating, 171. See also Embedding; Hyperlinks
Logos: creating, 141

Master Slide
formatting objects with use of, 69-71
formatting text in presentation using, 64-66
formatting with, 63-66. See also Slides
Menu bar: in PowerPoint window, 6
Microsoft Clip Gallery, 112
dialog box, 109
Microsoft Office Update Web site, 40
Microsoft Organization Chart window, 154, 155, 157
Microsoft Photo Editor, 115

Microsoft Windows Metafile (wmf), 115
Moving
    objects, 69
    organizational charts, 155
MS Organization Chart 2.0, 141, 154

Netscape Navigator, 128
New Line command, 62
New lines: creating, 62
New presentation: creating from existing slides, 178-179
New Presentation dialog box, 8, 9
    Design Templates tab in, 32
New Slide dialog box, 9, 118
    autolayout choices/format in, 33, 125
Normal view, 20, 32
    find and replace in, 50
Notes: header, footer, and date inserted in, 91-93
Notes pages: printing those selected at Print dialog box, 13-14
Notes pane: in PowerPoint window, 7
Numbering
    applying, 89
    for speaker notes, 91
Numbering button: on Formatting toolbar, 87
Numbers
    formatting with, 86-89
    inserting, 87, 88

Object boxes
    formatting applied to, 60
    rearranging in slide, 55
    sizing, 55
Object dialog box, 154
Object linking and embedding (OLE), 169
Objects
    deleting, 69
    distributing and aligning, 76
    drawing, 68
    embedding, 173-177
    flipping and rotating, 75
    grouping and ungrouping, 75
    linking, 170-173
    moving and copying, 69
    selecting, 68
Office Assistant
    help from, 36-37
    turning off, 38
OLE. See Object linking and embedding
On-screen presentations, 3, 21
Open dialog box, 16
Organization charts
    adding boxes to, 157-158
    commands review for, 163
    creating, 154-161
    creating in Word, 155-156
    creating with Autolayout, 160
    customizing, 141, 159
    customizing in PowerPoint presentation, 161
    editing existing, 157

keying information in, 155
    placeholders, 9
    sizing and moving, 155
    view changed in, 159. See also Charts
Outline pane
    deleting slides in, 51
    in PowerPoint window, 7
    text rearranged in, 54-55
Outline view, 14, 21
    deleting slides in, 51
    find and replace in, 50
    keying text for presentation in, 33
    preparing presentation in, 31-35
    text rearranged in, 54-55
Outlining toolbar buttons, 33-34
Oval button, 66

Paragraphs
    alignment changed in, 61
    increasing/decreasing spacing before/after, 62. See also Text
Paste button, 52, 54, 55
Paste Special dialog box, 171
Pasting. See Collecting and pasting; Copying and pasting
Pattern: specifying in WordArt, 150
Patterned Lines dialog box, 151
Pen: using during presentation, 22, 23
Photographs, 3
Picture Bullet dialog box, 87
Pictures: in Web page, 128
Picture toolbar
    Format Picture button on, 109
    Image Control button on, 116
    Recolor Picture button on, 115
Placeholders, 9
    for slides in PowerPoint template, 66
PowerPoint dialog box, 8
PowerPoint Help dialog box: hyperlinks in, 38
PowerPoint presentation
    creating/shaping WordArt text in, 146-148
    editing and formatting, 49-101
    embedding Word table in, 176-177
    fonts replaced in, 177-178
    organizational charts customized in, 161
PowerPoint presentation preparation, 3-48
    with AutoContent Wizard, 19
    closing, 16
    creating PowerPoint presentation, 4-9
    deleting presentation, 36
    expanding drop-down menus, 15
    Help feature, 36-41
    opening document, 20
    in Outline view, 31-35
    planning, 4
    printing presentation, 9-15
    running slide show, 21-31
    saving, 15
    viewing presentation, 20-21
PowerPoint window: understanding, 5-7

Presentation documents: opening, 20
Presentation formatting, 60-91
    autoshape creation, 68
    with bullets and numbers, 86-89
    creating blank presentation and applying design template, 83
    creating new line, 62
    design template changes, 81-82
    distributing and aligning objects, 76
    drawing objects, 68
    flipping and rotating object, 75
    formatting objects, 69
    formatting slide color scheme, 78-81
    formatting text in slide, 60
    formatting with buttons on Drawing toolbar, 66-68
    formatting with Format Painter, 83-84
    formatting with master slide, 63-66
    grouping/ungrouping objects, 75
    headers/footers insertion, 89-90
    increasing/decreasing spacing before/after paragraphs, 62
    moving/copying object, 69
    object deletion, 69
    object selection, 68
    sizing object, 69
    text box creation, 72
Presentations
    animation effects added to, 103, 105-106
    build technique used for, 107-109
    clip art inserted in, 109-117
    copying slides between, 52
    embedding/linking objects to, 171 folder, 16
    inserting date, time, slide number and footer in, 90
    publishing to Web, 127-129
    sent as e-mail, 130-131
Previewing: slides in grayscale/black and white, 15
Print button, 37
Print dialog box, 9, 10
Printing: presentation, 9-15
Programs
    embedding objects from one to another, 174
    steps in linking, 170-171
Promote button: on Formatting toolbar, 33
Publish as Web Page dialog box, 128

Recolor Picture button, 115
Recolor Picture dialog box, 116
Rectangle button, 66
Rectangles, 66
    drawing, 159
Rehearsal dialog box, 30
Replace dialog box, 50
Replace Font dialog box, 177
Rotate button, 75
Rotating: objects, 75

Save As dialog box, 16, 128

Saving
    presentation as web page and previewing presentation, 129-130
    presentations, 15
ScreenTips
    for buttons on toolbars, 7
    using, 40-41
Second rank options, 15
Select Objects button, 66
Self-repair, 40
Self-running presentations, 29-30
Set Page dialog box, 128
Set Up Show dialog box, 28, 29
Shadow: with WordArt, 141, 151
Shapes: changing in WordArt, 145-148
Show button, 37
Show Formatting button, 34
Sizing
    object boxes, 55
    organizational charts, 155
    in WordArt, 143
Slant of text: changing with WordArt, 143
Slide Finder dialog box, 178
Slide Layout dialog box, 125
Slide pane: in PowerPoint window, 7
Slides, 3
    adding with hyperlinks, 120
    build added to, 106-107
    copying, 52-54
    creating hyperlinks from, to Web, 119-120
    creating new presentation from existing, 178-179
    editing, 49-60
    finding and replacing text in, 50
    formatting color schemes for, 79
    guidelines in preparing of, 4
    inserting and deleting, 51
    linking within same presentation, 123
    linking with presentation with action buttons, 123
    previewing in web page, 128-129
    rearranging, 55
    rearranging object boxes in, 55
    rearranging text in, 54-55
    sending via e-mail, 130, 131
    speaker notes for, 91-92
    table creation in, 118-119
    text formatted in, 60
    watermark creation in, 116-117
    WordArt text inserted in, 143. *See also* Slide shows
Slide Show, 21
Slide Show button: on View toolbar, 22
Slide show controlling commands, 22
Slide Show menu icon, 23
Slide shows
    automatic running of, 28-30
    commands for controlling, 22
    pen use during presentation of, 22-23
    running, 21-31
    sound effects and transitions added to, 25-27
    starting, 22
Slide Sorter, 51
    and copying slide, 52

Slide Sorter toolbar, 26
    Slide Transition Effects button on, 106
Slide Sorter view, 21, 55
Slide Transition dialog box, 26, 28, 30
Slide View, 21
Slide view: find and replace in, 50
Slide View button, 64
Sound: adding, 25-27, 107
Source program, 169, 170
Spacing: increasing/decreasing, before/after paragraphs, 62
Speaker notes: adding, 91-92
Spelling check: completing, 57
Squares, 66
Standard toolbar
    Copy button on, 125
    E-mail button on, 130
    Grayscale Preview button on, 18
    Insert Hyperlink button on, 120
    Paste button on, 125
    PowerPoint buttons on, 55-57
    PowerPoint Help button on, 36
    in PowerPoint window, 5, 6
    using buttons on, 55-57
Status bar: in PowerPoint window, 7
Straight lines, 66
Symbols: inserting with Office Assistant, 37

Table autolayout, 118
Table placeholder, 9
Tables: creating in slides, 118-119
Tables and Borders toolbar, 118
Technical support, 40
Templates, 40
    creating presentation by using, 7, 8
    formatting options for slides from, 4
Text
    bulleted, 62
    customizing in WordArt, 152-153
    entering in WordArt, 142
    finding/replacing in slides, 50-51
    formatting inside box, 72
    formatting in slide, 60
    importing from Word, 124-127
    inserting/deleting in slides, 50
    rearranging in slides, 54
    selecting, 50
    wrapping in Autoshape, 72
Text box: creating, 72
Text Box button, 72
Text & Clip Art autolayout, 118
Texture: specifying in WordArt, 150
Three-dimensional (3-D) effects
    adding, 141
    with WordArt, 148, 151
Time: inserting into presentations, 90
Timings: setting and rehearsing, 30-31
Title bar: in PowerPoint window, 6
Title Master slide, 64
Title Only autolayout, 118
Title placeholder, 9
Title Slide autolayout, 118
Toolbar buttons: outlining, 33-34
Transitions: adding, 25-27
Transparencies, 3, 21, 83

Vertical lines: drawing, 159

Vertical scroll bar
    elevator on, 21
    in PowerPoint window, 7
View: changing in organization chart, 159
Viewing: presentations, 20-21
View toolbar
    in PowerPoint window, 7
    Slide Show button on, 22
Visual aids: for presentations, 3
Visual effects
    adding, 103
    animation, 103-105
    clip art, 109-116
    watermarks, 116-117

Watermarks: creating in PowerPoint slide, 116-117
Web
    creating hyperlinks from slide to, 119-120
    publishing presentation to, 127-129
Web browser: displaying presentation in, 128
Web page: previewing, 128-129
Web Page Preview, 128, 129
Web toolbar: displaying, 119
What's This option: using, 40
Word
    collecting text in, then pasting in PowerPoint slide, 126-127
    importing text from, 124-127
    MS Organization Chart 2.0 used in, 154
    organization charts created in, 155-156
WordArt
    changing font/font size in, 144
    commands review for, 162
    customizing, 144-148
    customizing, with buttons on Drawing toolbar, 148
    customizing text in, 152-153
    sizing and moving, 143
    text entered in, 142
    using, 147-153
WordArt gallery: displaying, 142
WordArt Shape palette, 145, 146
WordArt toolbar
    buttons for customizing on, 144
    customizing WordArt gallery choices with buttons on, 145
    Format WordArt button on, 144-145
    WordArt button on, 142
Word documents: linking to PowerPoint presentation, 122-123
World Wide Web. *See* Web